D0712764

WITHDRAWN
UTSA LIBRARIES

WITHDRAWN
UTSA LIBRARIES

Migrant Women of Johannesburg

AFRICA CONNECTS

Garth Myers (University of Kansas) and Martin J. Murray (University of Michigan), *Series Editors*

This scholarly series stands at the intersection of globalization and development studies, examining the social, political, and economic effects of these processes on the African continent. For advocates and critics alike, globalization and development are inescapable "facts of life" that define the parameters of social action not just in Africa but throughout the world. Yet while academic debates and policy discussions careen between praise and criticism, too little attention is given to how these processes actually operate in African settings. Rather than simply reacting to the mainstream scholarly literature, books in this series seek to creatively engage with contemporary debates as a way of developing new perspectives that establish and analyze the linkages between globalization and development.

PUBLISHED BY PALGRAVE MACMILLAN:

Encountering the Nigerian State
  Edited by Wale Adebanwi and Ebenezer Obadare

Zambia, Mining, and Neoliberalism: Boom and Bust on the Globalized Copperbelt
  Edited by Alastair Fraser and Miles Larmer

Fixing the African State: Recognition, Politics, and Community-Based Development in Tanzania
  Brian J. Dill

Migrant Women of Johannesburg: Everyday Life in an In-Between City
  Caroline Wanjiku Kihato

Migrant Women of Johannesburg

Everyday Life in an In-Between City

Caroline Wanjiku Kihato

palgrave
macmillan

MIGRANT WOMEN OF JOHANNESBURG
Copyright © Caroline Wanjiku Kihato, 2013.

All rights reserved.

First published in 2013 by
PALGRAVE MACMILLAN®
in the United States—a division of St. Martin's Press LLC,
175 Fifth Avenue, New York, NY 10010.

Where this book is distributed in the UK, Europe and the rest of the world,
this is by Palgrave Macmillan, a division of Macmillan Publishers Limited,
registered in England, company number 785998, of Houndmills,
Basingstoke, Hampshire RG21 6XS.

Palgrave Macmillan is the global academic imprint of the above companies
and has companies and representatives throughout the world.

Palgrave® and Macmillan® are registered trademarks in the United States,
the United Kingdom, Europe and other countries.

ISBN: 978–1–137–29996–3

Library of Congress Cataloging-in-Publication Data is available from the
Library of Congress.

A catalogue record of the book is available from the British Library.

Design by Newgen Knowledge Works (P) Ltd., Chennai, India.

First edition: November 2013

10 9 8 7 6 5 4 3 2 1

Library
University of Texas
at San Antonio

In memory of Sibongile Gumede

Contents

List of Figures   ix

List of Maps   xi

Preface   xiii

Acknowledgments   xix

1   Introduction: Welcome to Hillbrow, You Will Find Your People Here   1

2   The Notice: Rethinking Urban Governance in the Age of Mobility   25

3   Between Pharaoh's Army and the Red Sea: Social Mobility and Social Death in the Context of Women's Migration   47

4   Turning the Home Inside-Out—Private Space and Everyday Politics   71

5   The Station, Camp, and Refugee: Xenophobic Violence and the City   95

6   Conclusion: Ways of Seeing—Migrant Women in the Liminal City   113

Notes   131

Bibliography   153

Index   169

Figures

1.1 Johannesburg's dazzle—big brands and
    city lights in the Central Business District   4
1.2 The city as we live it, cooking in the corner
    of a studio apartment in Hillbrow   7
1.3 From the hawkers table, women traders' street world,
    Central Business District, Johannesburg   10
1.4 Street life, Central Business District   12
1.5 Woman in a taxi at the edge of Johannesburg's
    Central Business District   15
1.6 Weaving connections: Hair salons as nodes of
    social interaction, economic opportunity, and beauty   18
2.1 Yeoville market and taxi rank   26
2.2 The notice   29
2.3 Johannesburg Central Business District, opportunity
    and opportunism   42
2.4 On the corner of Plein and Klein   44
3.1 "One day I will be rich" aspirational images sent
    back home project success, which is yet to be
    accomplished   65
4.1 Mothering and nurturing an important marker
    of achievement   80
4.2 The structure and safety of domestic rituals   81
4.3 Pride in accomplishment, the family meal in Berea   82
4.4 "My happy family": Unguarded, tender moments
    between father and children   82
4.5 Blood stains in the bathtub after a violent
    quarrel in Hillbrow   86
4.6 The aftermath of violence, Hillbrow   87

Maps

1.1 Locating Johannesburg within Gauteng
 and South Africa   3
1.2 Map of Johannesburg and the study area   6

Preface

"Where are you from sister, where is your home?"

"Nairobi."

"You do not come from Nairobi...I mean where is your *real* home?"

It was May 2008. Violent attacks against foreign African nationals across South Africa had seen many flee to police stations for safety since the start of the violence. I had been volunteering at Primrose police station, east of Johannesburg, where displaced people from the Democratic Republic of Congo, Zimbabwe, Kenya, and Mozambique were seeking safety. On one of my visits, I overheard a Kenyan man and woman speaking Kiswahili. I approached them introducing myself in Kiswahili as "Caroline from Kenya."

Edward, in his mid-twenties, seemed irritated with my response to his question "where are you from?" Neither my name, nor Nairobi betrayed my ethnicity. But I had given him just enough information to indicate that I was not South African (essential against the backdrop of the violence), and that we shared a nationality. It was months later, after he had moved to Glenanda camp where makeshift United Nations High Commissioner for Refugees (UNHCR) tented homes for displaced people had been set up south of Johannesburg, that I told him the answer he had wanted to hear.

My interaction with Edward took me back hundreds of miles north and decades back to my childhood in Nairobi. Growing up, I remember numerous uncles or aunties asking "Where do you come from?" The scene was typically a backyard gathering in one of Nairobi's many housing estates. In between political discussions over beer, sodas, and meat, one of the adults would ask a child hovering around the proverbial "Where do you come from?" question. Instantaneously, other discussions would suddenly halt as all attention diverted to the child—as if the very essence of their existence was hanging on the thread of the child's response.

From early on, I began perceiving this as a trick question. I learnt that depending on how much attention I required from the adults, I could manipulate the conversation and get what I wanted. In those few seconds when I held everybody's attention, I had a number of choices.

"Mūramati!" where my paternal parents lived, was the "correct" answer and would solicit claps and words of praise. One of the uncles would exclaim, "What a clever girl, mom you must give her another Fanta!" My parents would beam because this was as much a test for me as it was of their parenting.

"Ihūrūrū!" would be my next option. This would raise some confusion and a few eyebrows. Those who did not know where my parents came from would wait to hear whether this indeed was the correct answer. "No, that is where your mommy grew up," a close aunt would say. I happened to like the place where my mother grew up, so why couldn't I come from there? While I loved my paternal grandparents dearly and had a huge fascination for Kikuyu traditional family structure (my grandfather lived with all his four wives, and he died when he was over a hundred years old. As a child, this made him my hero), Mūramati did not interest me that much. It is a semi-desert with not much appeal to a young city girl. On the other hand, I had fond memories of climbing plum and peach trees, milking cows, picking tea, and growing cabbages in Ihūrūrū. True, I enjoyed jumping into the crystal clear waters from the melted snow of Mount Kenya in Mūramati, but if I had to come from a village, it would be Ihūrūrū. Seemingly, the answer to the question was not a matter of my preference, any more than it was tied to where I was born and bred. I lived in a patriarchal society and I was to assume my paternal home, Mūramati, until I married. Once an adult explained these facts to me, I got my Fanta.

It was the third answer that would solicit the most interesting dialogue.

"Nairobi!" would be met with disapproving, pained looks that seemed to say, "The poor child has lost her roots." My parents would be mortified. "Nobody comes from Nairobi," an aunty would say pityingly. "Where does Cūcū[1] Wanjiku stay?" my mother would ask, trying to salvage her reputation as a good parent, something now seriously in question. If I wanted to be intransigent I would say: "But you asked where I come from. I do not stay with Cūcū, I was not born there, so how can I come from there?" After more head shaking, accusing glares, and embarrassed shrugs, one of the neighbors would exclaim: "The children of these days do not know their roots." "It is a very serious problem." Another parent would interject, "You need to send them there for three months during the holidays, that is what we do with ours." I would then be forgotten as our parents discussed how difficult it was to bring us up in the city and shared some remedies for rooting us to our "real home."

These discussions and debates fascinated me, and I would sit silently listening to my parents' generation grappling with notions of identity and belonging. Being pioneer migrants from rural Kenya to the city, they carried a huge burden of sustaining traditional values and culture. They also carried with them the guilt of not having done a good enough job transferring these to their urban children.

Once I had had enough of the conversation and wanted my Fanta I would shout "Mūramati!"—playing along in what I understood as communal deception, where the correct answer was, as I saw it, the wrong one. There would be a palpable sigh of collective relief, the adults' guilt appeased, at least temporarily. "All will be well with you," a graying uncle would whisper, "all is well with us."

With the advantage of hindsight I think that the question "Where are you from?" was aimed at the adult audience as much as it was directed at their children. It was a question on belonging, place, and identity that pioneer migrants often ask themselves, rooted as they are in both rural and urban worlds. Our responses (as children) would affirm or reject *their own* sense of belonging as much as it would ours as first generation urbanites.

Decades later, having migrated to Johannesburg, Edward's question "Where are you from" brought me face-to-face with some of the dilemmas my parents' generation face: the contradictory, even paradoxical, notions of belonging and dislocation, rootedness and uprootedness, in this South African metropolis. Indeed I straddle multiple worlds: rural/urban; Nairobi/Johannesburg; ethnic/cosmopolitan; local/global. And I am not alone. Through the lives of African migrant women living in Johannesburg, this book explores the experience of living between geographies. Their everyday lives are examined through this fluid location where they live "between and betwixt," multiple worlds, suspended between a past "back home" and an imagined future elsewhere. Around them, they create a social world that reflects these tensions, risks, and the opportunities it provides. By revealing the lives of people who are often hidden from view, this book tells the story of women's migration to Johannesburg as they experience it. In this interstitial city, we uncover how their relationships with the state, economy, place, and community shape contemporary urban life in Johannesburg and elsewhere.

I began my Johannesburg life selling Kenyan crafts to passers-by on the streets. Lured by the city's promise of a brighter future, I left Kenya with little more than an address and a conviction that Johannesburg was the place to be in. And indeed it was. In 1994, South Africa's new political and social landscape had endless offerings for African migrants. Much has changed 19 years later. I graduated and found work in a growing non-profit sector. But the recent slowdown in the country's economy has meant fewer opportunities for foreign migrants and also for South Africans. I write this book in the context of growing inequality and poverty, disillusionment with the ruling elite, and rising hostilities toward foreign migrants. My position as a black, African, middle class, migrant woman actively shapes my research. I am not an objective bystander, fragments of my own life are present in this work. Who I am, my history and experiences interact and relate to the subject matter and respondents in ways that affect my questions, the interviews, and the substance of my analysis. With this recognition, I side firmly with an established branch of feminist research that recognizes the importance of reflexivity and foregrounding the researcher's positionality in relation to the groups s/he is working with.[2] This stems from both an ethical and an epistemological commitment to research. On the one hand, it is about unmasking the research process and revealing the underlying assumptions and social context within which it occurs—being "truthful" about the researcher-"research subject" dynamics. In doing this, feminists reveal that assumptions of "objectivity" in the research process are often inconsistent with the reality. Moreover, uncovering the dynamics of the research process allows for a more nuanced reading of the research results and provides an opportunity to theorize knowledge and its formation.

The relationship and dynamics between the women I spoke to and I, as researcher, influenced the information that they chose to reveal, or not reveal. Being a migrant woman from Kenya meant that I had relatively easy access to the community, particularly Kiswahili-speaking women. While my proximity served as an advantage in some ways, for positivists it poses a methodological danger to "objectivity." Some scholars argue that closeness raises problematic ethical issues if researchers become complicit in illegal activities.[3] Whatever the position on the researcher's relationship to the respondent, the key question is whether the research findings can stand up to scientific scrutiny. My data collection method provided a mechanism for me to verify, in a number of ways, women's responses in interviews and group sessions. The advantage of an engaged relationship with respondents is that it provides a way of seeing that reveals the complexities of urban realities among migrant women in a way that a more "objective" methodology may not allow.

I also formed personal bonds with some of the women, which may have shaped the research process. I met one of the Ugandan women at the Yeoville market during a very traumatic period of her life. Her brother-in-law and sister had died, leaving her with three children, one of which was her own. She could not afford to support the three and made a difficult decision to put her sister's two in a state shelter. She called me one day to tell me that a bus had crashed the five-year-old girl on her way to school. Faced with this, I found that I could not remain "distant." I provided food, books, clothes, and financial support to her. I do not see this as a failure, but embrace those feminist traditions that welcome interviewer-interviewee relationships because they lead to greater trust and candid content. In these contexts, personal connections and assistance in the research process is considered acceptable.[4] Moreover, I do not believe that the nature of my interaction with interviewees was a barrier to the quality, integrity, and veracity of the research. Some may find this relationship problematic, not only because I am empathetic, but also because it raises issues of unequal power between the researcher and the research "subject" in the research process. That I offered material assistance when she required it may indicate that I have more power. In some ways this may be true. But just as she needed my material assistance, I needed her participation in the project. Without her acquiescence, I would have had to find another participant—a process that often took time. To view the interview process as a uni-directional power relationship where the researcher has the power and the research subject has none is to simplify notions of power. Power dynamics are not static; the balance shifts at different points in any relationship. Reciprocity may not be completely balanced, but it is unrealistic to expect that it ever is. To acknowledge that power dynamics are unequal does not mean that one actor possesses all the power while the other has none.

One reason I embarked on this research was to give voice to women migrants, who have no platform in South Africa's current political milieu. However, as I started on what I thought was a "worthy" cause, I realized my own arrogance. That I thought that *I* could make "invisible" women visible and give the "voiceless" a voice implied that I had power where they had none. As I discuss later in the book, it also reflected a fundamental misreading of their world. For sure, silence was sometimes a choice and necessity, not a curse. The women in this book are complex—life's obstacles may discourage them, but they are not defined by their discouragement. Yet, stereotyping them as powerless is as problematic as celebrating them as heroines. Both images, positive and negative, create cardboard characters—objects that lack the agency or failings of human beings. Indeed, women's actions may not always lead to the desired outcomes for themselves and others, but are nevertheless attempts to overcome the barriers they encounter.

While most of the women in this study had immigration papers allowing them temporary residence in South Africa, they remain vulnerable to police harassment and the threat of deportation. Because of this, I have used pseudonyms. All the images and material used in this book have been used with their consent.

Acknowledgments

Like many of life's journeys, this book would not have been completed without the encouragement, patience, (and sometimes frustration) of many who I encountered along the way. I am greatly indebted to the migrant women who gave of their time to participate in this study. Through tears and laughter, they told me their stories in ways that have had a significant effect in shaping me as a scholar and a human being. For their patience, courage, and generosity, I am truly grateful.

I have Martin Murray to thank for his belief in this project and his tireless motivation and patience. Raymond Suttner gave generously of his time, reading drafts and providing moral support along the way. With a keen ability to theorize African women's experiences, Nomboniso Gasa was always at hand to help me make sense of the data and provide some perspective. Without the support of Abebe Zegeye, Greg Cuthberston, and Pamela Ryan at the University of South Africa, this book would not have come to fruition. Over lunch in "old" China town in Johannesburg, Brahm Fleisch encouraged me to use my own story and voice, which forms an important part of this book. After my graduate studies, Phil Harrison provided an institutional home at Wits and funding support from the National Research Foundation. In Washington DC, Susan Martin, at the Institute for the Study of International Migration (ISIM), Georgetown, generously provided funding from the John D. and Catherine T. McArthur Foundation. For a year, ISIM provided a home and financial support to complete this manuscript.

I owe a particular debt to Terry Kurgan who worked with me on the Visual Diaries Project, to Sue van Zyl who is one of the best writing mentors I know, to Bikoko Mbombo who assisted with some of the research. Courtenay Sprague, Delia Harverson, Ellen Papciak-Rose, Laura Yeatman, Felicity Nyikadzino-Berold and Clare Loveday all read versions of this book and encouraged me to complete it.

Loren Landau walked beside me on this journey, and believed in me even when I had lost faith in myself. As my husband and friend, he tirelessly read multiple versions of this book providing critical yet compassionate insights, all the while tolerating my unpredictable moods without complaint.

Thanks to my parents without whose support I would not have found the courage to come to Johannesburg. Over the years they have provided an anchor and home in Kenya that I can always go back to. An undertaking such as this cannot be done alone. I had the support of my community—friends, family, and colleagues. While the achievement is shared, any shortcomings remain mine alone.

Introduction: Welcome to Hillbrow, You Will Find Your People Here

"Get out! GET OUT!"

Tired, hungry and disorientated, Fazila squinted in the bright light streaming through the truck's back door. The driver cut a large figure, and his silhouette offered her some respite from the glaring afternoon sun. As her eyes adjusted to the light, she asked "Are we there?" barely recognizing her own voice. She had not spoken for days in her full voice and her mouth was dry. Had she left Lubumbashi for South Africa four, five days ago? She could not be certain and had lost count. Her journey to South Africa seemed like one long arduous night cramped at the back of the truck with no windows.

Fazila's journey had, in fact, started not four or five days before, but a few months before, in 2000 in a Kinshasa jail. She had been taken in for questioning by the Kabila regime because of her links to a man who had worked for the deposed president, Mobutu. After a few days in jail, she bought her way out and flew to Lubumbashi where she found a driver who, for a fee, would smuggle her into South Africa. Without a passport or a change of clothes she climbed aboard the truck with all the money she had, and left for Johannesburg. "I abandoned everything. I am going to a country where I don't know what is going on there. I left my studies, family, my life. I lost everything," she had said to me in the livingroom of her Berea apartment. From Lubumbashi, the truck entered Zambia. Fazila and seven others, including a woman with a two-year-old child, travelled through Zambia, Mozambique, Zimbabwe, and South Africa in silence. The border guards and the police at roadblocks could not know that the driver was carrying human cargo. They were crossing the borders illegally. Under the cover of darkness, they made pit stops once a day to go to the toilet in bushes.

"What day is it?" she heard someone in the truck ask the driver.

"Same day it is where you came from. Welcome to Hillbrow, you will find your people here."

Fazila gathered herself and stepped tentatively into the commotion on the streets. She blinked as her eyes adjusted to the light. As she straightened the creases on her clothes, a heady feeling of excitement and fear came over her. "I am here, I am in Johannesburg," she thought to herself. For a few moments, she forgot her anxieties and listened to the banter of street life—cars honking, a police siren, and people buying and selling. After the hushed silence and the irregular rhythm of the truck's overextended engine, the cacophony of the city's sounds accosted her ears. She stood on the sidewalk and looked up at the towering apartment blocks. Down the street, she noticed traffic lights, each set turning green and then, moments later, red, as if in a synchronized dance. The smell of fried chicken mingled incongruously with the exhaust fumes from a nearby taxi. How far she had come from the place of her birth, Bukavu! As reality began to creep in, her fear returned. She needed to focus on survival, finding food, accommodation, and work, in that order. Looking around her new host city, she caught a glimpse of a cylindrical skyscraper, the iconic and infamous Ponte City. She did not know then, but at 54 stories high it is the tallest residential building in Africa. With a history of suicides, gangs, international drug cartels, and stories of revival, Ponte, Norman Ohler writes, "is Johannesburg's infamous landmark."[1] She remembers noticing its rooftop, a gigantic blue and white billboard advertising VODACOM.

Johannesburg: A City Between and Betwixt

For those living in Johannesburg's wealthy northern suburbs, its inner city is perplexing, impenetrable, and dangerous. Stories of crime, drugs, the concentration of "illegal aliens," and poverty lament the decay of what was once the symbol of South Africa's gold wealth and prosperity. But these stories of despair are only a partial rendering of Johannesburg's infamous center. In truth, Johannesburg's inner city is an ambivalent place—a site of both opportunity and lack, hope and despair.

In many ways, this has been Johannesburg's story since its founding as a mining camp in the mid-nineteenth century. After the discovery of gold in 1886, the city became a magnet for people seeking

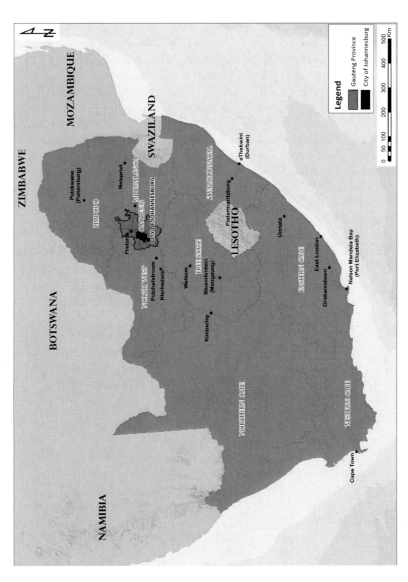

Map 1.1 Locating Johannesburg within Gauteng and South Africa

their fortune in its mines, industries, and growing service sector. By the 1900s, Johannesburg had a class of black contract laborers living in single-sex dormitories or overcrowded slums, who needed permission to be in the city.[2] They became the city's workhorses who never belonged. Wealth and success is almost always accompanied by poverty and misfortune. And Mongane Wole Serote's poem "City Johannesburg" captures this paradox in the story of a migrant worker who leaves the warmth of "his love, comic houses and people" in search of the city's wealth in an unforgiving, alienating, and racially segregated environment. At the height of apartheid and its industrial glory, Serote's Johannesburg is at once the source of life and of death to those who ventured to work in its mines and industries.

Johannesburg is located in Gauteng province. Most of the country's internal and international migrants find their way to Gauteng because of its dominant economic position in South and Southern Africa. With a population growth rate of 2.7 percent between 2001 and 2011, Gauteng is the fastest growing of South Africa's nine provinces.[3] It is also the country's most populous province, with 12.3 million people, representing 23.7 percent of South Africa's population.[4] It is estimated that about 3.75 million people live in the city of Johannesburg.[5]

Figure 1.1 Johannesburg's dazzle—big brands and city lights in the Central Business District

The history of Johannesburg's inner city and its surrounding areas has been covered elsewhere[6] and is not the focus of this book. But its beginnings as a mining town, and the subsequent racialized nature of its industrialization, had an impact on how migrant labor and, in particular, black populations saw themselves in the city. The apartheid city produced a group of people who lived and depended on it, but could not claim it as their home. Blacks were temporary sojourners to the city of gold. And although they toiled in its mines, industries, and streets, they had no rights to live in it or make decisions about its future.[7] Those allowed temporary domicile could not live with their families because of restrictions on movement.[8] These were people useful only for the duration of their economically active years. Like the protagonist in Serote's poem, their lives straddled Johannesburg and their homes in South Africa's rural areas and neighboring countries. Today's cross-border migrants may not face apartheid's harsh racial policies, but, like the migrants of yesteryear, they continue to live between their countries of origin and the city of gold—never fully at ease in their adopted city.

The Setting

This book is set in Johannesburg's inner city—the Central Business District (CBD) and areas northeast of it where the residential suburbs of Berea, Hillbrow, and Yeoville lie. Unlike most of Johannesburg, the inner city has a high-density residential stock that was built in the 1930s during an economic upturn.[9] The apartments, particularly in Hillbrow and Berea, were built to house the city's well-to-do, providing shops and services to match a sophisticated urban lifestyle. It is the availability of accommodation, the retail opportunities that high-density living provides and the inner city's central location that continues to attract new migrants today. But, like cities elsewhere, Johannesburg's center has seen periods of booms and busts. At the culmination of the CBD's decline in the early 1990s was the flight of big capital. The exodus of the Johannesburg Stock Exchange, De Beers, and Gold Fields, and the closure of the iconic Carlton Hotel sealed the city's fate. Although today there are signs of the city's revival with the development of new art, knowledge, and lifestyle precincts like Arts on Main, these investments remain small, niche, and exclusive, appealing to artsy, green, and urbane lifestyles.[10] In their midst however, remains a sea of decaying, overcrowded, poorly managed buildings and infrastructure.

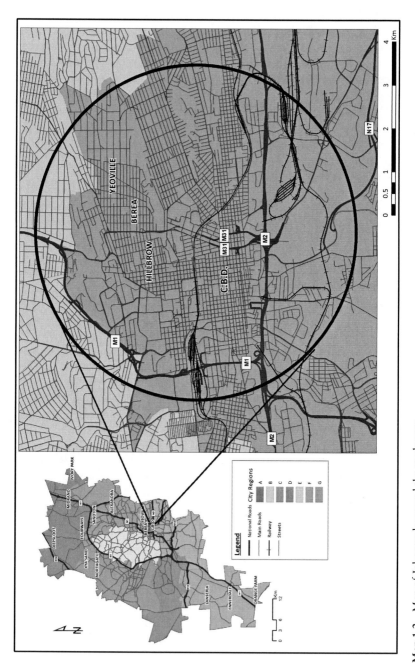

Map 1.2 Map of Johannesburg and the study area

Figure 1.2   The city as we live it, cooking in the corner of a studio apartment in Hillbrow

As the CBD was experiencing capital flight, the adjacent residential areas of Yeoville, Berea, and Hillbrow were also undergoing their own demographic and economic changes. The early 1990s saw an influx of people from South Africa's rural areas and other African countries into the inner city, which urban authorities were ill-prepared for. The timing seemed right for Africans from both within and outside of South Africa. The dreaded pass laws that restricted blacks' residence in the city had been repealed, allowing them to become *bona fide* residents in the city. For international migrants, the lifting of travel sanctions after the release of the African National Congress leader Nelson Mandela made it legal for foreign Africans, whose countries had participated in the boycott against apartheid, to travel to South Africa. Moreover, the devastating impact of Structural Adjustment Programs on African economies and livelihoods;[11] and the growing political and civil unrest in parts of the continent propelled people to travel to places that were safer and had economic opportunities. South Africa became such an option for international migrants.

The number of foreign-born migrants in Johannesburg remains an intense point of debate. City officials tend to exaggerate the numbers, some believing that up to 86 percent of Johannesburg's population comprises of illegal foreigners.[12] Far from these estimates, the 2011 census puts the number of foreign-born nationals in country at 3.2 percent.[13] Although the number of foreigners in Johannesburg is likely to be above the national average, it is unlikely that eight out of every ten people in the province is foreign born. Measured estimates seem to suggest that between 13 and 14 percent of the city's population are foreign-born.[14] Whatever the numbers, the inner city provides many newcomers from South Africa and beyond a foothold into the city. Population figures in 2010 show that the CBD, the area where this research took place, has the highest population densities in Gauteng—with 64, 623 people per kilometer.[15] A combination of factors—pressure on infrastructure, the lack of investor confidence, poor building maintenance, absentee landlords, and overcrowding—have resulted in the physical decay of many residential blocks and the infrastructure that serves them. The presence of international drug syndicates and gangs[16] has sealed inner city Joburg's reputation as an area riddled with "crime and grime."

It is the transitional aspects that drew me to inner city Johannesburg to study women from other parts of Africa. Hanging out with them, I became aware of the fluid nature of Yeoville, Berea, and Hillbrow. These parts of the city seemed to be places that migrants passed through rather than settled in. A place where newcomers saw themselves living for only a short duration of time—their sights set on Johannesburg's northern suburbs or on cities in North America or Europe. In 1999, Morris found that many cross border migrants "saw South Africa and Hillbrow as a temporary stop."[17] A few years later, in 2006, a survey conducted by the University of the Witwatersrand (WITS), Tufts University, and the French Institute of South Africa (IFAS), came to similar conclusions, confirming broader trends in what I witnessed in my fieldwork. The survey showed that the majority of respondents in the study, both local and foreign, imagined their lives elsewhere in the city, or outside the country.[18] Both South Africans and foreign-born migrants keep strong ties with kin and communities elsewhere, even as their everyday lives are physically rooted in the city. Few who live in the inner city stay there longer than three years, perceiving it as inappropriate for raising a family or living with a spouse.[19] Those who do stay on live as if suspended in society, aspiring for lives elsewhere. It is within these broad population dynamics that foreign-born migrant women's experiences of the inner city are located. Honing in on the particularity of their experiences allows for a deeper exploration of these trends and a better understanding of how women's mobility, both real and imagined, shapes urban processes in Johannesburg and elsewhere.

This book is about urban life. It examines this through cross-border women's relationships with host and home communities, the South African state, its economy, and the city of Johannesburg. It explores their fluid lives against the backdrop of a city that is also in flux, transitioning from an apartheid to a postapartheid city. It looks at what it means to live in Johannesburg, yet remain dislocated there; what it means to be in the inner city, yet aspire to live elsewhere; and what it means to be both visible and invisible in the city. The book holds these in-between spaces long enough to uncover the texture of urban life and the relationships that constitute it. Through this fluid and transient location, women's everyday lives and relationships unveil a world that has a profound effect on the city they live in. Migrant women allow us to see how populations living in society's margins influence urban practices. Their lives show us how significant they are in shaping the actions of state agents, and overturning common understandings of urban governance as a state-led project. As we follow them through the city's streets, the boundaries between legality and illegality, formal and informal, official and unofficial city collapse—rendering these categories inaccurate descriptors of the city or their lives. The women in this book compel us to rethink the twin frames that have for so long shaped how we plan and govern cities: the legal versus illegal city, the formal versus informal city, the visible versus invisible city. What we see instead is a city where these realities are intertwined and city life becomes a hybrid of formality and informality, legality and illegality. But the call to revisit our planning and governance frameworks requires more than simply tweaking what exists. It requires more than incorporating the informal city into the formal one or applying "good governance" principles to ungoverned spaces. Indeed, it calls for a transformation of urban planning and governance, and a redefinition of what these might mean in twenty-first-century African cities.

Through Their Eyes and Words

I met Fazila and the other women in the pages that follow, between 2004 and 2008, hanging out at hair salons while having my hair done, or at markets in Yeoville and the CBD helping to sell at their stalls. As a participant in their world, I witnessed their interactions with each other, listened in as well as participated in their conversations. It is

Figure 1.3   From the hawkers table, women traders' street world, Central Business District, Johannesburg

through their stories of love, illness, fears, children, violence, family, and money that I collected some of the most rewarding data on issues that they cared about. Taking my cue from them, I let their lives lead me through the city, with their words and snapshots forming the nucleus of this book. The women had left their countries of origin in Cameroon, the Democratic Republic of Congo, Congo Brazzaville, Nigeria, Rwanda, Burundi, Kenya, Tanzania, Uganda, and Zimbabwe in the late 1990s and early 2000s, in search of a better life. Many had come to Johannesburg as young adults in their early twenties. When I met them, their ages spanned between the mid-twenties and late thirties. Most of them had a basic level of education, and a few had tertiary and university degrees. The circumstances of their migration to Johannesburg differed. While some had fled their countries because of war and have harrowing memories of their journeys to South Africa, others were attracted by Johannesburg's economic promise. As the coming chapters reveal, many of them crossed the South African border overland, entering through Mozambique or Zimbabwe. Their family circumstances differed—some were single mothers, others had husbands and children in Johannesburg, while others supported their children and sometimes husbands in their home countries. Some had no children, but remained obligated to supporting the families they had left behind. All came to the city in search of safety, economic opportunity, and the possibility of upward mobility for themselves and their families.

After four years of conducting interviews and writing field notes, I decided to add a visual component to the data of photographs taken by the migrant women themselves. I had become increasingly frustrated with what I saw as the limits of language. Working with oral techniques, I was consistently aware of some of the failings of spoken language to convey women's experiences. My first reaction was to blame language barriers—particularly where I could not converse directly with interviewees because we spoke different languages. As the research progressed however, I became convinced it was not just that there were language barriers, but that there were times when no words *in any spoken language* could have articulated the women's feelings, memories, and ideas. This is not an uncommon observation, particularly when interviews relate to, or trigger, traumatic events.[20] Feminist authors have written about the importance of reading bodily and spatial practices[21] and silence[22] to gain insight into women's lived experiences. These writings formed the basis for my decision to develop an accompanying visual method in my data collection.[23]

Cultural and media studies have drawn our attention to the importance of the "image" as a communication tool.[24] Just as words are accepted as an evocative interface in communication, so too is the visual image, particularly in an era where digital technology and mass media continually produce and circulate images across space and time. John Berger writes: "Seeing comes before words...It is seeing which establishes our place in the surrounding world; we explain that world with words, but words can never undo the fact that we are surrounded by it."[25] The photographs taken by migrant women of their everyday lives provide a novel way of seeing the city from a viewpoint that is rarely acknowledged or seen by scholars and policy makers. The women's snapshots did not replace oral evidence, but complemented our verbal interactions. My initial objective was simply to use images as visual confirmation of migrant women's material conditions—opening us up to spaces in the city that are often invisible to outsiders. As the research progressed however, I realized that women's photographs went beyond their material dimension, constructing meanings that lie beyond the two-dimensional image, constituted as part of a complex meaning-producing system.[26]

Using the camera, women took authorial control over how they are represented. Their photographs uncovered the complex relationships that exist between a population living in the margins of the city, and the city in which it lives. Knowingly or unknowingly, their images overturn iconic representations of displaced and marginalized populations, depicted in the press as victims who are vulnerable, weak, and desperate.[27] They produce images of resistance, in which they overtly project how they want us to see them in the city—as respected members of the community with a self-consciousness about looking "good" in front of the camera. Images of wealth and aspirations not only show us migrant women's dreams for material wealth, but also the way mobility is tied to dignity, honor, and status in their communities. The photograph therefore transcends its opaque two-dimensional form.[28] Its layered meanings expose the politics of representation in the city, allowing us to reflect upon the unequal power relations embedded in the production of images of marginalized urban communities.

By taking control of the camera, these marginalized women "talk back" to society, sometimes resisting stereotypical representations and sometimes reinforcing them, but all the while choosing how to they want us to see them in the city. The images of women's everyday lives presented in this book not only provide glimpses of their world

Figure 1.4   Street life, Central Business District

in the city, but also overtly challenge us to look and see them, and the city, differently.

The City from Below

This ethnographic account of urban life examines the city from the point of view of migrant women's everyday lives. It approaches the city from "below," through their visual and discursive constructions of Johannesburg, and the social worlds they have helped create. Rather than ask how political forces and global capital shape Johannesburg, it turns the dominant urban question on its head, and interrogates how cross-border women shape Johannesburg's politics, regulatory systems and local economies. To borrow Simone's turn of phrase, the focus here is on what migrant women, who are considered marginal in the city, "actually do in order to enlarge their space of operation."[29]

By focusing on women's interpretations of the city, I do not discount the importance of the broader socioeconomic and political forces that condition their lives and the spaces they inhabit. Whether the economy is doing well or not affects employment and the circulation of money in the city, which impacts upon women's businesses or chances of finding work. Moreover, state immigration laws condition migrant women's rights to work, just as city bylaws determine where they can or cannot locate their businesses. No doubt the broad structures of the economy and the state remain significant in people's lives. But by approaching the city through the everyday lives of a group of marginalized women, I shed light on these broader processes, exploring what their lives reveal about the nature of the contemporary African city. Tonkiss makes the point that "people's experience of the city is not only or always determined by larger social or economic structures, but also fashioned by their individual perceptions, mental maps and spatial practices."[30] Looking at women as productive agents in the city, we see them not as victims of forces beyond their control, but as actors that manipulate and shape urban life. This approach to Johannesburg is counter-hegemonic. Scholarly writing on Johannesburg has tended to read the city from "above," using approaches that analyze the macro socioeconomic and political forces that shape urban spatial form and social relationships. Political economy analyses, for instance, explore the intersection of race and capital in the city's sociopolitical geography.[31] In the last two decades, the focus on "governance" has tended to see Johannesburg from the way in which institutions of the state and civil society are configured in the city.[32] A large focus of this literature reflects on urban service delivery and the state's responsibility toward ameliorating inequality and ending poverty.[33] While seeing like a state (to borrow from James Scott) provides a powerful explanatory framework for understanding changing political, economic, and spatial processes in the city, its vantage point hides as much as it reveals. By their very nature, analyses from above smooth over the local variations inherent in urban processes, capturing only the dominant narrative that is often presented as a coherent or uniform story. This viewpoint is unable to explain the "anomalies"—in Kuhn's[34] sense—that exist, as it erases individual experiences, particularly those of marginal groups.

The question on how to approach the city, whether from above or below, is not new to sociology—the discipline is divided into two broad camps. Soja argues that "studies of the local, the body, the streetscape, psycho-geographies of intimacy, erotic subjectivities, the micro-worlds of everyday life—[are] at the expense of understanding the structuring of the city as a whole, the more macro-view of urbanism, the political economy of the urban process."[35] While each approach provides different ways of seeing and understanding urban life, it is the polarizing way in which they are pitted against each other that remains unhelpful in understanding processes of urbanization. Short makes this point, writing that "[no] single method or approach is able to capture the complexity of the new urban forms.[36]

Rather than seeing approaches from above and below as diametrically opposed, this book explores their *interplay* through the lives of migrant women in Johannesburg. The city is, after all, the productive outcome of the interaction of broader structural processes with local (even individual) actions. Socioeconomic and political processes no doubt have an impact on the lives of men and women in the city. But no less important are their everyday actions, which reconfigure, tweak, and sometimes transform the nature of urban institutions. While building on approaches that read the city from below, my work stresses the iterative nature of the theory/practice, subjective/objective, micro/macro dualities.[37] These varied aspects of urban life are in constant dialogue, continually producing hybridized urban landscapes as they interact with each other. An analysis of the city can therefore not ignore the ongoing interactions between the self and the built environment, official and unofficial cartographies, formal and informal economies and the interaction of structure and agency. Processes of self-worlding are intertwined with broader structural processes, both of which intersect to produce new forms of urban life.

It is not just the rich detailed narratives of migrant women's experiences that are important in this study. It is how these experiences readjust our lenses to provide new tools to explain the contemporary urban condition in Johannesburg, and their implications for other cities. Migrant women's actions provide insights into the nature of the state, urban authorities, and power. They also present alternative ways of explaining analytical concepts like social mobility and governance in contemporary African cities. What we know as "the city" is thus inter-constituted by a variety of macro and micro practices in dynamic relationship to each other.

Liminality and the City

"Being in between is not good. We are somewhere and nowhere"

—A migrant from Cote d'Ivoire

The women in this study speak of seeking freedom from social oppression, yet linger amid oppression in South Africa. They long to go back

Figure 1.5   Woman in a taxi at the edge of Johannesburg's Central Business District

home to their countries of origin, yet also share a fear, and sometimes shame, of doing so with little to show for their time in Johannesburg. Women discuss the harshness of South African society, its hostility toward foreigners and their inability to participate in the economy, but also recount how they are ostracized by their own communities because they are divorced, belong to a different ethnic group, or are HIV positive. Not unlike the city dwellers of Douala and Kinshasa that Dominique Malaquais writes about,[38] the women we meet in the following pages live in flux, aspiring to be elsewhere geographically, socially, and economically, while remaining bound by their circumstances in Johannesburg. Although they are sometimes able to achieve some of their aspirations, the thresholds that prevent them from fully emerging into a higher socioeconomic status nevertheless plague them. They dwell in the liminal, a space that, as we shall see, both limits and expands their opportunities in the city.

In setting out to capture these spaces in the city that were transient, often contradictory, and not immediately visible, I was confronted with the difficulty of finding a concept that encapsulated the complexity of migrant women's lives. Sociology has a tradition of developing concepts that are "fixed and immutable" and has a historical mistrust of "inexact" concepts.[39] The unpredictability and ephemeral nature of what I was witnessing in my work made finding the vocabulary to describe it, difficult. John Law's question aptly describes my dilemma: "If much of the world is vague, diffuse or unspecific, slippery, emotional, ephemeral, elusive or indistinct, changes like a kaleidoscope, or doesn't really have much of a pattern at all, then where does this leave social science?"[40]

To some extent, the globalization literature has made this possible by describing the intensity with which goods, capital, information and people flow, in the twenty-first century.[41] Thus, appropriated from the language of globalization, Johannesburg first appears to be a "space of flows"(to borrow Castells term)—a place where people, goods, and capital move through. A closer look however, reveals a stickiness to space characterized by structural obstacles that limit migrant women's social, spatial, and economic mobility. While the imagery of flows may be apt for an elite minority, the movement of women in this book remains constrained by border regulations, bureaucratic struggles to get passports and obtain travel visas, and policing. In the celebration of the global transgressor of time and space, globalization literature misses these "in between" spaces—the interstices—which the majority, who are not part of the elite, struggle to cross.

While globalization literature refers to people who live beyond thresholds, this research is about "threshold people": ordinary women on the African continent who have in common their desire to travel, but encounter barriers. It is the thresholds encountered, negotiated, and sometimes crossed that sets the women in this book apart from the Bauman's "weightless" or Sassen's "deterritorialized" elite. Those living in society's margins call to question the appropriateness of analogies of effortless movement. A minority elite may transgress boundaries, but their experience cannot be universalized for a majority of people who remain in conditions of material poverty. Those who travel without legal documents use their wit and negotiating skills to navigate border guards or cross electric fences and crocodile infested rivers, risking their lives in the process.

If globalization's vocabulary of flows did not fully capture migrant women's experiences, Turner's concept of liminality seemed to offer a viable, if inexact alternative. When studying the Ndembu's rites of passage in northwest Zambia, Turner observed a phase where initiates no longer held their previous social status, but had not yet emerged into a new one. They were in a "limbo of statuslessness."[42] He described this phase as liminal, a word derived from the Latin word *limen,* meaning threshold.[43] Turner's limbo phase seemed to capture women's "suspension" in Johannesburg, living between and betwixt their host country and country of origin, between a romanticized past and an imagined future elsewhere.

But Turner's liminality is structured, embedded in social rituals that are located in a well-defined phase in an individual's life trajectory. In interactions with migrant women, I realized that their narratives of leaving Johannesburg to improve their social status were often more imagined than real. Women often told me they were leaving "next week" or "soon." While a few have left, I continue to see, and talk to, many of those who were leaving "next week," even five years on. Cross border women may live in limbo, but their experiences are emblematic of a paradoxical liminality—one with an uncertain life trajectory and an undefined structure.

Yet, liminality brings into relief the notion of thresholds in the city—the physical, social, and psychological boundaries that migrant women encounter in their everyday lives. These thresholds are the socially constructed boundaries between individuals and groups—gender, ethnicity, and nationality. They are the geophysical political lines drawn between two nations, such as the border between South Africa and Zimbabwe, or Botswana. Thresholds are also self-created as when women draw boundaries of safety and trust around domestic spaces. The fragility of these boundaries is evident when violence breaks through their domestic walls. Thresholds are psychological when migrant women live between a romanticized past and an imagined future elsewhere—permanently in-between. The thresholds are visible and invisible, porous and solid. These bordered lands are sometimes like prisons where women are trapped, unable to go back or move forward. Yet the liminal space between these thresholds can be empowering, providing a place of respite outside of the state's gaze. It is a space where agency and structure are in constant interrelationship. But being in permanent limbo has its price—as a place where aspirations never seem fully realized, life in the city remains perpetually incomplete.

Gendering the City

Although Johannesburg has a long history of women's migration, their urban lives have remained invisible in much of the literature. This is true not just for Johannesburg. Feminist scholars have long argued that urban studies have tended to be masculinist—eliding women's experiences and perspectives of city life.[44] Where urban women are

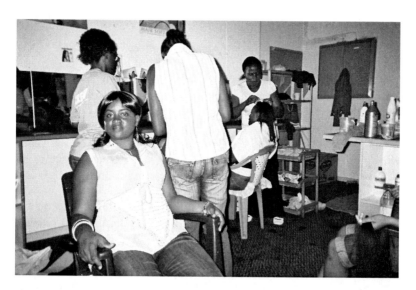

Figure 1.6 Weaving connections: Hair salons as nodes of social interaction, economic opportunity, and beauty

discussed in African scholarship, they tend to be add-ons[45] and few studies have stressed women's roles in shaping the urban environment, economy, and geography.

Drawing from authors who highlight women's agency in cities,[46] this book disrupts urban scholarships' bias toward the *Flaneur*[47]— the male stroller—choosing to privilege women's experiences in the city. The women move from the "margins to the center,"[48] beyond mere case studies, becoming sources of knowledge of the city in their own right. These writings push the boundaries of urban literature by overturning commonly held assumptions about urban economies, domestic life, and women's roles in cities. They provide important clues about the sociocultural values and stigmas that affected women. Hellmann's[49] landmark socio-anthropological study in Johannesburg, undertaken between 1933 and 1934 in what is now New Doornfontein, shows how single or widowed women were, through trade, prostitution, and domestic work, able to support their families. Similarly, Luise White's[50] historical treatise on prostitutes in colonial Nairobi shows how economically significant women were as landlords in the city, and in supporting rural economies. But this economic independence was not restricted to single women. With men's income too low to support their families, married women entered the wage economy either as businesswomen selling beer or doing domestic work for white people.[51] And, contrary to assumptions about women's passivity in making household decisions about money, they jointly, with their husbands, decided how household earnings were spent.[52]

While there are shared urban experiences between men and women, how women interpret, encounter, and navigate the city differs from the way men do this.[53] In developing its epistemological location, this work is indebted to feminist standpoint theory and the idea that women's specific gendered, class, national, and ethnic location permits a way of seeing that would not otherwise be visible from other viewpoints. In other words, women's specific locations produce particular knowledge related to their contexts and the place from which they look. It draws from Collins's thesis that black women's social locations "have created independent, oppositional yet subjugated knowledges."[54] Standpoint theory acknowledges women as "knowers," and their experiences as producing and shaping theoretical understandings of social dynamics.[55]

By analyzing migrant women's experiences through their gendered, ethnic, class, and national locations in the city, this book provides insights that explain urban processes: the nature of the state, space, and belonging in Johannesburg. Exploring women's lives allows us entry into the domestic realm and the private spaces that they occupy, which are often hidden from view in discussions on the city. Using women's life experiences as entry points, we overturn commonly held assumptions that they do not participate in or shape public life. By exploring their lives on the streets, relationships to the state and communities in the city and elsewhere, we draw a new map of the city—one in which women modify notions of the state as sovereign and highlight the diffuse nature of power and the shifting boundaries of sovereignty in the city. Their movements and relationships in the city illustrate how they produce urban spaces that are off official cartographies. Their domestic lives teach us how influential private spaces are in constructing the city's public life. Indeed, cross-border women demonstrate that they are shaping the urban environment—its politics, economy, social life, and geography.

Structure of the Book

In chapter 2, "The Notice: Rethinking Urban Governance in the Age of Mobility," we see how this dynamic relationship between the state and its legal instruments on the one hand and street sellers on the other, reconfigures the boundaries between legal and illegal practices. But rather than simply displacing city bylaws with alternative regulatory regimes, the interactions between street traders and the city police produce syncretic regulatory practices that neither replace the authority of the police nor abolish illegal street trading. By focusing on the dynamics between the state and its margins, the chapter reveals a fragile hybrid social order held in balance as much by an acknowledgment of state laws, as by a recognition of "street laws." So, while the state plays an important role in the city's present and future, looking at migrant women's everyday interactions with it allows us to see how urban dwellers continually reconfigure the nature of urban governance.

Chapter 3, "Between Pharaoh's Army and the Red Sea: Social Mobility and Social Death in the Context of Women's Migration," highlights the contradictions of migration and its productive abilities. Migration is often linked to economic and social mobility, and the promise of a better life elsewhere. Neoclassical economists speak about the migrant "maximizing utility" by moving to those regions that yield the highest income. While migrant women move to South

Africa to maximize their earning power, their decisions are embedded in cultural and institutional norms and expectations that sometimes undermine their own economic well-being. Exploring this dilemma through the experiences of a Burundian refugee Rosine, we come face-to-face with the tension between social obligations and moral pressure on the one hand, and personal well-being on the other. This tension means that women live a double life. Celebrated in their home communities because of the images and stories of success they send to family and friends left behind while living in impoverished circumstances in Johannesburg. The social pressure to be successful results in women being marooned in Johannesburg—too ashamed to go back home, and unable to move elsewhere because of lack of legal papers or money to do so. Caught in this space, migrant narratives and imaginations become productive, developing alternative ways of measuring success, and repositioning their relationships with communities in multiple sites. As what it means to be "a success" shifts over time and space, the reading of class and social hierarchies become illegible, begging us to rethink what social mobility really means when it is embedded within social norms and moral economies.

Honing in on migrant women's domestic spaces, chapter 4, "Turning the Home Inside-Out: Private Space and Everyday Politics" reveals aspects of the city often hidden from the view of policy makers and planners. Through the focus on domestic space, this chapter explores how what happens "out there" in the city affects the private sphere, and conversely how domestic practices shape urban life and relationships. Urban literature generally has tended to separate the private from the public sphere, allocating each with discreet functions and actors. Through the focus on migrant women's domestic lives we see how the separation between the public and private spheres collapse, highlighting the way city form, urban relationships, and politics run through the walls of domestic space. When Linda, a Zimbabwean woman, finds her house upside down and her sister in hospital as the victim of domestic violence, she avoids going to the police, opting to deal with the matter with her Zimbabwean network. Although this network cannot guarantee the family's safety, she makes a tacit reciprocal arrangement with them. She will not "rat" on her sister's Zimbabwean boyfriend, as this provides unwanted attention on the community, which she may need help from in the future. These sometimes unspoken, sometimes overt deals, negotiations, and relationships have consequences on the nature of the city. For an outsider, life in the city may seem unintelligible, insecure, and precarious, yet beneath the surface is a complex labyrinth of moral codes and obligations that govern urban relationships. For policy makers and planners concerned about the rule of law, urban regulations, and safety, understanding these complexities is significant in building appropriate responses to violence.

Das and Poole write, "though certain populations are pathologized through various kinds of power/knowledge practices, they do not submit to these conditions passively."[56] Chapter 5, "The Station, Camp and Refugee: Xenophobic Violence and the City" makes this evident. Exploring the xenophobic violence that broke out across South Africa in May 2008, the chapter uses three vignettes to bring to life the characters in Cleveland police station and Glenanda camp where displaced refugees were relocated. When marginalized populations brush against power, as those displaced in the xenophobic violence did, they allow us to reexamine our assumptions about the relationship between the center and the periphery. Despite the structural odds, refugees' actions prompted state response. Although this may not have always been in their favor, it illustrated how populations in the margins can change the nature of the center through their actions. Life in camps also magnifies the abstruse nature of the state's policies and actions. Yet it is not only about the state's affinity for drawing biopolitical boundaries of inclusion and exclusion. Through Sergeant Khumalo, a policeman at Cleveland police station, we yet again come face-to-face with the complexities of policing the city: the disjuncture between law and police practice; and the paradoxical nature of state power that sits both within and outside the law.

So what *is* this liminal city? The Conclusion makes the argument that we need to move beyond the simplistic dichotomies that characterize our understanding of urban processes in Johannesburg and elsewhere. In the liminal city, women's experiences defy binary, either/or logics. Their lives reveal that they are *both* legal *and* illegal; occupy *both* the official *and* unofficial city; interact in the formal and informal economic sectors; and remain rooted to their sending countries while located in Johannesburg. Yet even the "both/and" logic of women's lives does not adequately explain their lived experiences and can consequently be misleading. In many ways, the logic of living in multiple social worlds implies that these worlds are discreet, and women experience these worlds, each with its own set of norms, values, and ways of being, separately. This is not what I mean. These seemingly contradictory social worlds are experienced seamlessly, as one reality, in everyday living. In other words, the liminal city is a productive, hybrid space, where this liminal stage is, as it was in Turner's work, constantly about becoming. But unlike the clear life stages of these cultural rituals, we do not know the next stage, nor do those passing through the liminal city. Edward Said once wrote, "For an exile, habits of life, expression, or activity in the new environment inevitably occur against the memory of these things in another environment. Thus both the new and the old environments are vivid, actual, occurring together contrapuntally."[57] And it is in this sense that the chapters ahead approach city life in Johannesburg.

2

The Notice: Rethinking Urban Governance in the Age of Mobility*

Ungoverned spaces are not merely areas lacking in governance; rather, they are spaces where territorial state control has been voluntarily or involuntarily ceded to or shared with actors other than legally recognized sovereign authorities.

—Clunan and Trinkunas, 2010, 275

Introduction

All too often, policymakers and urban theorists use state weakness to explain persistent urban poverty, inequality, and conflict. Embedded in this approach is a Manichean cognitive frame that constructs African cities and urban spaces in binaries: as well-managed versus mismanaged, as formal versus informal, legal or illegal, or governed versus ungoverned. The resultant analyses suggest that the crises facing many African cities lie with state failures and governments' inability to provide services, manage diversity, and enforce the law across Africa's fast growing and fluid cities. If a weak or failed state is the basis of the urban crisis, it stands to reason that a strong state is the cornerstone of good governance, order, effective regulation, and the amelioration of poor socioeconomic conditions.

Since the late 1980s, the term "urban governance" has gained fashionable repute and a considerable following in urban studies.[1] Defined loosely as "the relationship between civil society and the state, between the rulers and the ruled, the government and the governed,"[2] governance has become a catchall concept on which varied ideological fronts have hung their strategies for better-managed cities. Set

Figure 2.1   Yeoville market and taxi rank

against growing urban poverty, inequality, collapsing infrastructure and mounting social and political crises, "good governance" has become the means through which the state builds relationships with urban actors to resolve urban problems. From the decentralization of government[3] to the devolution of decision making to communities.[4] From the democratization of local government[5] to the privatization of government and New Public Management approaches.[6] Good governance—the mantra for ailing cities across the African continent—has come to mean something for everyone.

Working from the association of strong, state-centered governance, much of the practice-oriented literature indicates that managing the urban crisis entails building a "strong" local government.[7] This state-centric understanding of urban governance works on presumptions that (a) the state is weak or absent in "ungoverned" areas, and (b) that ungoverned spaces are coterminous with the absence of regulation and collective, potentially positive, and socially legitimate enterprise. It is true that the lack of state capacity to provide urban services, poor levels of tax collection, corruption, and a weak human capital base, all lead to cities that fail to remedy crumbling infrastructure, poverty, and the growth of slums. But viewing the urban crisis as simply a function of technocratic challenges and institutional weaknesses obscures our understanding of how cities really work. Mobile populations highlight that there exist multiple governance and regulatory processes in cities, which at times compete and at other times collaborate to define urban territory.

With the state constructed as so central to urban governance in both policy and planning circles, we miss the opportunity to see how other urban actors influence the character of urban relationships and regulations. Lindell[8] writes that "an exclusive focus on the relations between civil groups and the state seems to be insufficient to capture the complexity of governance in African cities today." Indeed, by locating governance within regimes of knowledge that underpin how the state and other modern institutions order and make sense of the city, we miss the ways in which ordinary urban dwellers recalibrate the nature of the terms of engagement with the state.[9] More importantly, we are blinded to the ways in which the state itself unwittingly produces "ungovernable" cities. True, weak institutions are ill-prepared to direct planning and investments in ways that build a successful city. But the ability of state actors to position themselves both inside and outside of the law makes the state a powerful actor in producing informal and extralegal urban spaces—precisely the kind of practices that good governance aims to get rid of.

In South Africa, debates on urban governance have been dominated by literature that defines how the city *ought* to work, the kind of *formal* relationships that are needed to enhance transparency, participatory decision making and economic progress. Local government has featured prominently in these analyses, not least because of its pivotal role in transforming the racial, geographic, and economic inequalities bequeathed by apartheid. Given the magnitude of the task of restructuring the postapartheid city, it is unsurprising that "good governance" came to be equated with a "strong local government"—a government that would work with citizens to actualize its "developmental" objectives.[10] To enable this, legislation was created to transform local government from "a tier to a sphere,"[11] a status that indicated that local government was not merely the administrative arm of higher levels of government, but was also a "driver" of development in its own right.[12] If Johannesburg's success rests on the strength of the state, its failure is also traced back to the state's ideological misdirection[13] or its poorly configured administrative structures.[14]

Cross-border women's interactions with the state on Johannesburg's streets invite us to reflect upon local practices of urban regulation and political life. Their lived experiences of regulation and law enforcement on sidewalks, roadblocks, and markets confound state-centered analyses by revealing that urban governance is inter-constituted among a variety of actors in ways that blur the governed-ungoverned, legal-illegal and center-periphery boundaries. We often see a state that is present and complicit in the production of illegality, ungovernability, and informality. Through interrogating local per-formances and expressions of bureaucracy and the law, we come to understand that the state is not a homogenous site where rational bureaucratic procedures are negotiated with a participating citizenry. And underneath what often seems to be chaotic and unregulated urban spaces, are codified disciplinary and regulatory practices that are continually being made and remade. In the in-between city, polit-ical space is configured by the interaction of competing relationships in ways that both fragment and consolidate state authority.

The Notice: Law Enforcement in Johannesburg's CBD

"Your name?"
"Hannah"
"How do you spell it?"
"H-a-n-n-a-h"

H|A|N|N|A|H, the policeman wrote painstakingly.

"Your ID number?"
"I don't have a South African ID...but my passport number is A470."
"When were you born?" interrupted the officer, glaring at Hannah.
"I was born on twenty-three March, nineteen eighty-six."

|1|9|8|6|0|0|9|2|3| | | | | | There were blank spaces left in the form, *this would have to do*, I imagined the officer thinking. Few migrant women had local identity documents.

"Nationality?" he asked brusquely.

M|A|L|A|W||AN he wrote squeezing the last three letters together. The form only provides six spaces for this entry.

"Address?"
"Flat 103, Fatis Mansion Jeppe corner Harrison street Johannesburg."

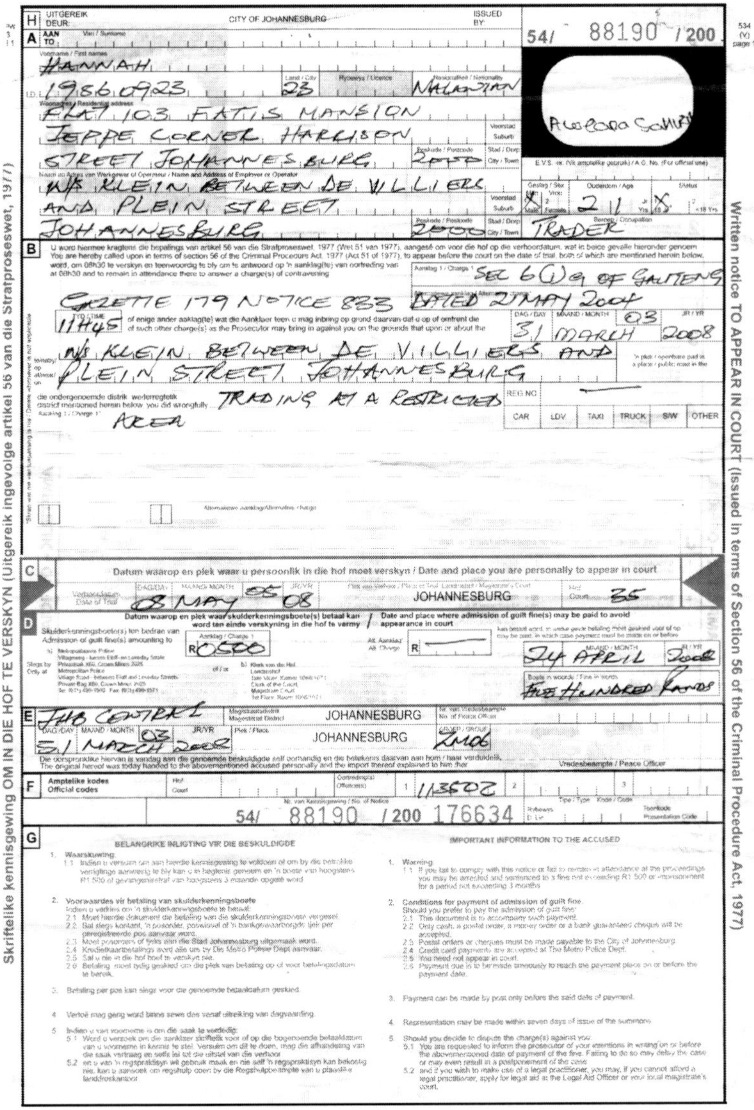

Figure 2.2 The notice

F|L|A|T| |1|0|3| |F|A|T|I|S| |M|A|N|S|I|...continued the officer. His left hand moved slowly, making jerky movements with the strokes of his pen. Each letter was carefully written in the spaces. I could not tell whether he had conviction in what he was writing, but he did seem to take pride in his written work.

Hannah and the officer stood on Klein Street, on the pedestrian path between Plein and De Villiers. It was a late summer morning on the last day of March 2008. The painstaking ritual of writing out the notice was made even more taxing by the midday sun that pounded them with inescapable heat. The area is close to the Noord street taxi rank, one of the busiest transport nodes in the city. It was easy to understand why the illicit traders set up here—the number of people passing through daily guaranteed them a ready market. Moreover, it was the end of the month, and business is always good at this time. As hoards of commuters go home with monthly earnings in their pockets, they may buy a few extra tomatoes, the pair of sunglasses they have been eyeing all month, or some imitation jewellery for a loved one. "Month-end" pronounced "maanzy-end," is a good time for traders and their customers alike.

I was sitting next to Hannah's makeshift stall when the police arrived. Their arrival had disrupted the rhythms of street banter, negotiations, and trade, causing the illegal traders to take what goods they could and run. It looked like a tornado had come through this part of Johannesburg's CBD leaving destruction in its wake. On the sidewalks were abandoned cardboard boxes. Alongside them were bright orange crates—one half-filled with maize was lying on its side with a few of the green cobs spilled over into the street. Strewn across the pavement were newspapers, plastic bags, sweets, oranges, beads, cigarettes, and cooked *mielie pap,* which the wind and people's feet were helping distribute to other parts of the city. Even though it was the last day of the month, the street was eerily quiet. On this day, the police Superintendant was issuing notices to appear in court, while his colleagues confiscated the goods left behind by some of the traders who had not been quick enough to make a clean getaway. I heard a woman crying foul, wailing that the police should have mercy on her because she was pregnant and needed the money to buy food for her children. The woman, Hannah, who was talking to the Superintendant, and a few others were the unlucky ones—caught before they could escape "the metro." That is what the traders call the Johannesburg Metropolitan Police Department—"the metro."

The written "Notice to Appear in Court (issued in terms of section 56 of the Criminal Procedure Act, 1977)" is one of the legislative mechanisms empowering the city to regulate what can or cannot be done in a given space in the municipal area. The act provides guidelines to officers who work in the policing, justice, and correctional services departments on the procedures available in criminal proceedings. Section 56 presents an officer of the law the option to hand an accused a written notice to appear in a magistrate's court. The legal document outlines that the notice should:

(a) Specify the name, the residential address, and the occupation or status of the accused;

(b) Call upon the accused to appear at a place and on a date and at a time specified in the written notice to answer a charge of having committed the offence in question;

(c) Contain an endorsement in terms of section 57 that the accused may admit his guilt in respect of the offence in question and that he may pay a stipulated fine in respect thereof without appearing in court; and

(d) Contain a certificate under the hand of the peace officer that he has handed the original of such written notice to the accused and that he has explained to the accused the import thereof (RSA, 1977).

As Hannah and the officer continued their conversation, I wondered about the bureaucratic ritual taking place before me. I am no expert on the city's geography, but I questioned whether F|L|A|T| |1|0|3| |F|A|T|I|S| |M|A|N|S|I|O|N| really did exist and whether Hannah in fact lived there. I noticed that the form had an incomplete identity number. The notice provides 13 spaces for the identity number—the officer only inserted eight digits. (South African identity documents typically have 13 digits). The first six digits are the individual's birthday—comprising the last two digits of the year of birth, month, and day—written in that order. |1|9|8|6|0|9|2|3| | | | | | was not only incorrect, but also incomplete. I wondered why the officer continued the charade of writing up the notice. Surely even he realized it would be impossible for the state to enforce illegal street trading with such incomplete information? He may have fulfilled section 56 b, c, and d of the Criminal Procedure Act, but without Hannah's residential address, and identity number, the local police would be unable to collect the fine or summon her to court.

The lives of migrant women reveal the alternative structures of governance at work on Johannesburg's streets. We come to understand that urban regulation and authority is not based solely on legal statutes and the letter of the law, but on socially embedded codes derived from relationships between actors in the state and outside of it. In the performance of local bureaucratic practices, we see how state power is configured and reconfigured, and how categories that seem so clear in official parlance—legal-illegal, official-unofficial—collapse into each other. This conception of urban regulation shifts how we understand dominant ideas of governance and presumptions that government can codify and regulate its territory in ways that result in predictable outcomes. It also reveals how those living in the city's margins are agents in the making and unmaking of the rules that shape people's relationships to the law, state, and urban territory.

The Uncaptured Urbanite[15]

Here I am nobody. I hide from the police, I hide from the South African government, I hide from my government at home. Sometimes I even hide from my own countrymen… you see, this is how I survive.

—Florence, Congolese market trader in Yeoville.

Raids against illegal trading, illegal immigrants, crime, and grime are part of Johannesburg's inner city renewal strategy. The regulation of the inner city includes on the one hand encouraging urban investment, and on the other enforcing municipal bylaws on informal trading, building codes, policing, and health regulations.[16] Ostensibly, the raid on illegal trade on Klein and Plein streets was an attempt by the city to enforce municipal bylaws. Illegal street trading presents urban government's with numerous problems.[17] City officials argue that trading on sidewalks interrupts the flow of pedestrian traffic, creating overcrowded streets that can potentially harbor criminals. Unregulated street trading also affects formal businesses in the city in ways that could result in capital flight and the loss of a tax base for the municipality.[18] The presence of informal street traders signals the inability of the city government to control its area of jurisdiction. Hygiene and public health are another concern for local authorities, and unplanned markets that have no ablution or cleaning areas present a potential health hazard for not only the traders, but also their customers.

The police officer's interaction with Hannah highlights the limits of the state to enforce local bylaws. In particular, it highlights the inadequacies of the state's disciplinary apparatus in capturing mobile populations. Hannah represents an "uncaptured urbanite,"[19] an urban migrant class that is able to use its mobility and uncertain legal status to escape some forms of state disciplinary power. Borrowing from Hydén who described the "uncaptured peasantry" as a population that derived their autonomy from the state from their reliance on subsistence farming and their ability to exit the market and state system,[20] I argue that cross-border women's ability to escape state sanction derives from their structural-legal invisibility and their agility—their capacity to move quickly and leave no bureaucratic trace of their existence in the city. My use of the term "uncaptured" does not imply that migrant women are fully autonomous from the state or other forms of social discipline. Like Hannah's encounter with the police shows, even a population that seems invisible to the state encounters state regulation in one form or another. Although the uncaptured urbanite cannot always dodge the state or live completely autonomously, away from its disciplinary powers, Florence's quote above suggests that they can and do employ tactics to "hide" from the state and other forms of social discipline.

Legal Limbo

Unwittingly, part of Hannah's illegibility is shaped by South Africa's visa, asylum-seeker and refugee protocols, but not in the way envisioned by those who made the laws ostensibly governing it. Many of the women in this study had asylum-seeker permits, which puts them in a precarious state of legal limbo. A section 22 permit allows women to work and study while awaiting their refugee status determination. While the law (the Refugees Act of 1998) indicates that status determination should take six months, in practice it takes years for the state to establish whether an asylum seeker qualifies for refugee status.[21] In the meantime, migrants are unable to access services as few employers or service providers—landlords, banks, clinics, schools—recognize their asylum-seeker papers as legal documentation.[22] This has direct and often dramatic consequences on women's everyday lives, as Rosine's story illustrates.

When Rosine and her husband arrived in Johannesburg after an arduous journey from war-torn Rwanda, she arrived convinced that she would be able to find a job that would let her raise a family. After all, South Africa was the only country she had been to where she would not be indefinitely marooned in a refugee camp. She had received an asylum-seeker permit that allowed her to live and work in the city while she waited for her refugee status to be confirmed. She soon found out however, that state recognition as an asylum seeker on paper meant little on the streets.

> Every month I have to go to renew my permit at Home Affairs. This asylum seeker permit can't allow you to get a job; can't allow you to open a bank account. Asylum seeker permits can't allow you to even to rent your own house because you have to have an address...Even the flat where we are living is in another person's name because they don't allow us to rent the house.

Fazila, an asylum seeker from the Democratic Republic of Congo shared similar frustrations "there are many, many barriers here in South Africa. First I'm not a South African; second, I don't have a document like South Africans. That's what is...not allowing me to go far."

A straightforward reading of law and policy suggests that asylum seekers should be administratively legible. The section 22 permits they receive when applying for protection not only list applicants' names but also reproduce an identity photo, thumbprint, residential address, and country of origin. However, many of these documents have outdated, incomplete, or false addresses making many in the asylum system invisible to the state, because records are poorly kept and not updated regularly. Moreover, at the macro level, the asylum system is not linked to national population registers[23] and while there are ongoing efforts by the Department of Home Affairs to link population registers with refugee and visa systems,[24] this had not yet taken effect at the time of this research. In addition, census data do not have "asylum seeker" or "undocumented migrant" categories, making it impossible to capture these populations accurately. Even if these categories existed, migrants documented and undocumented alike are unwilling to give their true details for fear of deportation or police harassment. This structural-legal invisibility works against state efforts to regulate and enforce urban laws.

From the Margins to the Center—Migrant Women as Agents in Shaping Urban Space

Although the state's legal and administrative regimes structure women's invisibility, part of their illegibility is produced by their own agency and ability to use their legal limbo and mobility to avoid state capture. As elsewhere, Africa's cities are spaces of intensified movement of goods, people, and capital in ways that continually challenge the primacy of the nation state.[25] This movement "has been appropriated as a multifaceted strategy of urban survival—accumulation, but also control."[26] In a society where "one cannot stay put in moving sands,"[27] mobility becomes a resource that not only shapes the nature of state-society relations, but is also an integral ingredient in the (re)constitution of urban territory and its regulation. In many ways, Hannah and other street traders live a nomadic life that has no fixed coordinates. Unable to open bank accounts, sign leases, or find formal work, they live as if suspended in South African society. They walk the streets with the fear that the police will detain them or that they will have to pay a bribe.[28] With their permits not recognized on Johannesburg's streets, integrating and participating in South African society is difficult. They are permanent outsiders claiming usufruct rights to the city, but unable or unwilling to root in its political and social institutions.[29] On the streets, they plan their everyday lives around being able to make a quick getaway in the event of a police raid. Like Emma, also a trader on Plein and Klein, once said to me, "I don't put all the things on display…most of the stuff is in a sack which we hide somewhere else in case the cops come, they cannot take all your things." With indeterminate coordinates, everyday survival is about mastering mobility and using it as a resource for survival. It is about how fast you can move your wares, how quickly you can change your business strategy, and how swiftly you can rebound from a "metro hit."

Coming back to the scene on Klein Street, the police officer was writing up the offense for which Hannah was being charged:

TRADING AT A RESTRICTED AREA.

The officer continued to write that Hannah had the option to pay a fine of R 500 or appear in courtroom 35 at the Johannesburg's magistrate court on May 8, 2008. When he was finished, the officer handed the notice to Hannah, and I wondered where it would end up. Maybe she would crumple it and throw it in a bin in a back-street alley? Hannah mindlessly shoved the notice into her purse as she watched policemen load her goods into the back of the police van. Making a quick calculation of her day's losses, she looked around for her friends and approached them two blocks away where they were putting what they had managed to save in the ubiquitous plastic "Ghana must go" bags.

"Eish, today they caught me...I couldn't run fast enough."

"Ag, shame! How much is your ticket for?"

"About five hundred Rands...my stuff is not even up to five hundred. That fine is just too much!"

"Just leave your stuff with them and start again my sister."

"Eish, now where shall I get money for new stock to sell tomorrow?"

Hannah did not appear in court, nor did she pay the fine. Instead, she offered me the notice to appear in court:

"Keep it as a souvenir for your research" she had said as she handed me the folded legal document.

"What if they catch you for being in contempt of court?" I protested.

"Who will catch me?" she said mockingly "Where will they find me? Who am I?" she laughed, making her point.

Resisting State Capture: Circumnavigating the City

Hannah's experience of the police raid was similar to one I had heard often about how women use multiple strategies to avoid state capture on Johannesburg's streets. Fazila, from the Democratic Republic of Congo (DRC), described her experience at a police roadblock in the city. "I do not like going down that street, Joe Slovo...you know it?...because under the bridge there are always police there. If I have to go to Bertrams, I rather take another route through Yeoville. It is very long, but it's better than meeting the police." Fazila was speaking to me in her flat in Berea, and her statement took me back to the late 1990s, when I lived in Yeoville and worked in New Doornfontein. For six years I approached the same roadblock on Harrow Road (now Joe Slovo) with dread. It was not an issue of illegality—I carried all the documents I needed to avoid deportation. When I bought a second-hand car, I made sure to carry my driver's license and the documents proving that I was the legal owner. Nevertheless, when approaching a roadblock, my heart rate would quicken, as my mind raced through the people I could contact if things went badly. In the end I opted to avoid those places where I knew the police would be, not because I had anything to hide but because an encounter with them was unpredictable—there was always the threat of incarceration and violence. Being a woman driving a private vehicle, I may have been less vulnerable than Fazila to police harassment, but the similarities in the strategies we employed raised questions about our trust in the police and perceptions of our safety at roadblocks. Migrant women's tracks in the city are formed by their knowledge of police roadblocks or presence. Unlike Benjamin's *flâneur* or De Certeau's rendition of walking in the city, women's navigation through urban space is shaped by "fear and risk."[30] Because of this, women's movements in the city avoid encounters with the police, which undermines not only the legibility of urban space, but also questions the efficacy of programs to improve urban safety.

Hannah and Fazila represent an enduring problem for urban planners and policy makers. "Bureaucracies," writes Scott, require populations that are "legible and administratively convenient."[31] Within the framework of an all-seeing, omnipresent state,[32] there is an expectation that local authorities ought to know who lives in the city and where they live; which areas in the city are growing; whether people are young or ageing; and whether communities are stable or transient. All these questions have a bearing on the kinds of urban services needed by urban dwellers, and the nature of public investment required in the city. Indeed, these normative conceptions of urban governance are dependent on the ability of city policy makers to collect and maintain bio-data and population registers,[33] because these data allow governments to plan for services such as health, education, housing, water, and sanitation. It also makes taxation, and finding criminals or law-breakers, possible. These tools of government are the technologies that the modern state has "to gain control over the transparency of the setting."[34] But migrant women's illegibility undoes the script of the all-seeing state. Urban development is predicated upon knowledge of urban populations. But the state-society interactions described above illustrate that these relationships sometimes frustrate formal urban renewal and governance efforts while generating alternative, experimental, and yet remarkably enduring systems of governance and regulation. Mobile populations, living as if "in-between" the city—present but not fully resident in it—allow us to confront the diffuse nature of state power in one of Africa's strongest states.

State as Anti-state

In classic Hobbesian readings, the modern state exercises the monopoly over violence, defining the boundary between orderly state territory, and disorderly violence "out there." In this vein, the notice symbolizes urban order, defining the boundary between a disorderly, poorly governed city, and a rule-bound, well-governed one. The police officer's lack of concern for the omission of critical information about Hannah's identity and physical address, and Hannah's indifference to the charges compel us to revisit our understanding of urban governance and state regulation. *What we see in the performance of the law is the collapse of the boundaries between disorderly and orderly, governed and ungoverned city.* Rather than a static instrument of law and order, the notice becomes a productive site of the making and unmaking of urban codes, continually revising the ways urban law is interpreted, created, and enforced on city streets. If we move beyond a state-centric model of governance, and understand urban governance as comprising competing authorities, regulatory regimes, and moral codes, we may find that it is not always in the state's interest to enhance the legibility of its urban spaces.

The Notice as the Making and Unmaking of State Law

In the bureaucratic performance of the notice, it is not just Hannah's illegibility that frustrates state laws. The state's agent, the police officer, is complicit in ceding space for the remaking of urban regulations, and the unmaking of state law. Hannah did not intend to go to court or pay the fine. In fact, she planned to be back at her trading spot on the corner of Plein and Klein Street as soon as she could find money to replenish her stock. In fact, few traders pay the fine. Fewer still try to retrieve their confiscated goods from police warehouses. The traders are aware that the police officers do not always declare all the goods they confiscate. Either they sell what they can or take what they want for themselves. Police "siphoning," as it is sometimes known, is seen as part of a street tax that traders must pay to trade. There is an informal system of exchange at work. In addition to the confiscated goods the police help themselves to, every month street traders pay a protection fee to a designated leader who in turn pays the police. While the R 50 (approximately USD 7) cannot guarantee full police protection, it allows traders some respite from constant raids. On the one hand, the police tolerate some level of illicit street trading because it gives them an added source of income through bribes and the theft of confiscated goods. On the other, informal traders are aware that they are breaking the law by trading illegally and therefore see the exchange as part of a business expense. They may complain about the unfairness of police harassment and the amounts they have to pay, but they also recognize that the police, who possess the authority to execute official regulations, also have the power to turn a blind eye to their illicit trade.

The grandstanding between Hannah and the police officer is not an isolated event, but an interaction that occurs often in the city.[35] In this fragile system of exchange, the notice becomes a space where formal rules meet informal ones. Without the backing of the state's laws and regulations, the police are powerless to enforce urban order. But *because* of their location in the state, they are able to facilitate an illicit sub-economy that allows illegal trade in the city. It is precisely because official rules occupy a position of power in state officialdom, that the police are powerful actors in the informal economy. As James Scott points out, part of the power of the official over the subaltern "is the strategic use of 'the rules'."[36] Urban authorities represent law enforcement, yet at the same time they are complicit in its undoing. In this zone, where the boundaries between legal and illegal are blurred, it is possible to see the extent to which extralegal practices run through the institutions of the state.[37]

State technologies like the notice shed light on the complex nature of relationships between the state and society in cities like Johannesburg. Indeed, if we look carefully, we can no longer speak of a city in which firm boundaries exist between official regulation and enforcement on the one hand, and unofficial and extralegal practices on the other. These practices collapse when we scrutinize local relationships between the state and urban actors. The notice may not always result in the enforcement of state law, but the ritual of officialdom endures where neither the police nor the traders take street-trading regulations seriously. Traders and officers alike may not pay much attention to the contents of the notice, but state law nevertheless remains a powerful, if symbolic instrument in shaping the nature of urban spaces.

Roadblocks as Generative Urban Spaces

Just as the notice is as much about the law as it is about its unmaking, roadblocks that are meant to make the city legible to the state become illegible and unpredictable spaces in the city. As spatial installations, police roadblocks are somewhat perplexing spaces.

I had met Sibongile, a Zimbabwean woman in her late twenties at a restaurant in Johannesburg's northern suburbs where she worked as a waiter. I invited her to join the women's visual diary group that artist Terry Kurgan and I ran with migrant women in the inner city. We provided disposable cameras to women in the group and asked them to take pictures of "a day in their lives."[38] Every two weeks the group would meet and discuss the images that the women had taken. At one of our workshops, Sibongile expressed her frustration at not being able to take pictures at the police roadblocks she encountered frequently on her way home from work.

> You know, we are supposed to show you what is happening in our lives, but there are some things that happen all the time that I cannot put on the camera. Many times when we are going home from the restaurant in the evening in a taxi, we find a lot of police roadblocks. We all know these police are just there to target Zimbabweans because they know we have just finished working and we have money from tips. I would really like to take a photograph of a policeman taking money from us, but I don't know what they will do if they catch me.

Jeganathan writes that "the checkpoint works betwixt and between the recollection and anticipation of violence."[39] On the one hand, these spatial nodes of policing are supposed to ensure the safety of urban dwellers. On the other, for migrants they evoke fear, the possibility of deportation, and violence. Police roadblocks are unpredictable. Even with your "papers" up to date and legal, passage is not guaranteed. This privilege depends on the whims of those manning the roadblock. At the roadblock you are guilty until proven innocent and your innocence is often hanging on a thread. The "wrong" word, or gesture, a smile, or even how you make eye contact with the police officer could mean trouble. Rather than enforce the law, they disrupt our understanding of the boundaries between legal and illegal, existing as they do in paradoxical zones of legality and illegality.[40] Sanford suggests that:

> the use of paramilitary forces to control checkpoints highlights the manner in which control is vested into agents who are in one sense outside

the law but in another sense are inside the law, for they are able to function precisely because they enjoy the protection of the state.[41]

It is precisely the way roadblocks break down the boundaries between legal and illegal that makes them productive spaces for the exercise of state power that is at once within and outside of the law. Migrants' everyday encounters with state agents at roadblocks, and on Johannesburg's streets highlight the paradoxical nature of state power. The governance mechanisms employed to ensure legibility, law, and order in the city, become part and parcel of breaking it. This is not simply that some corrupt agents exist within the state bureaucracy. Nor is it just a practice that deviates from a legally defined norm. Rather, this is a socially embedded if dynamic practice with its own rules and norms. Ironically, roadblocks' location within the state make extralegal activity possible. These are parts of the city where local practices of regulation take advantage of and co-opt state laws in an attempt to ensure the political and economic survival of populations."[42] So to understand governance we need to see how the state is itself implicated in the production of the "ungoverned" city.

Beyond the blurring of the lines between urban order and disorder is a more telling demonstration of the nature of the state, which moves beyond the romanticism of its "all seeing" imperative. Scott,[43] Foucault,[44] and Bauman[45] make the argument that the *raison d'être* of modern states has been to make their sovereign territory transparent, codifying it with rules and norms that shape behavior. In fact for Foucault, state disciplinary power is so pervasive in our everyday lives that we live in a panopticon society, where not just surveillance, but even the *idea* of surveillance controls how people behave.[46]

Yet, by examining local instances of the state's interactions with urban dwellers, we unsettle these idealized renditions of the state's disciplinary reach. It is not simply that the state is complicit in the illegibility of mobile populations or the undermining of its own legal frameworks. It is that there are parts of the state that flagrantly thrive on such illegibility. Landau puts it this way "We begin to see that this mobility is not so much a threat to current state practice. Indeed…African states rarely have the capacity and often not even the desire to regulate and fix their populations."[47] If we move beyond the normative cloak around which we dress the state, we realize that the threat of "illegibility" does not shake the foundations on which it stands. In fact the opposite is true. By willfully obfuscating migrant identities on a legal form and taking advantage of the fact that many of them do not have identity

Figure 2.3   Johannesburg Central Business District, opportunity and opportunism

documents that are traceable in the legal system, the police become coconspirators in creating an invisible population. This may undermine the effectiveness of the law. But it does not shatter the state's symbolic power as an institution that can mete out violence. Women traders dread the thought of appearing in court, deportation, and encounters with state authorities, as much as they articulate their frustration with police corruption. Indeed it is this unique location that the state occupies as a "double agent"—both inside and outside of the law—that guarantees its continued presence as significant actor in shaping urban spaces.

Inter-constituted Urban Governance

Even as the liminal city creates a dislocated urban class, their presence has far-reaching consequences on the government's urban renewal strategies, and urban governance more generally. Migrant women are both objects and agents of urban regeneration programs, actively shaping their outcomes. On the streets, women's interactions with the state produce hybrid local practices, where competing authorities and regulatory practices influence the outcomes of regeneration efforts in unforeseeable ways. These outcomes shift how we understand governance, particularly presumptions that government can codify and regulate its territory. Migrant women illustrate that urban space should be understood as configured by the interrelationship of competing authorities operating on different moral codes.

Although these street practices are, according to state law, illegal and corrupt, there is a moral discourse that justifies their necessity as everyday means of survival. During my interviews I would sometimes ask women whether they felt guilty for trading illegally and bribing police officers. Ruth, a shy and mostly law-abiding woman said quietly, "Everybody does it. And anyway how would I feed my child if I did not have my business?...I am not selling drugs, just earrings. According to God, I am not breaking the law." Making similar justifications, Jean, a Cameroonian, said to me that "killing is a crime, selling my body is a crime, selling clothes or food to eat is not a crime. I am trying to be a good woman and support myself and my family." Supporting one's family is associated with being a "good woman" and in a sense this is a noble and moral thing to do. For, as long as a boundary considered immoral—such as killing another being, or prostitution—is not crossed, breaking a bylaw to meet social obligations is an acceptable practice. Writing about practices of corruption in Nigeria, Smith explains that everyday corruption makes "moral sense" when people are meeting their social obligations to kin or friends.[48] "Many instances...people are doing what seems right, necessary, or imperative to fulfil their social obligations."[49] Indeed, everyday circuits of exchange are located within defined cultural norms and moral boundaries. They are technically illegal, but are infused with a rich "moral pulse which regulates recognized codes of conduct, expectations of appropriate behavior and patterns of conflict mediation."[50] In these everyday interactions, the law seems too abstract and disconnected from what is considered necessary and socially acceptable.[51]

The local regulatory practices I had witnessed between Hannah and the police officer highlight the dynamic and productive nature of urban regulation. Governance and the law are not static. In fact, legal instruments like the notice are part and parcel of the production of a hybrid regulatory system created not just by the formalism of state rules and regulations, but also by the intersection of these rules with the alternative logics of non-state actors. In the survival pressures of everyday life, they become productive sites for the creation of new urban codes and regulatory systems. In this context, regimes of urban practice cannot assume the supremacy of the state or the location of power in "one individual or group exercising power over another."[52] Nor can we presume the dominance of extralegal practices. Writing about governance and security, Clunan points out that

> the state is joined by a number of other actors, benign and malign, who sometimes compete and sometimes collaborate in providing governance and security through bottom-up and horizontal forms of organization. In many places, states are themselves a main contributor to insecurity at the human and global levels.[53]

What we see is the creation of hybrid practices that meld official with unofficial, formal with informal, legal with illegal. In the end,

Figure 2.4   On the corner of Plein and Klein

the outcomes make it impossible to disentangle the "official" from the "unofficial" city. In this hybrid and productive landscape, the nature of urban governance shifts as state power is subverted, reconfigured and reinforced in uneven and arbitrary ways.

Through migrant women's experiences, we begin to understand urban governance as comprising multiple moral and regulatory codes that are inseparably bound together. So when state-centered models of urban governance read urban space through contours of power that define the state as *the* actor that shapes, controls, and determines spatial hierarchies, they fail to reveal how everyday spatial practices diffuse and fragment state power in ways that create alternative and enduring, albeit fragile power regimes. Moreover, condemning unofficial practices as resulting from ineffective enforcement or weak local states, overlooks the dynamic and inter-constitutive relationship between state and society. To be sure, strengthening state enforcement agencies, rooting out corruption, and improving systems of registering migrants will go toward improving the state's control over the inner city. But this is not entirely up to the state. There are other social norms, values, and codes that determine acceptable and disagreeable behavior, which compete alongside official behavioral codes.

Conclusion

But what do these dynamic local practices mean for urban planning, investment, and regulation in cities like Johannesburg? At a policy level we need to recognize that multiple authorities shape urban development, access to services, and forms of disciplinary practices. This recognition would entail understanding the incentives, social obligations, and rationalities of different urban actors and using this "intelligence" to develop strategies for change. In certain parts of the city, this may mean working with local institutions that are considered socially legitimate, but not necessarily linked to the state. If policy makers retain a commitment to normative principles of what governments in the city should look like, they need to consider and address the fact that state agents are social actors. While addressing corruption, improving the conditions of service, and career opportunities within state bureaucracies may strengthen the state's regulatory capacity, it is still essential to acknowledge that state agents are embedded in social obligations and moral codes that are not always bound by material needs. Understanding what these incentives and disciplinary codes are is critical, if any form of urban transformation is to take place.

On an analytical level, the language of "good governance" and its Manichean "good" versus "bad" outlook ignores the potential opportunities that emerge out of structural failures and economic need. This is not to deny that some forms of sociality can make those at the margins of society even more vulnerable. But there are instances where these social experiments serve to expand spaces of inclusion in the city, where mechanisms within the formal system fail to do so.

As authors elsewhere show, there is often a disjuncture between state intentions and actual outcomes.[54] Policy makers' efforts to control urban spaces are often confounded by the actions of urban dwellers.[55] The enduring faith in statutes and law enforcement seems even more misplaced when we consider urban areas with mobile populations. At a theoretical level, the state faces a two-sided challenge. On the one hand, we see how its agents undermine its legal frameworks. On the other, we confront the reality that migrants are not just the victims of a predatory state, but also play an active role in shaping urban regulations. Migrant women's experiences allow us to see how those at the margins influence urban governance. Governance is not simply the realm of the state, it is co-constructed by the state and other actors. Yet, migrants' power does not lie in the politics of representation or in social movements, but in the everyday tactics they employ. Their day-to-day choices to not go to court, to take advantage of their legal invisibility, their ongoing negotiations with police, and their ways of circumnavigating the city highlight a sense of power that we do not normally associate with people at the political margins of society.

3

Between Pharaoh's Army and the Red Sea: Social Mobility and Social Death in the Context of Women's Migration

Going home is like being between Pharaoh's army and the Red Sea. You hope to God that there is a rescue ship. If God does not answer your prayers, you have only one choice—to negotiate with the army. Jumping in the Red Sea is sure death...The Red Sea is going back home with nothing in your hands; that is social death.

—*Ayo, Nigerian migrant*

A non-impoverished life means the freedom "to appear in public without shame"[1]

Introduction

It was around 6.30 in the morning when my cell phone started ringing. Still half asleep I picked it up, trying to remember where my family was, if anyone was travelling or sick, and dreading the emergency that waited on the other end. Rosine's distressed voice interrupted my thoughts. She was calling from the street where, until a few hours before, she had had an flat. She and her three children had been evicted and their belongings were spewed on the pavement. The building superintendent had not given her enough time to pack things into bags. Now homeless and desperate, she needed shelter.

The last few months had been difficult for Rosine. Her husband, who had deserted her and his children, was in hospital with pancreatic cancer. She made a living selling bananas, running a telephone line and illegally subletting a room in her two-bedroom Yeoville flat. But even when times were good, she could not meet the costs of feeding, clothing, and taking her children to school. Her husband no longer contributed to the household. Even before he fell sick, they were having difficulties in their marriage and he had moved out of the house to live with his father and brother. He had made it clear to his children that their mother Rosine was inferior, a "cockroach," as he often called her—a term redolent of the mass killings of Tutsis in the Rwandan genocide. A few hours later, we sat at the *Nandos*, a fast food chicken restaurant on Raleigh street, the heart of Yeoville's commercial strip. Rosine had convinced her two older children to go to school. The younger one, who shadowed his mother, was uncharacteristically silent, eating quietly in his chair. As she ate, Rosine and I weighed her options. Her in-laws in Rosettenville were not one of them. She had married a man from Rwanda and she was Burundian, and over the course of the years, their relationship had slowly disintegrated as a result of ethnic pressures. "But surely they will take care of the children, I said." "Yes, these are their children. But if they take my children, I will have nothing left. I may never see them again." A few months before, I had found a shelter willing to take her and her children. She and I had driven to the city's outskirts to see it. Rosine seemed reluctant to move her life there, expressing concerns about being away from her support network and her church. We had visited the shelter a few months after the xenophobic violence had spread across townships in cities across South Africa. She had felt safer in inner city Johannesburg where many of the inhabitants were foreigners. She worried that moving to a township (where the majority were South Africans) would make her and her children a target of antiforeigner violence. The children's schooling would also be affected. With few options left, I asked her if she would consider going back home, to Burundi. I pushed a little, "What if money for transport and your in-laws were not a problem, would you consider going back?" I knew that she had recently made contact with her mother and sister in Burundi, after years of not knowing where they were. "Burundi was now rebuilding," she had told me, the war was over and there seemed to be no immediate threat to her life.

"But if I go, what will I show them? How will I go with nothing?"

"What do you mean nothing?" I said. "You have your children, and your experience."

"You don't understand," she laughed bitterly, "I will be a failure, I will be nobody because I do not have money to help people at home, to help even myself and my kids."

Rosine's fear about going home as a "nobody" is common amongst migrants. As Ayo from Nigeria put it "going home with nothing in your hands is social death…there is no way I am going home to tell my parents I came empty handed. Do you want me to shame my family?" In the social sciences, the term "social death" is associated with the process of dehumanizing individuals, negating them as social beings.[2] It manifests violently in situations of genocide, apartheid, and slavery, but can also refer to processes of excommunicating or marginalizing people from their communities.[3] Ayo and Rosine would rather live in Johannesburg's misery than experience the humiliation of being labeled worthless by their sending communities. Social death amounts to being a "nobody"—less than human—and this castigation seems far worse than the troubles women face in their everyday struggles in Johannesburg.

Whether they leave their countries for economic reasons, or as refugees fleeing wars, going back home is always complicated by assumptions that the migrant's inevitable success will benefit the family and community left behind. Like Ayo's quote about being between Pharaoh's army and the Red Sea, even in the face of significant hardship in the host country, returning home is almost always not an option if one is unable to fulfill material obligations to family. Migration, whether made possible by familial resources or not, is a communal process that is located in a "migration economy" where systems of exchange, reciprocity, and status circulate. In this context, going back home without fulfilling familial expectations amounts to being a "nobody." The personal shame, and the shame upon the family that this represents is considered so grave that women are prepared to live in alarmingly difficult conditions in Johannesburg, or go through great lengths to weave tales of their success.

My conversations with Rosine and Ayo resonate with a long-standing debate about the socioeconomic opportunities that migration presents to those who move and their families. Although much is written about why people move, analysts have tended to focus on the movement of male labor.[4] Where women are discussed, it is often as passive participants in the process who are "left behind" or "tag alongside" their male counterparts.[5] The surge of research on gender and migration since the 1990s has began to overturn this bias.[6] Much of what is written about women's mobility in southern Africa has been descriptive, filling the gaps in our knowledge of how they move, their motivations, the livelihoods they draw from such mobility, and the differences in migration experiences between men and women.[7] Women's mobility has drawn attention to aspects of migration that economic theories have previously ignored or deemed unimportant, focusing as they do on the economic costs and benefits of mobility. Although scholars who study women's mobility do not discard the importance of economic calculations, their research shows that social ties greatly influence where and whether women move.[8] Because of women's centrality in social networks, their decision to move is often linked to their roles in social networks, and their desire to be considered important actors in their community.[9] It is not that social standing is unimportant for male migrants, indeed ethnographic research shows that men are concerned by how they are perceived in their communities.[10] But the social aspects of migration were not the focus of the dominant labor migration literature, and highlighting women's mobility has provided the opportunity for complicating the economistic narrative. Given that women's migration in sub-Saharan Africa accounted for 47.2 percent of total migration in 2000,[11] and there is evidence to show that they are migrating independently of their spouses or male guardians,[12] it is essential that we understand how mobility impacts their life trajectories. While the scale of female migration is itself significant, the numbers alone do not tell us about women migrants' life chances, and the possibilities they have of upward social mobility.

By interrogating how migrant women, moving from other African countries to South Africa, understand their own social mobility—we explore what it means to be respectable, where obligations lie, and what success may ultimately mean. Women's upward mobility moves beyond conventional indicators of success and well-being—like income, education, and health—revealing a conception of success that is embedded in collective cultural practices and moral discourses. Looking at the moral and social measures of success does not mean that objective measures like education, income, and health do not matter. Indeed, such achievements as graduating from university or getting a job are celebrated as important milestones for the individual. But they are more than just individual milestones, these achievements are embedded in social values and obligations to kin and the community. Women's discussions of moving to Johannesburg show

how these cultural values are internalized and codified in ways that shape their everyday behavior in the city. To be a "good" woman, to rise up the social hierarchy, requires accumulating material wealth in ways that will improve their well-being and that of the family left behind. If income opportunities or material wealth are not accessible, they live dual lives. On the one hand, creating appearances of success back home, while on the other barely holding it together in Johannesburg.[13] Migration provides a lens through which the complex and contradictory processes of "success" can be analyzed and understood—drawing attention to the fact that what it means is not always so clear in real life.

Improving Whose Life? Migration and Social Mobility

The notion of being "mobile" carries connotations of improvement, escape from poverty, modernity, and even success. Migration literature makes the assumption that people's decision to move is linked to opportunities for this kind of upward mobility. Indeed, migration across the world is replete with narratives that evoke heroic and successful endeavors, that improve the life chances of the émigré and his/her family. In fact, recent debates on migration and remittances are embedded in these assumptions. That the income from migration helps reduce poverty; provides capital for small-scale enterprises; provides income for consumption during times of crisis, and leads to increased household investment in education and health in migrants' home countries.[14] Writing for the World Bank, Ratha and Shaw presume that these investments lead to uplifting the community and, eventually, to the community's upward social mobility.[15]

For neoclassical economists, wage differentials between regions constitute the most important causal factor for human mobility. Economists in this school argue that individuals move to "maximize utility" by going to areas where they are most likely to draw the highest income, and have the greatest chances of improving their economic status.[16] Migrants are located in an "immigration market."[17] Using the information available they weigh the costs and benefits of moving, comparing different possible destinations, and selecting the one offering the highest wages. Todaro's Migration Model makes the primacy of the economic argument clear. He starts from the assumption that

> migration is primarily an economic phenomenon which for the individual migrant can be a quite rational decision...the fundamental premise is that migrants consider various labor market opportunities available to them, as between rural and urban sectors, and choose the one which maximizes their expected gains from migration.[18]

Through higher wages, migrants experience upward social mobility as they invest in goods and services such as education, health, and economic investments that allow them to improve their life trajectories.

These viewpoints are not without their critics. First, claims that remittances lead to development are contested and debates abound as to whether remittances can replace development aid and public investment in social and economic infrastructure. Further, this point of view remains relatively silent on the quality of life and dignity of the migrants who send money home. In other words, it fails to consider the personal consequences of remitting for the senders.[19] Moreover, even fewer studies look critically at how migrants define their own social mobility in the context of the real and perceived obligations toward sending families and communities.[20] Second, Castles and Miller[21] argue that neoclassicists' economistic explanatory frameworks overshadow other noneconomic reasons for why people move. Uni-dimensional income measures such as the GNP fail to capture nonmeasureable variables that enable upward social mobility.[22] Aggregated income measures are also silent on the nature of distribution within households and countries, and are unable to provide an explanatory framework for why inequality exists. Income measures also say little of the nature of work and the conditions of the worker. Nobel Prize–winning economist Amartya Sen argues that the measure of social well-being is not simply about the income earned but also about the capabilities—political freedom, economic facilities, social opportunities, socioeconomic rights, and deliberative democracy—that allow an individual to lead the life they value and have reason to value.[23] This is not to deny the importance of income measures. Indeed, both Sen[24] and Nussbaum[25] point out that income remains an important measure of social well-being, but on its own it is unable to tell us the quality of lives people lead. In Sen's words, "Income may be the most prominent means for a good life without deprivation, but it is not the only influence on the lives we can lead...We must look at impoverished lives, and not just at depleted wallets."[26]

Being a Nobody: The Social Embeddedness of Success

Sen's approach—to look at a life without deprivation as the freedom to lead the life you value and have reason to value—draws on the importance of considering individuals' broader socioeconomic and political contexts in understanding poverty. Although freedom is an important aspect of this definition, I am drawn to the *embeddedness* of social mobility in the social values and practices of one's community. What this means is that definitions of success/progress/development are contextual and cannot be separated from the sociocultural institutions that shape people's everyday lives. The idea that people's decisions are influenced by their social contexts is not new. Curran and Saguy[27] show that the nature of migrants' ties and their positions in social networks influence their remittance behavior. Cultural and social relationships will affect how people save, remit, what they buy, and even how much they send back home. Economic behavior is thus embedded in complex sociocultural contexts.[28] Even some economists admit that social context matters. Granovetter's[29] work on individuals' market behavior, makes the point that decisions and preferences are shaped by social relations. Unlike the presumptions that inform neoclassical economists, he shows that individuals rarely act autonomously in their own self-interest.[30] By questioning the materialist and individualistic foundations that link migration solely to improved economic well-being for the migrant, this chapter opens up the possibility of seeing social mobility beyond the measure of wealth or income alone, allowing us to explore how social and cultural institutions shape not only meanings of success but also its everyday manifestations.

Looking at women migrants shows that conceptions of social mobility are located within a social system of reciprocity and responsibility toward kin and community. Nussbaum[31] reminds us that human striving consists of multiple elements, which need to be understood within everyday relationships. To understand this, let us dwell on Rosine's story for a moment, considering where she is located in her community, and how this affects both her well-being and decisions. Despite multiple attempts to make a living, she has few sustainable income opportunities in Johannesburg. Part of the reason for this is her refugee status, which works against her finding work. But as already discussed, migrants live in a world not structured by law alone. Being Burundian, and married to a Rwandan from a different ethnic group, taps into long-standing ethnic feuds and differences that make her vulnerable to domestic violence and abuse. After her husband abandoned the family, she not only lost potential income, but also bore an unequal burden in raising their children.

Theoretically, Rosine could have pursued child support through the courts, but a combination of a lack of knowledge of the resources available to her, her fear of the state and being deported, and her reliance on her community (which may ostracize her for sending her husband to court) prevented her from doing so. Instead, she opted to use mediators through her church and community to smoothen her relationship with her husband and obtain some support. An effort that bore little fruit. Her husband's death did not heal the rift between her family and his. The fear that her in-laws might take away her children prevented her from asking them for help. Finally we see how the social pressure to "succeed" and the shame of returning home a nobody mean that Rosine remains in Johannesburg in these precarious and impoverished conditions. Rosine is a second-class citizen: her nationality; ethnicity; and gender mean that she has unequal rights to work, lacks state protection, and has no access to justice. Despite living under these conditions, going home is not an option for her for fear of being branded a failure. To be sure, there are other reasons that make going back home difficult. There is the fear and trauma of returning to a country that she fled because of war. There are unknown factors—would she be able to establish a social network? Would her children find good schools? Would she find means for supporting them? The issue of going back home raises many practical and emotional questions. Yet it was the fear of going back "a nobody" that weighed on Rosine's mind when we spoke about returning to Burundi.

Rosine's decisions in the city are influenced both by her structural location in South Africa's legal framework and economy, and the values of the community she belongs to. Being in legal limbo no doubt affects how she relates to the law, accesses jobs, housing, and other urban services. But this is compounded by her obligations and responsibilities to kin and social networks in Burundi and Johannesburg. In the end, being a nobody both in a legal and social sense, keeps her in this liminal state not only unable to go back home but also incapable of rising up the socioeconomic ladder in Johannesburg.

The Contradictions of "Success"

Rosine's experience shows us that social mobility is linked to individuals' relationships to, and social standing in the community as much as it is determined by their economic status. Yet if notions of success and doing well are linked to the social values and aspirations of your social networks, we are likely to encounter what Nussbaum calls "adaptive preferences."[32] This is a situation where people living in deprivation adjust their horizons and aspirations to adapt to their "second-class status."[33] Julius Wilson makes a similar argument elsewhere about the "underclass," pointing out that in predominantly lower-class and poor American neighborhoods, people's capacity to move out of their situations of poverty is significantly reduced because they lack the appropriate role models to aspire toward.[34]

Although measures of well-being must include participation in social relations and the ability to be in public without shame,[35] they cannot be divorced from objective criteria such as income, education, and health. Subjective or even socially embedded notions of success are therefore not always accurate measures of mobility. Rosine's aspiration to be someone in her community inadvertently further jeopardizes her family's already precarious economic position because it limits the options she has to get out of a difficult situation (for example the possibility of going home). She may "save face" by not going home, but saving face does not translate into a safe home for her children, a steady job, or food on the table. Migrant women's locations at the margins of the city's legal and economic structures also limit their capabilities. But when their marginality intersects with their social obligations and aspirations, the notion of success becomes complex and contradictory. While I do not deny that there is a tendency toward adaptive preferences, migrant women's experiences show that they have not necessarily "settled" into their poverty. They dream of prosperity, possibly finishing school, building homes, and travelling the world. Nevertheless, because women's standing in the communities they have left behind is at times more important than their own material well-being, their aspirations to be respected as upstanding community members back home sometimes result in their material impoverishment in Johannesburg. Juggling their obligations in these multiple locations, women project multiple life trajectories concurrently. To use Adam Smith's words, while they may appear to be without shame back home, they feel the shame of failure in Johannesburg. In the context of migration, notions of social mobility, well-being, and "doing well" are complicated and contradictory. As the following sections show, women construct false narratives of their great accomplishments in Johannesburg while hiding their real living conditions from kin and friends in their countries of origin. At times, they remit what little money they have while struggling to put food on the table in Johannesburg. These projections of success, while at odds with their everyday experiences, are integral to maintaining their social standing in their communities. And while it undermines their material security, social respect and recognition is, ironically, an important aspect of their social mobility.

Migrant Livelihoods in Johannesburg

Women's experiences forging a livelihood highlight how restrictions in South Africa impact the work opportunities available to them. After arriving in Johannesburg, women face numerous legal and economic obstacles finding work. Their statuses as nonnationals, and their vulnerability to criminals and the police on the street frustrate their efforts to participate in South Africa's economy. Chipo from Bulawayo remembers how she imagined her life in Johannesburg, and how different the city's reality was when she arrived:

> My picture of Johannesburg was...I was expecting a very beautiful country with a lot more opportunities than in Zimbabwe; a place where I could make a lot of money and call for my son. Unfortunately, the reality is different in the sense that life is very difficult and for that reason I cannot ask my son to join me here. I prefer to take care of him in Zimbabwe and every month I send some money to my mother for food and other things. But I am telling you this is a very huge responsibility for me, given that I am very limited financially.

With few opportunities in the formal economic sector, many women turn to informal trading to support themselves and their families. According to a Wits-IFAS-Tufts 2006 survey[36] conducted in Johannesburg of cross-border migrant populations without access to formal job opportunities, migrants, both men and women, are equally likely to be involved in petty trading and hawking when they first arrive in South Africa. In another study, the Southern African Migration Project (SAMP) found that women were just as likely to be entrepreneurial as their male counterparts.[37] These studies overturn beliefs that men are more likely to be involved in activities that "matter" while women participate in domestic activities. Moreover, their economic activities move beyond the commodification of domestic work typical of the women that Bozzoli[38] and White[39] write about in their research. Rather, the informal and small business sector provides women a range of retail opportunities. In addition to selling vegetables and other household and beauty products, they own or work in migrant owned hair and beauty salons, restaurants and Internet cafés. Those with capital enter the import-export business, trading arts and crafts, second-hand clothing, and household goods. But success in these enterprises is dependent on access to capital, and women often have to rely on their family networks to raise funds, as May, a 21-year-old Zambian woman, explains:

> Currently, I do small personal business at my sister's place, such as plaiting hair and other jobs related to women's beauty. Apart from that, I do also import and export business; I go sometimes to Zambia to sell clothes with the money I receive from my brother who lives in the US. I have also a boyfriend from the Democratic Republic of Congo; he is among those who gives me money for my business. He is also a refugee in SA.

Cross-border trading seems to be a niche that migrant women occupy, and other studies corroborate this. Research by SAMP in Lesotho, Zimbabwe, and Mozambique in 1997 showed that women dominate cross-border trading.[40] In personal communication, Donatien Dibwe, professor at University of Lubumbashi, told me about how Congolese women traders dominate the import trade between the Middle East and the Democratic Republic of Congo (DRC), arguing that this has shifted family dynamics, especially with the loss of male work on the mines in Eastern DRC. Women's businesses vary in scale and in the levels of capital required. Some are more successful than others, and cannot be compared to very small survivalist businesses. May's various business initiatives—a hair and beauty salon, the import and export of clothes—show the resourceful ways in which women attempt to create a livelihood. But the success or failure of these initiatives is in some way linked to external support and access to cheap goods and capital. Jinnah[41] points to the strategic importance of local and international social networks for information, access to cheap goods, and credit for the success of Somali businesses. May's brother and boyfriend provide much-needed finances that allow her to support her export business. While they may have the business ideas, not all women have access to networks and funds to invest in their businesses.

Migrant women's business trajectories and levels of success are mixed. Although all the women interviewed in this study were involved in small businesses, mostly petty trade selling vegetables, hair products, or other small items at council markets or on the street, their success levels varied. Many just managed to make ends meet in the precarious informal economy. However, over the three years that I have been visiting and talking to these women, some businesses have grown remarkably. Betty, a 30-year-old Kenyan woman who owns a hair dressing salon in the Yeoville market, began her business as a single-woman operation, working on the sidewalk, hassling for street customers. As her clientele grew, she found premises in the market and hired two other women, a Tanzanian woman, and her own sister whom she "sent for" from Kenya. She had also saved enough money to invest in hair-drying equipment and to fit wash basins in her shop. Two years later, her sister was running the salon while Betty managed her import-export business between Zambia, Kenya, and Tanzania.

While there are success stories like Betty's, many of the women that I interviewed say that Johannesburg has not turned out as they imagined. Neema, a Tanzanian woman with two children, explains:

> Since 2003, I started a small business in Hillbrow where I live. I sell clothes, ladies bags, and some other small stuff. But the money I make is not enough...I have to send my first born who is two years old to the crèche and every month I pay R 250 for her. My husband and I have to pay R 1600 every month for the rent. My last born doesn't have someone who can look after her and I cannot send her to the crèche because of the lack of money.

On the one hand, we see an opening up of women's work in a range of informal economic activities, on the other there is the phenomenon of "brain waste." Brain waste occurs where skilled migrants are unable to obtain jobs commensurate with their professional skills and qualifications. In these situations, the obstacles around obtaining work permits and translating qualifications into the South African environment, force migrants into semiskilled or unskilled work. This is by no means peculiar to South Africa; in 2008 it was estimated that in the United States, more than 1.3 million skilled university-educated immigrants worked in unskilled jobs.[42] In objective terms, brain waste seems to indicate downward mobility. Like Flore, a qualified nurse from Cameroon who worked as a nurse at a public hospital in her country. She came to South Africa because she saw how many of her friends in the health profession, working outside Cameroon, were able to build houses and buy cars for their families back home. Without legal documents and South African qualifications she was unable to find work as a nurse. Her only option she says, was to start a business of her own.

> I do it [street trading] because I do not have choice; this is not what I want. Let me tell you something: if you are running a business that you do not like, even if you are making money, you cannot be happy. This is what I always feel in this country. Because this is not a kind of business that I am supposed to do; my place is in hospitals, helping people. Sometimes I cry in the market simply because I don't believe what I have become. In my country, I couldn't do such business.

Flore explains the difficulties she has registering in the South African Nursing Council with her foreign qualifications. She argues that obtaining a South African certificate is not a viable option given her responsibilities to her family in Johannesburg and at home. Yet, remarkably, she has managed to obtain some work as a translator in public hospitals.

> I work also part-time in different public hospitals, not as a nurse but as interpreter for HIV/AIDS patients. There is a French organization dealing with HIV/AIDS patients. As a member of this organization I used to interpret for doctors and patients, especially from the rest of the continent, because I can speak English and understand French. Usually, I deal with patients from Francophone countries. I receive small money just for the transport. The most important thing in this job is it allows me to keep contact with my profession. I learn so many things about patients; it is very helpful.

If the lack of entry into formal employment in South Africa, and pressure from families back home to provide material support, has led women into creating their own work, many seem discontented with the levels of their success and professional fulfillment. Only a handful of them seem to have succeeded in growing their businesses. The precarious nature of the informal sector and their legal status, and the difficulties translating foreign qualifications, reduce their earning capabilities, making economic success a distant dream.

Barriers into the labor market reinforce women's liminal condition in Johannesburg. The possibility of women investing in the city and seeing themselves as part of its future diminish with limited work opportunities and precarious earning opportunities. Moreover, women are always striving to meet goals that seem beyond their reach, even as they redefine meanings of success in the city. Stuck between meeting their goals and their social obligations, women remain caught in a revolving door, unable to break through the threshold, yet not willing to quit because of the social consequences.

Becoming a "Real" Woman—Migration and Social Recognition

One of the questions that women's migration to Johannesburg raises is why, despite their difficult experiences, do they continue to stay in Johannesburg, particularly when going back home is an option? The answer to this lies less in economic explanations than in the social pressures that migrants face. More and more, we are beginning to understand the role that mobility plays as a rite of passage. Wentzel, Viljoen, and Kok[43] write how this is true of Mozambican migrants whose migration to Johannesburg allows them to transition from "boys to men." Other authors[44] show how migration has become the functional equivalent of traditional ceremonies of rites of passage in the DRC. In continuing with the imagery of ritual, Johannesburg has to be seen as the liminal space, a place where the émigré transforms or at least expects to transform their social status. A place where migrant women become "real women." The appearance of success, and the promises of income transfers to families make migrant women's rise up the social hierarchy a possibility. It is in this context that geographic mobility becomes part of a process of social mobility. Yet what "growing up," becoming "a real woman," or achieving "success" mean, is fluid, allowing social mobility to be made and remade in everyday life.

Women's movement occurs in the face of significant legal obstacles. Such movements may also entail considerable material, emotional, and sometimes physical costs. Further, the material rewards in Johannesburg are not guaranteed and many struggle to make a decent livelihood. As Sibongile, a Zimbabwean woman said, "Here we live like dogs, sharing a room with so many people…strangers who can take your things. It is not like home, where you are safe and you have your own space. We can be poor there, but at least we live like human beings." Yet, despite the hardship and numerous setbacks, women remain in the city, and social pressure, both perceived and real, seems to play a significant role in explaining why. Economic models alone cannot explain why women continue to remain in situations that do not result in "optimal" economic returns. While economic calculations are an important factor in decision making, strong kinship ties and communal sanctions on "expected" behavior sometimes override what would appear to be viable decisions. Women are actors in social institutions that judge them heavily if they have not fulfilled community expectations. The resulting shame of this failure seems so grave that they would rather "live like dogs" than go back home.

When speaking to migrant women, I often asked why they had moved to Johannesburg. Responses like "to make money," "to escape war," "to escape economic crises," or even "to look for better opportunities" fit within well-known explanations of migration. A set of push factors cause people to leave their homes, and pull factors attract them to greener pastures.[45] But it was responses such as "to become independent," "to become a real woman," or "to grow up" that piqued my interest. Not only did these responses not fit standard push-pull explanatory frameworks, but it was not always clear what a "real," "independent," or "grown" woman meant and how migration aided this social process. This is not to mean that the push-pull schema does not apply to women's decisions to move. Rather, it is to suggest that there are also social motivators that are not always factored into economic calculations, which compel people to move. In making sense of their mobility, women use language and metaphors that suggest that migration is embedded in social values and expectation and, in some cases, is also an important rite of passage.

Women move to South Africa in the hope of growing their wealth and becoming important social actors in society—particularly in their communities back home. While economic reasons often seem to underpin their mobility, migration cannot be fully understood without considering women's social positions. As Esperance, a 26-year-old woman from the DRC points out:

> As you know yourself, in DRC, people have a good image of South Africa because they consider it like a place where there are a lot of opportunities, where people can make money and send back home. It was the same for my family, where my relatives, including myself, seemed to be happy with my move because they knew that I could become the "bread-giver" to them.

Esperance's response not only overturns traditional ideas of women's role in the family, it also allows us to see the social dynamics present in migration. Moving is located in a moral system of exchange in which a person is expected to provide materially for the family. It is an obligation that is not questioned—an exchange that is expected. This aspect of participating in social life is considered an important marker of social acceptability that enhances one's status in the community. If there is any social resistance to women migrating alone, it is mitigated by expectations of material support for families. To be sure, there are sacrifices that come with migration—the isolation and fear of leaving family and the loss of a support network. But the expected material and social gains seem to make these sacrifices worthwhile. Besides, success in the host country means that family reunification is a real possibility. Amidst failing economies, a deterioration of quality of life, civil wars, and the absence of viable choices, the migration of women, and their role as breadwinners in the family, is fast becoming a normalized and significant livelihood strategy on the African continent.

The importance of how women are regarded in their community is a critical factor in the decisions they make when they migrate. Not only do their ties back home remain important, the nature of those ties is also vital. In some instances, women's discussions of how their economic activities have reversed gender roles and overturned traditional hierarchies in the household because they are breadwinners reveals the socioeconomic transformations occurring in contemporary African societies. Some women talk about how their brothers and male relatives' requests for money makes them feel important. Blanche is often irritated by this expectation, but nevertheless relishes the power it gives her in the family:

> I avoid to speak to my brothers because they used to ask me for money and to come here. Usually, I tell them that life is very hard in this country and I cannot help someone to come here, especially if he does not have enough money...But even if they disturb me I am happy that they look up to me now as someone who can give. When in Congo they never used to treat me like this...like I am somebody.

Hellen, a 28-year-old Ugandan woman who has her own stall at Yeoville market, has similar experiences with her older brothers:

> Sometimes, I send money back home for my mother. My father understands my situation because he knows how I survive in this country

since my sister passed away, but my brothers do not understand. When I phone them, they ask for money and other things. If I tell them that I do not have money, they do not trust me. That is why I don't like to phone them, except my father and mother who understand me very well. But since when did my brothers ask me for something? I am the one who used to ask them! Things change when you move.

Even when women migrate because they have been ostracized by their communities, they remain concerned about their reputations back home. Kinship ties remain a significant part of their everyday life in Johannesburg even as they decry the cruelty of these relationships. This is true for Sarudazai a 45-year-old Zimbabwean woman who left her home to escape the social stigma of being a divorced woman. Her financial independence earned her respect in her community, which may have not been possible had she remained in her own community:

I returned home after many years of sending money to my mother's village. I dictated that I wanted the money spent on building a house. I went back home a hero because of the house I built. These were the same people who accused me of being a bad woman because of divorcing my husband. Yes...to move was the best decision I made; it earned me respect.

Despite the geographical distance from home, migrant women's familial and communal ties remain an important part of their everyday life in Johannesburg. They care about how they are regarded back home, in ways that have consequences on their relationship to, and behavior in the host city. Considering women's economic positions, their social relationships, and the moral economies of exchange in our understanding of social mobility provides a more dynamic explanation for how we understand the motivations and outcomes of contemporary migration.

Migration Myths and the Story-Telling Economies

Namwene's reasons for leaving her home in Zambia echo the burdensome obligations that fall on migrating women. As a 29-year-old single mother who has a small business plaiting hair in a park in Yeoville, she speaks of both the expectation and the social importance of supporting the family left behind:

Coming in this city [Johannesburg], my purpose was to look for a job and a lot of money in order to improve my life and take care of my daughter. Zambians who live out of Zambia used to send a lot of money to their relatives, build good houses and make a lot of contribution with regard to the improvement of the life of their relatives back home. This was also the expectation of my own family: seeing me improving the social and economical situation of all my relatives with the money I will make in Johannesburg. For these reasons, no one in my family regretted to see me leaving Lusaka because I was considered as the one who will help my family, following the degradation of the socio-economic situation of Zambia. I can also add that all my family was convinced that I was old enough to take care of myself out of my country. That is why nobody was afraid about me leaving.

As Namwene's testimony highlights that the relational aspects of decision making in the context of migration do not discount the underlying economic motivators. Nevertheless, she helps us see how myths around mobility and its accompanying wealth are constructed. The stakes for the individual and the family are high, and they move beyond the realm of economic empowerment. The social aspects attached to migration, the importance of gaining respect and recognition in the community, play a significant role in the dynamics of migration. If respect and recognition are important in the constellation of factors considered when people migrate, so too are stigma and shame. Memory, a Zimbabwean woman from Bulawayo says she had no choice but to leave her community because of the stigma attached to her husband's untimely death, and the rumors that she had killed him with HIV. Although one of her reasons for moving to Johannesburg was to find work to take care of her son, the other was to avoid the shame and humiliation of being branded a husband killer.

People in my community started saying that my husband died of AIDS although we did not tell anybody. Then his family started to blame me for his death, and said that before he met me he was "okay." They said that I gave him that disease that caused death, and I could stay there no longer because there was no way I could get another husband in that community, and I was scared that everyone would think I was sick. How would I be able to walk in the streets with my head high after such rumors. No... I had to go.

Turning to other kinds of myths and storytelling, the bounds of migrants' creativity move beyond looking for innovative ways of making money. Indeed storytelling and identity building become strategies for projecting a successful image to people back home, even when the reality is far from it. The image below of Jean, taken at a mall in front of a luxury car is revealing. As Jean explained the picture at our bimonthly workshops, it was clear that it was intended for the audience back home as much as it represented her aspirations in Johannesburg. "I took this picture to remind me of things I want when I am a successful business woman," she explained. "I will send this picture home, because it shows me being happy and successful." To her family in Cameroon, the car that she stands in front of is a symbol of her success. She may not explicitly claim that it is her vehicle, but she may not deny it either. When sent home, the "staged" image becomes an important talking point for her father, a source of pride when speaking to neighbors and extended family. That he has a successful daughter in Johannesburg increases his own status in the community. For Jean, the image earns her respect, even though the

Figure 3.1   "One day I will be rich" aspirational images sent back home project success, which is yet to be accomplished

remittances she sends home are irregular and not commensurate with her successful image. Her living conditions in Johannesburg may be far from the flashy lifestyle she projects in the snapshot, but it buys her, at least for a while, some status in her community.

Jean's performance of success to people back home is echoed in other studies. For some Congolese migrants, the symbol of "having arrived" is paying a small fee to the DJ at a local radio station for a mention of their name on radio.[46] For others, social recognition comes through dressing up in expensive designer clothing, despite living in conditions of poverty.[47] These displays of conspicuous consumption may be dismissed as a form of false consciousness or capitalist oppression, but are a means of claiming dignity and markers of social mobility among young urban Congolese migrants. These practices not only make the reading of class and social hierarchies illegible, they also both complicate and create new registers of what it means to "do well."

Migration is replete with tales of the journey, the glamour of life abroad, and the migrant's great accomplishments. Over time, the very act of moving, of "travelling abroad" becomes a source of status. Sometimes, the mere fact that the émigré lives in *Johannesburg* may be enough to elicit a tacit respect (and envy?) from people who once shunned them. Travelling, particularly to another country and across seas comes with a certain social prestige and status. Whether it is the "weightless" elite that Bauman refers to, or Sassen's "deterritorialized" globe-trotters, mobility has become a celebrated preoccupation of the twenty-first century. This is true too for those not considered the global elite—the category of people Bauman refers to as "vagabonds," for whom crossing borders is beset by visa requirements, prohibitive costs, or the lack of passports. Travelling overseas has incredible symbolic value for those courageous and prosperous enough to leave their country of origin. "When you have travelled," Pat, a Kenyan woman said to me, "people see you as somewhat sophisticated even though you may not be richer." Yet, even amongst those who have ventured outside their country's borders, there exists a social hierarchy that awards respect accordingly—the further you go and the more restrictive the location, the more one's status grows. "I think Europe and the US and Australia earn you most respect" she continued, "especially the United States. People wonder, if she can go [to the US] and come back *here*, she must be doing well. Then the other countries come after that, like maybe South Africa, Dubai...something like that." The act of travelling itself evokes admiration. Even when it does not result in a significant material payoff, the ability to transcend borders claims a status more typically ascribed to a globe trotting elite. Ayo does not deny that she came to Johannesburg for its economic opportunities, but she says:

> One thing I was afraid of is to live and die in Nigeria. Growing up, most of my friends wanted at least one qualification outside of Nigeria. And it is not only about books or studying. I wanted my own travel degree, my own paper which shows I have travelled in the world.

Beyond the perceived financial rewards, the ability to travel "outside" has a cache amongst peers that evokes a sense of having achieved something akin to a diploma in World Affairs. Given the media images of migration, with sponsored advertisements to discourage Africans from migrating to Europe, showing people starving to death as they attempt to cross the Sahara, or drowning in the ocean, the diploma seems well-deserved. Yet, the knowledge of the brutality at border posts, targeted xenophobic violence, and incarceration in inhumane conditions only increases levels of admiration for those who have left. Sitting in her home in Yeoville, Hellen said to me:

> I talk to my brothers in Kampala often when I am here. I am even frank with them and tell them things are difficult. But they keep telling me, "but you have left home, you are in South Africa." It's as if they think being here is like amazing. Even when I am low, they still think it's amazing to travel. I pity them.

In the extreme, the migration dream can cause those who left to lose touch with reality, resulting in mental illness.[48] The heroic travel narrative can result in such extreme deprivation that it can undermine one's own health and well-being. Making "going home" conditional on economic success makes women vulnerable to exploitative relationships and to living in appallingly difficult conditions. Vocalizing what may seem an extreme viewpoint, Ife points out:

> No-one cares how you make the money. Every time I go to Nigeria everyone is like this [she reclines in her chair with arms raised and her mouth open]. Even if you live in a gutter, they don't care. But, of course if you go home, you do not say you live in a gutter now. What are people going to say? Just bring the goods, and shut up about your circumstances.

Sharing a similar point of view, this Cameroonian woman, a student in Johannesburg, points to how accomplishing her studies and getting degree is not enough for her to go home:

> I remember when my father came back from being a student in France in the seventies; he brought back only his certificate degree. Everyone celebrated! Now if I went home with my degree, people would say, "I don't want to see your leg here. What is this paper you are bringing to us? You think we can eat paper?"

In the face of incredible social pressure to support their communities, women's decisions to remain in Johannesburg are driven as much by the continued hope that they will strike it rich in the city of gold as by the fear of "social death." The ultimate symbol of success is the "return" home with material "resources" that connote one's rise in the social ladder. The fear of going home is associated with losing one's dignity or bringing shame to the family, and women would rather live a precarious life of poverty than lose face by going home empty handed. The "fear of going home" is not a new phenomenon. In her work on Mexican migrants in America, Anzaldúa[49] shows how social pressure to conform to community values and expectations makes going back home, even where legally possible, a source of anxiety and great apprehension. Unable to go back home, women remain in limbo where they are, to use Turner's words, "no longer, but not yet."[50]

Conclusion

Women's mobility highlights the expectations, imaginations and hard realities of everyday life in Johannesburg. We learn from their experiences that moving is not simply an individual decision, but a process that is embedded in social relationships and cultural norms of exchange in which families' expect material benefit. For women, migration is also attached to gaining social recognition and respect amongst kin and the extended family. Notwithstanding women's reasons for leaving, they yearn for recognition in their communities of origin, and geographic mobility provides opportunities for asserting new social positions. The social aspects of upward mobility—gaining respect in the community, and becoming recognized as important actors—are important registers of success. Returning home empty handed is not an option because they are caught in an impossible conundrum of survival (in some cases literally) and saving their reputations.

But caught between these expectations and Johannesburg's jobless-ness, low wages, and discriminatory practices, women's imperative for success leads them to send fanciful messages of their achievements, maintaining or potentially inflating the ultimate expectations of what will be delivered. When making even modest economic gains in Johannesburg is a challenge, the need for these fictions makes wom-en's return home even more difficult. In some cases, keeping the cha-rade of their success means remitting what little money they earn, resulting in their self-deprivation in Johannesburg. Rather than reflect the "true" marker of their earnings, remittances become the mecha-nisms for projecting false images to family and community members of achievements and dignity that have yet to be actualized in host countries.[51] Even when women try to send messages of the austerity they find, these seem to get lost amidst familial expectations and the circulating narratives that depict Johannesburg as a place of golden opportunities.

With the real and perceived demands made by family members "back home," women find themselves stuck both geographically and psychologically. Johannesburg is a liminal space—they are caught in its vortex, unable to move onto other destinations because they lack the material means to do so. Psychologically, women are unable to meet their own goals—their aspirations of accumulating wealth remaining distant dreams. Stuck between Pharaoh's army and the Red Sea, they develop new imaginations and symbols of the Promised Land, shifting what it means to "do well" in the context of contem-porary migration.

4

Turning the Home Inside-Out—Private Space and Everyday Politics

Feminists' rallying cry that "the personal is political" has had an enduring effect in championing the idea that personal lives are intertwined with public and political issues. Claudia Jones's[1] 1949 essay *An End to the Neglect of the Problems of the Negro Woman!* argued that black women's personal circumstances cannot be separated from their economic and political struggles. In a later piece, Carol Hanisch's *The Personal Is Political,*[2] crystallized the argument that decisions about children, motherhood, intimate relationships, household incomes, which spouse earned more, and so on, were deeply political. But it was not only feminists that advanced the connection between personal life and politics. In 1959, Sociologist C. Wright Mills wrote about the intersection of public issues and private problems and in particular the intersection of personal biography and history.[3]

Behind the slogan "the personal is political" lie critical issues that remain important for our understanding of urban relationships today. Authors involved in breaking down the walls between the domestic and public spheres point to the unequal power relations between the sexes, where women's labor, decision-making capacities, and rights are always second to their male counterparts. Yet, beyond the classification of women as second-class citizens is an inimical tendency to use "private" space to perpetuate oppression, domestic abuse, and exploitation. All too often we hear that what happens in the home is a private matter, where the state or "outsiders" have no business to interfere. Arguing that what happens in the home is political opens domestic relationships up to public scrutiny. This not only highlights the inequality between public and private spaces, but it also allows the individuals' rights to be enforced. The conception that what happens in private lives is connected with politics is not only useful in understanding domestic life, private space, and even intimacy within the context of power relations, it also helps us understand the domestic sphere in relation to the city, state, and individuals' sociopolitical rights.

Extending the theme that the boundaries defining personal and public life are porous, this chapter uses domestic space as a heuristic to examine women's urban relationships and practices. With a focus on the places they call "home," the relationships between migrant women and the state, patriarchy, places of origin, and the city are examined. By honing in on the dynamics of private spaces, the chapter not only sheds light on how women negotiate everyday events and activities in their own homes, but also how their responses shape urban practices outside of it. For them, domestic spaces are a place of ambiguity and contradictions, resistance and conformity, fear and safety. In these spaces, they negotiate, shape, and recreate their lives in ways that challenge hegemonic ideas about space and gender—and have a profound impact on cities in contemporary Africa.

The construction of "home" does not happen in a vacuum. Rather, migrant women's gender, class, race, ethnicity, nationality, and sexuality have an impact on the meanings and aspirations they attribute to the notion of home. But the reality of home often reveals the complex ways in which women create and produce urban spaces in their everyday lives. Women's liminality—their legal limbo, the tension between their sense of obligation to their home communities and their own well-being manifests in the domestic realm in ways that have a broader impact on the city. Living in legal limbo for example, impacts how they address domestic violence. With women afraid to report abusive partners because of their precarious legal status, they resolve to address it through community networks in ways that shape the action or inaction of the police. Violence in domestic spaces not only transforms relations in the home, but also shapes women's engagement with the state and the communities they encounter. What happens in the home has repercussions "out there." Domestic relations are at once the product and the medium through which urban relations are produced and reproduced. The practice of domestic life not only counters the implicit tendency to view domestic space as unimportant in urban theory except as a basic need, or as a site of reproduction, it also highlights that domestic and public spaces are mutually constituted, and have interesting and unpredictable consequences for urban relationships.

The Public City and Private Home—
Debunking the Myth

Despite overwhelming evidence to the contrary, it remains a surprise that public and private spaces remain segregated in urban analyses, with domestic space viewed as the by-product of socioeconomic processes "out there" rather than an agent of social change in its own right. Whether it is the political economy paradigm, or the urban ecological approach, the domestic sphere is seen as the outcome of broader structural forces. In as much as there was any interest in understanding the private domain in the city, it was always represented as the outcome of forces beyond its control. For the pioneers of the urban political economy approach, Castells and Harvey,[4] the private domain was an important part of the reproduction of capital, and it was the particular nature of capital accumulation and its need for labor that shaped the nature of the private sphere. To the extent that urban ecologists studied the domestic realm, it was as part of a broader quest to understand spatial urban patterns and how competition for land between different uses influenced the location of workers' residences.[5]

But the idea of the delineation of the public and private spheres has its origins in eighteenth-century Europe and early nineteenth-century America. Against a context of rapid urbanization and industrialization, distinctive roles began to attach to each sphere in ways that continue to influence how we conceptualize these spaces today. Infused with Victorian values of family and gender roles, domestic spaces came to be represented as the locus of the nuclear, conjugal family, and the sanctuary to which working husbands could return and lock the door on the outside world.[6] The male occupied the productive public sphere, while a woman's role as mother and nurturer in the inward looking private sphere was idealized. Public/private, male/female spaces were positioned in a distinct hierarchy. The public male space was the arena of action and domination, whereas the private female sphere played a subjugated supportive role. It is important to note, however, that even at the time that these ideas were taking form, there was mounting evidence that the fixed boundaries between public and private had little empirical basis.[7] Indeed, for working-class families, home was a "malleable" space used as an economic resource, to supplement household incomes.[8] Nevertheless, these gendered boundaries of the public economic life and the private reproductive one continue to influence contemporary analyses of cities in ways that overlook women's agency, and reinforce public-private binaries that obscure a deeper reading of urban dynamics.

Further afield in Africa, the underlying normative theorizations of public and private space do not reflect the realities of the majority of urban dwellers living in them. Even historically, the boundaries between private and public spaces for urbanizing Africans were continuously tested.[9] Ideas of home as a sanctuary, protected from the world outside, may be alien to urban slum dwellers whose shelters cannot protect them from the elements, police, or criminals. Moreover, "private space" is nonexistent in a ten-square-foot one-roomed shack shared by a family of four children and their parents. The notion of the home as a dwelling for the nuclear family is mythical among many African urban families who frequently host and support new urban migrants and extended families.[10]

Additionally, African historical and contemporary urban practices and material conditions highlight not only the false dichotomy between public and private spheres, but also their significance in shaping urban spaces and economies. Deindustrialization and informal economic activities have erased the strict demarcation of domestic spaces as sites of reproduction and public spaces as sites of production. Indeed, urban anthropological and sociological studies show that even in colonial cities, domestic spaces were established as sites of reproduction and production as women raised household incomes through brewing, cooking, sewing, and prostitution in their homes.[11]

Contemporary urban policies tend to focus on how the public realm shapes or transforms private lives and spaces. Urban housing policy in South Africa, for example, focuses on the impact of the state's housing program on household poverty and the leverage it gives to poor households to climb the housing ladder.[12]. Other debates analyze the impact of state housing delivery on the fragmentation of the urban form and its impact on households' access to economic and social opportunities.[13] In Johannesburg's inner city, the appalling condition of residential buildings has turned the state toward finding remedies for safer, healthier neighborhoods.[14] Similarly, domestic violence statutes focus on regulating the nature of family relations, and economic policy on improving household incomes. In other studies, the scourge of HIV/AIDS has brought into focus the issue of child-headed households, the changing nature of the household structure and the increasing burden it places on children.[15] These policy debates are premised on a uni-direction logic that state action transforms private lives, but rarely look at how the private domain shapes public action and policy.

Where private space is referred to explicitly in urban studies, it is in relation to the "privatization" of cities with focus on the privatization of public spaces and the rise of gated communities,[16] and not on private domestic spaces *per se*. Elsewhere, scholars have written about the privatization of the state[17] to refer to the process of privatizing state economic and regulatory functions in ways that blur the line between private and public. But while these writings illustrate that the boundaries and scale of the public private divide are multiple, their point of analysis is not the domestic space or the home.

Is the relationship between the private and the public domains static? And is it a one-way street, where the dominant public realm impacts upon the private domain, with the latter having little influence on the former? The following pages illustrate how the domestic realm and the public domain are in continuous negotiation with each other—their interactions shaping the nature of the city. This is not a novel idea. Nor is it limited to contemporary urban life. In her book on Boston between 1870–1940, Deutsch points out that domestic spaces

> did not so much mediate between public and private for its female residents, as has been claimed, as eradicate the bounds between public and private—eradicate the notion of home as refuge from the world outside it and of women as limited in their proper sphere to the space within four walls.[18]

As women's lives show how porous the walls between public and private are, they also co-construct the city and its relationships. Domestic space is at once the product and the medium through which urban relations are produced and reproduced. The practice of domestic life counters the implicit tendency to view it as unimportant in urban studies except as a basic necessity that supports public life in the city. Women's domestic practices show us how domestic and public spaces are mutually constituted, with interesting and unpredictable consequences for urban relationships. As women navigate the city—living between sending and receiving countries yet belonging to neither—they show us how intricately intertwined the public and private spheres are, and how these interactions shape urban practices and policies.

Life between Homes: The Complexities of Living In-Between

There is home with a big capital "H" which is where I come from. And there is home...small "h" where I am living here in Johannesburg. The two are different; they are both my homes but one is more of my "Home" than the other...does that make sense?

—Harriet, Ugandan migrant

Is "home" where they [migrant women] now are, or where they have spent much of their lives? Is it the nation where they have now set up camp or it is the country whose passports they continue to hold? For many migrants, while they may be located in a new state, home remains elsewhere, the land they left behind.[19]

The extent to which the boundaries of domestic space are porous is evident in how women speak about home, and the meanings they ascribe to it. Harriet's quote above was the result of a conversation about domestic spaces, which we also referred to as "home." We were discussing what the notion of "home" meant in the context of migration, and these questions always produced complex and sometimes confusing stories. Women grappled with how they related to their domestic spaces—their homes with a small "h" in Johannesburg, and the one where they felt rooted in their countries of origin—their homes with a big "H." It was as if whatever happened in the big "H" home had implications for the small "h" home in Johannesburg, and vice versa. Harriet's quote illustrates how difficult it is to put a fixed boundary around private spaces from what is outside. In discursive acts, the boundaries that demarcate the private sphere are fluid and porous. Women's narratives uncover home's multiple geographic sites being at once the homeland and the house/domestic space in Johannesburg. Home, the space where domestic activities occur is used interchangeably with country of origin. Although the coterminous use of home to mean both domestic space and nation may seem an insignificant discursive way in which émigrés refer to where they come from, it points to the shifting boundaries between private and public. Khattak[20] illustrates this within the context of international relations. For a country among a polity of states, domestic policy would refer to its internal matters, so that home in the international context is synonymous with state. The collapse of home and nation has implications for how we conceptualize these boundaries particularly, as Khattak shows, in times of conflict.[21]

Living between sites has a significant impact on how women envisage their future in Johannesburg. Their multiple geographic locations mean that they make minimal social, economic, and emotional investments in the city, living in a way that allows them to pack and leave as soon as opportunities arise elsewhere. We see these trends illustrated in Ladi, a Congolese student. She had been living with her uncle and brother in Johannesburg for two years. Ladi had just completed her matric (equivalent to "A" levels) when I met her. While she was excited at having had the opportunity to study in South Africa, she wanted to go back home. In a muddled way, she tried to articulate the complexities of being between geographies. "Home is always home. I like my home. But South Africa is also good its nice, but I prefer my home," she said at one of our group meetings. "I could go back [to the Democratic Republic of Congo], because I like my home. South Africa also, I study here. I finished my Matric but I don't have a job. When I go to find a job, they tell me 'No! Here there is no job for a foreigner here'...But South Africa is also better here, but not as good as home."

These confusing emotions point to the paradoxical nature of belonging and the difficulties migrants face rooting in the city. Johannesburg provided Landi the opportunity to complete her Matric in a way that her homeland in the DRC could not. But as a foreigner in the city, finding work is difficult. Her exclusion from the labor market means that Ladi remains unrooted in Johannesburg, unable to envisage a viable future in the city. On the one hand, Johannesburg has provided education opportunities, but on the other hand its attractions as a better place prove elusive. Like Ladi, Juliette from Cameroon shares feelings of exclusion that make it difficult for her to claim South Africa as her home:

> I was at Wits [the University of the Witwatersrand based in Johannesburg]. I just finished my Honours [degree]. So it was good getting into school but what makes me feel that this place is not my home is because I can't get a job. Everywhere you go they ask for a work permit. I am not from South Africa and even if you have a work permit they will need to prove that the job has been advertised to South Africans first. That's a problem so up to now I don't know if I wasted my time because maybe I won't ever be able to work...So those are the kind of things that make you feel like an outsider here...if it can be okay at home, I will go back.

Although the notion of "going back home" is more imagined than real for many women, it nevertheless has significant effects on how they "root" in Johannesburg. As the previous chapter showed, returning is complicated by social expectations and obligations and their location within a moral system of exchange within kinship relations. But staying in Johannesburg does not necessarily offer the economic opportunities that women expect. The discrimination, exclusion, and violence against foreigners makes the possibility of investing in the city and seeing themselves as part of its future difficult if not impossible to imagine.

More Than a Curse? Domesticity in Everyday Life

Even as women navigate the complexities of living in multiple sites, their domestic lives, seem mundane—so rooted within daily rhythms that are incongruous with the idea that they are liminal, unrooted or suspended in Johannesburg. But being liminal is also about a tactical assertion of belonging, being able to assert oneself in a particular space in the city and disengage in another within the context of broader structural confines. Domestic space was a key protagonist in women's conversations, images, and everyday stories. A significant proportion of the time spent in women's workshops focused on discussions of the photographs they took of routine domestic tasks and ordinary house-scenes. Given my interest in women's engagement with the "city," these images and conversations seemed uninteresting at first. The images of women's traditional gendered roles as housekeepers, cleaners, and nurturers, were far removed from how I had imagined their lives in the city.

However, to dismiss domestic family scenes as too mundane to explore analytically would be to negate their importance in women's lives in Johannesburg. First, there is a performative aspect in the choice and composition of the photographs. Women's images actively "talk back" to stereotypes of refugees as dirty, poor, or diseased, unveiling ways in which marginal groups counter asymmetrical and unequal power relations.[22] In their ordinariness, these family snapshots, consciously or unconsciously, resist derogatory images of immigrants and refugees. Second, within the context of high levels of crime, the insecurity of being a foreigner, and a lack of control of what happens outside the home, domestic space becomes a place where migrant women can exercise their agency and create a level of security. With some having left their countries under conditions of war, having a home represents a place of security and belonging. Moreover, given a general hostility toward migrants, domestic images present a form of resistance to women's exclusion and dislocation. It is precisely because of their liminality that women's images of domesticity become a powerful source of resistance. Using the camera to contest racial, gender, and class stereotypes has a history.[23] bell hooks argues that "cameras gave to black folks, irrespective our class, a means by which we could participate fully in the production of images.... Access and mass appeal have historically made photography a powerful location for the construction of an oppositional aesthetic."[24] Yet whatever we think of domestic space and its activities, it remains clear that it is constructed as much by what happens within its walls as what happens outside it. It is a battleground for the politics of representation, gender inequality, class, and ethnic struggles, and its reputation as insular, protected, and inward looking has no basis in real life.

My initial ambiguity about women's domesticity resonated with modern feminists who have long associated domestic practices with patriarchal oppression, viewing domesticity as the ultimate symbol of the subjugation of women.[25] With the home seen as a prison, and household chores as an albatross to women's freedom and progress, domesticity came to symbolize women's subjugated status in society. The escape from domesticity seemed to symbolize an important step toward the equality of the sexes. But the contradictions in this discourse were evident even at the turn of the twentieth century. While middle-class women fought against staying at home to take care of children, working-class women had to work as cheap industrial labor and could not afford the the luxury of dedicating their days to raising their children.[26] Furthermore, constructing women as structurally oppressed problematically denies them agency in the home. Mohanty argues that while it may well be true that given a choice, women would not choose to spend their lives doing housework, it is impossible to assume that all women have identical desires and aspirations.[27] Indeed Pink's research on housewives in Britain and Spain[28] points to women's enjoyment of cleaning, cooking, and the performance of other household tasks. Writing about her interviewees she says:

> One might propose that Lola and Carmen are constrained by a patriarchal structure and have a false sense of consciousness. However, having listened to their self-conscious accounts, I would argue that they have a choice. Their lives are intimately interwoven with the multiple agencies of home and part of their business is to maintain a material and sensory equilibrium, or pattern, at home.[29]

But the domestic scenes we become privy to in migrant women's lives seem more complex than mere reproductions of social conservatism, or the celebrations of domestic heroism. Domestic space is imbued with multiple meanings attached to morality, belonging, and resistance. Through daily practices, socially marginalized groups create urban spaces that mitigate the effects of marginalization and domination. Their discursive practices, embodied cultural practices, and the creation of sanctuaries in the domestic realm, build private spaces as sites of resistance to various forms of oppression and exclusion.[30] These spaces, albeit fragile, become the redemptive sites of the city, places of belonging, safety, and morality.

Consider Jeannette's images below, showing her cleaning and getting her daughter ready for school. Talking about her images, she says, "I like to see my family because I don't have other family here. only my husband and children. I'm very much happy because when I see my family I just feel I'm whole."

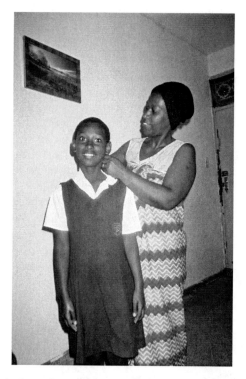

Figure 4.1   Mothering and nurturing an important marker of achievement

Figure 4.2 The structure and safety of domestic rituals

Jeannette escaped the war in Rwanda in 1994. It took her three years to get to Kenya, moving from one refugee camp to another. After meeting and marrying her husband in Kenya they decided to move to South Africa, spending more than a year on the road before arriving in South Africa as a refugee. Her images and discussions highlight the significance of domestic space. From the location of dislocation, having a home and a kitchen, and performing such humdrum tasks as cooking and cleaning take on a significant meaning. For refugees or people seeking asylum, being able to do the ordinary tasks of feeding, cleaning, and nurturing is a significant feat—one that women in stable political and economic contexts take for granted. Given this context, the women's snapshots elicit a sense of power and assert their self-worth. Showing us her food tray, Fezila's tone exemplified just this. "*I* cook for my kid and husband. *I* feed them."

Images of domestic harmony, smiling children, happy family snapshots were another mode of representation of domestic space. Below, the image of a father and three children sharing a couch in their living room while watching television portrays contentment and happiness. Fezila explains this picture as representing her happy family: "Here is my family, a happy family!"

Figure 4.3 Pride in accomplishment, the family meal in Berea

Figure 4.4 "My happy family": Unguarded, tender moments between father and children

Moral Boundaries

Everyday domestic practices are not simply about material realities, but are also sites of negotiating cultural and moral boundaries. In the domestic spaces women create, the reenactment of ritual practices are essential not only in reaffirming women's sense of belonging, but also in resisting the isolation and exclusion experienced living in South Africa. A Ugandan woman advised me:

> It is important to make your home here in Johannesburg to be nice. To remember where you have come from and what you are doing here. I like my home because when we have ceremonies, we come together and we do rituals that remind us about ourselves. Here we are free to talk in our language…we remember home, we pray, we laugh and we can forget how difficult it can be here. In my home I am not a *Kwerekwere*, I know where I have come from and I know that I can be whatever I want.

Domestic space is constructed as a moral space that not only strengthens women's bonds with their countries of origin, but also delineates them from South African society that they perceive as lacking in morals. One of the issues frequently brought up in conversations was of raising children in Johannesburg. Many of the women decried the way in which South African children are brought up and argued the importance of instilling "good values" and "respect" in children so as to distinguish themselves from South Africans. Jeannette's discussed how she ensured that her children growing up in Johannesburg, do not forget their "roots." She wanted to be sure that her children, who had never lived in Rwanda, grow up the way she did:

> In our home we used to eat sitting down together and eat not having tables. So I was so happy to get this mat, putting down and then I teach my children how we used to eat at home. We eat from one plate, at home we eat like this, but we enjoy it sometimes; we do it to just remind them. It is good because we teach them sharing, like the way we were taught at home. I want them to grow up remembering where they have come from.

Migrant women's narratives show how they resist and negotiate cultural boundaries. South Africans are constructed as being "too modern" and in having lost the respect that children should have toward their elders, men toward women and women toward men. Talking about dating and how men relate to women in Johannesburg, Harriet from Uganda had this to say: "Here you see young men proposing to women even if they do not know you. How can you propose love to a stranger? In Uganda you will not find that...first a man will ask to date you for a while before proposing marriage." Agreeing with Harriet, Juliette added "Yes, it is as if here men do not respect women. Look, here I am a woman with a child and yet you will find a man on the street proposing love to me. They do not respect me or my husband...the problem is when you have so much development you forget how to respect. At home there is respect."

Conversations with women of different ages and social circumstances reveal this moral code that is associated with the home, and how this is "spatialized " in Johannesburg. A single woman from Cameroon remarked, "I can never bring a man to my home, we date outside." Another, who had fought with her husband because of his infidelity, said: "I told my husband never to cross that door with another woman." Yet another unmarried woman from Kenya said that "my house is the shrine of God." These moral codes are not only demarcated by a physicality, they also shape how women behave outside the domestic space. "I do not date just anyone because many men think a single woman is raw meat for them; use them and never marry them," said the Kenyan. She continued: "My body is the temple of the Lord, and I will keep it safe for my husband...whoever the guy may be."

But, just as cultural mores and values give women a sense of belonging and dignity, they can also be debilitating. Rosine from Burundi married a Rwandese man, who she met in a refugee camp in the Congo. Her parents, seeing no future for her in the camp "gave her away" to the man, who promised to give her an education. Her husband passed away, leaving Rosine behind with their three children.

> I did not know that I was going to get married, I thought I was going to school and I was very happy. But I never went to school. I got pregnant, one time, two times and now I have three children. He never did what he promised...my husband is from Rwanda and me from Burundi and every time he tells my children "look the bad food your mother is making from Burundi. Don't eat that cockroach food"...We speak the same language but he is hating me for being from Burundi. Me, I ask him, why did you marry me if you hate me so much?

Rosine's experiences illustrate the interconnectedness of the public and private spheres. Rather than remaining static these domains of her life are continuously influencing both personal and public relationships. The ethnic divides that framed the Rwandese genocide in

1994 are manifested in her home in Johannesburg. Both her husband and his family refuse to provide support to the children, unless she gives them up to his family. Rosine often has to seek help from her church, yet even her networks at church are not always willing or able to assist her as her church community is also divided along ethnic lines. Women's domestic experiences invite us to move beyond analyses that celebrate the private domain as a symbol of empowerment or denigrate it as a site of oppression. Just as the private sphere can symbolize a space that resists the dominant cultures and discourses, it can also be disempowering and used to reinforce prejudices.

Navigating Domestic Violence and Safety

Far from being the idyllic sanctuary from the outside world, where embodied rituals remind children of who they are and where they belong, domestic life is a precarious balance of safety and violence, security and insecurity, belonging and dislocation. Violence in domestic spaces not only transforms relations in the home, but also shapes and is shaped by the action (or inaction) of the police, community, church members, and society as a whole. In other words, what happens in the home has repercussions "out there," just as what happens in the public sphere affects the dynamics in domestic spaces. As the following events reveal, the mechanisms through which violence in the domestic sphere is addressed are produced by the nature of social relations both in the home and outside it.

It was late summer, and all of Johannesburg's heat seemed to have been bottled in the stuffy room at the Yeoville community hall where the women's diary group met every two weeks (see chapter 1). Rosine was trying to keep her two-year-old son quiet so that we could hear Sibongile tell us about the pictures she had taken the last two weeks. Sibongile was discussing her "home" pictures showing images of her one-room apartment in Hillbrow where she lived with her sister, daughter, and niece.

Domestic pictures were commonplace in the group, but some of the ones Sibongile had taken were particularly brutal. She had come home at 3 a.m. after her shift at a restaurant in the northern suburbs of Johannesburg, to find her child and niece whimpering in a corner of the apartment. The door to her apartment was open, the lock had been broken and it looked like a fist or a hammer had made a hole through the chipboard. The apartment's contents had been turned upside down. There were clothes strewn all over the floor. The table where she kept her household utensils and food had been tipped over, with all its contents, including a microwave and a stove, landing on the floor. It was the image of the bathroom, with blood splattered across the white tiles and tub, that really brought home the extent of the violence that had occurred in the flat just a few hours before.

> My young sis had a fight with her boyfriend...he hit her with a hammer and destroyed my property. He was hitting my sister against the bath, you can see the blood there...They couldn't, you know, stitch her head because it couldn't come together. He was hitting her against the tap and he also used a hammer.

By the time Sibongile arrived home, a neighbor had already taken her sister to hospital, and the building security had called the police. She found out the next day from Zimbabwean friends that her sister's boyfriend had paid the police the equivalent of USD 100 to avoid being charged.

> He bribed the police. We fear for our lives but he was banned from the flat. We paid the building security guards and he is not allowed here any more...but you know the system can let you down.

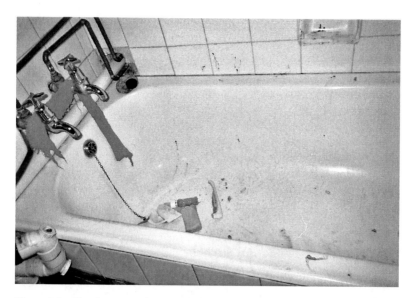

Figure 4.5   Blood stains in the bathtub after a violent quarrel in Hillbrow

Figure 4.6   The aftermath of violence, Hillbrow

As the rest of us absorbed what we had just heard, Sibongile looked angrily at her pictures, perhaps recognizing that they may be the only leverage she had for ensuring that the perpetrator never returned to her home.

> So I have got these pictures, and I am just thinking to go to the police and show them and ask them, where is the person who did this to us? He never went to court, he never even slept in a [police] cell for one night.

Sibongile never went to the police with her pictures, nor did she follow up the case. Instead, she paid the security guard in the tenement building where she lived to provide extra security—a practice that is common even in wealthier areas where the middle class pay private security companies. But a few weeks later, she reported that her sister's boyfriend had been let into the building and had attempted to come into the flat to "reconcile" with her sister. With nowhere else to go Sibongile decided to speak to an elder in the Zimbabwean community, a woman who was from her hometown in Plumstead. Although the woman was sympathetic, she castigated Sibongile and her sister for involving the police. "That is not how we handle these things here, this is not home." Sibongile had not directly been involved in calling the police—she had been at work when the incident happened, but her community judged her disapprovingly for reporting one of their own to the law. "Here, we stand together and solve our own problems together," cautioned the matriarch.

Sibongile's response to addressing domestic violence is not unique. Both foreign and South African women confront a corrupt and insensitive justice system that makes them vulnerable to intimate partner violence.[31] A variety of factors such as poverty, culture, limited access to support services, and an ineffective and corrupt police and justice system exacerbate all women's susceptibility to domestic violence. But Sibongile's immigration status, xenophobia, and a general hostility toward foreign nationals further heightens her risk when compared to domestic populations.[32] At the time of the incident, Sibongile possessed an asylum-seeker permit, which, *de jure,* grants her permission to stay legally in South Africa, work, go to school, and access social services such as public health care. Nevertheless, discrimination by some service providers who refuse to provide services to foreigners imply that members of her family are unable to go to a shelter where they can be protected, or access counselling services to deal with the trauma.[33]

Being in legal limbo and not having their papers recognized on the city's streets not only affects women as they move around the city and try to make a living in it, the barriers they face also reconfigure the nature of urban relationships generally, and women's relationships to the state and their community. Moving beyond state institutions and private service providers, social networks play an important role in shaping practices around domestic violence in the city. Fezila's discussion at another of our fortnightly workshops tells us how.

As the wife of a pastor, Fezila who hails from the Congo, often finds herself mediating domestic conflicts within her community. At one of our workshops, she showed us images of domestic violence, where a husband had beaten his wife, and thrown her and their children out of the house. "The husband said the wife was impolite," Fezila explained, "and that she had answered bad in front of people, and that day he said he can't support it anymore. She called me to give them advise and pray with them and everything was normal again." When asked why they had not reported the violence to the police, Fezila's response was revealing:

> You must understand how we live in our community. The police are
> not safe…we have complications if that woman went to the police she

could have been rejected by the community because she went to report one of us. Also, she does not have "real" papers, only this refugee papers and the police can tear them up and send her to jail because she is an illegal alien. Before she go to the police she has to find a way of sorting it out among the community. That is why they called me. I am known and from their church.

At a glance, migrant women's experiences seem no different than those of many South African women. A recent report on the extent of violence against women shows that between 40 to 50 percent of women have been victims of intimate partner violence.[34] Earlier studies report that at least 80 percent of rural women have been abused by an intimate partner.[35] In a study of domestic migrants in Johannesburg, Vearey[36] points to the ethnic forms of discrimination in the city among new South Africans migrants to the city from different ethnic groups. The way in which Sibongile and Fezila handled domestic violence seems no different either. Intimate partner violence is underreported, with studies showing that the community "very often" protect perpetrators.[37] While South African and foreign women may have similar experiences, the fears of non-South Africans are heightened by the threat of deportation and the fact that they "do not belong" in South Africa. For South Africans there is a discourse of entitlement of rights and services from the postapartheid government. Foreign women however, are less able to hold the South African state to account, and prefer to avoid it all together. Women's experiences of violence and attitudes toward the police may be similar across nationalities. However, the risks that this entails including the possibility of deportation, because they are not a political constituency with influence in South African politics, differs from native populations.

Between a Rock and a Hard Place

Like Sibongile, Fezila's story of violence illustrates how migrant women negotiate these complex social codes within their communities. On the one hand their actions are constrained by an administrative system that discriminates against foreigners even when they have documents that allow them access to support services and state protection. (Besides, safety from violence should not be a protection extended only to citizens or legal denizens). On the other hand, even if going to the police was a possibility, it is often ruled out by the moral codes that regulate women's actions as members of their communities.

Reporting domestic violence may bring unwanted scrutiny into the home and family. Involving the police can result in being exiled from the group and losing the support it provides at critical times in Johannesburg. Belonging to a community secures some form of protection in times of crisis. The church and other forms of associational life may provide food, money and nonmaterial assistance in difficult times. Associations sometimes pool money for burials, to send a dead body home, or to pay medical bills for a sick member. Groups can also facilitate networks that may assist in obtaining asylum seeker permits, space in markets, or business opportunities. Yet, despite the advantages, membership in a community also exacts a toll on members. So, just as membership in their communities offers women some level of protection, it can also make women vulnerable to its violence. Like Sibongile's sister, for women facing violence in the home, belonging and adhering to communal behavioral codes may increase their exposure to domestic and other forms of violence within the community. By protecting perpetrators for fear of being labeled traitors, they become susceptible to continued violence. While these practices protect domestic spaces from penetration by the state, they also protect perpetrators of violence within communities. Although women do not necessarily condone the acts of violence, their fear of losing the "protection" of their own communities is often much greater than that of facing violence at home, or unduly drawing police attention to themselves. These tensions are not limited to migrant women married or living with foreign men. In a study of undocumented women living with South African men, Kiwanuka[38] shows how foreign women endure abuse from their partners because of fear of being reported to the police and getting deported.

The Tension Between the Collective and the Personal

Both Sibongile's and Fezila's accounts of domestic violence illustrate how migrant women walk a tightrope between protecting themselves and protecting "the community" in ways that affect the character of urban relations. Yet, the concern about the consequences of disloyalty to the community may seem to make little sense in inner city Johannesburg where research shows that low levels of social capital and reciprocity exist. Survey data in the inner city reveals that few people have strong social ties in the city, nor do they seek any. A large part of the population's sense of belonging or community is located elsewhere.[39] Elsewhere, Gotz and Simone[40] highlight the mobile and ephemeral social associations in inner city Johannesburg, and the tactical practices of survival and self-interest. In this context, Sibongile's and Fezila's anxiety about maintaining a connection to their community in Johannesburg seems surprising given the apparent atomistic nature of life in the city. Migrant women's interactions with their communities invite us to move beyond the weak social capital thesis. In fact, what we see is the continual tension between autonomy and community, a condition Simmel[41] so cogently characterized in his seminal work on the city and mental life at the turn of the twentieth century. Women's relationships with group members, whether ethnic, national, or religious, remain essential in Johannesburg as a source of support during times of crisis. The family and community are involved in deaths, births, weddings, baptisms, naming ceremonies, and other rituals and events. These networks are activated when women have no money to buy food, or need start-up capital to buy goods to trade.

But membership in the group is not always liberating. Ties to community networks can exact responsibilities or loyalties that compromise migrant women's financial and physical security in the city, eroding their capacity to support themselves. While being part of a community in Johannesburg is important, it also requires that women undertake responsibilities that they do not want, or are unable to fulfill. It may mean contributing financial resources to community needs, which deplete much-needed individual resources. It could also mean entering into relationships, sexual or otherwise, that are not ideal as a means of "paying back" for security in the market or at home. As Devas[42] points out, "social networks can be characterized as much by exploitative relationships and antisocial behavior as by reciprocity, support and cooperation." Women may want support from the community, but not the responsibility that it exacts. They may need community ties, but do not necessarily want to be tied down to them. The process of immunizing against collective responsibility is one that Louis Wirth described in the early twentieth century:

> The contacts of the city may indeed be face-to-face, but they are nevertheless impersonal, superficial, transitory, and segmental. The reserve, the indifference, and the blasé outlook which urbanites manifest in their relationships may thus be regarded as devices for immunizing themselves against the personal claims and expectations of others.[43]

Yet, while distancing oneself from collective responsibilities is a significant aspect of urban life, its everyday manifestations are more accurately described as a continual tension between the collective and the personal. Women's relationships are a balancing act between personal and communal responsibilities.

Women migrants' lives show the tension between building social relationships and remaining autonomous. In the city, they actively avoid capture by the state on the one hand, but nevertheless seek to engage with it on the other when they perceive they can draw benefits from it. Their relationships with other groups and associations are similar, seeking assistance when they need it and "hiding" when they deem the costs of engagement as too high. The city then holds the tension between familiarity and unfamiliarity, the individual and the communal,[44] in ways that shift our normative understandings of cities as spaces of stable communities that seek lasting relationships to people and space.

Conclusion

Using domestic spaces as the theatre through which the city and its relationships are explored, this chapter illustrates the interconnectedness between the private and public realms. What happens "out there" has implications on domestic relations, just as what happens in people's homes influences urban practices in the public sphere. Through discussions of home, women unpack the meanings of belonging and dislocation, bringing insight into how their gender, nationality, sexuality, class, and race affect their inclusion and exclusion in Johannesburg. For them, home is a fragile space, at once a site of empowerment and disempowerment, a place of safety and violence. Amid the structural frameworks that prevent their full participation in South African society, women create sites of inclusion in the city that affirm their sense of belonging. Indeed, the greater the structural barriers, the more likely the culture of resistance develops and persists.[45]

Migrant women's experiences break down the artificial separation between the public and private spheres. The moral and cultural boundaries that determine behavior, obligations to kin and community, and circuits of exchange have significant consequences on what happens in the home, and outside it. Migrant women use their homes to create moral and cultural boundaries that strengthen bonds with their countries of origin, and sets them apart from South Africans. The enactment of mundane everyday practices such as eating, or rites of passage rituals like naming ceremonies, open up a geographic connection between their homes and their countries of origin. Yet, while enacting cultural practices from countries of origin can have an anchoring effect in a new city, historic ethnic divides, for example, permeate through the domestic walls, ripping apart the sanctuary and safety often associated with "home."

It is through the experience of domestic violence that we see how the handling of violence in the domestic sphere shapes state, community, and domestic practices in ways that highlight how inter-constituted public and private lives are. In these situations, there is an implicit, and sometimes explicit system of exchange that shapes how communities respond to violence, and the extent to which the state is involved in its resolution. It is not just that women make calculating decisions about how they deal with conflict in private spaces in ways that provide the least disruption to their lives, but it is that in doing so they reconfigure how violence is addressed by society at large. Women's actions are informed by the nature of the public sphere, the extent to which the police are perceived as trustworthy, or effective mediators of domestic violence. They are also shaped by the relationships with kin and community associations. Both the public and private spheres shape local practices around domestic violence.

This has direct implications on the city and the rule of law. Through Sibongile's and Fezila's experiences of domestic violence we see that urban regulation is shaped less by the statutes than by people's own sense of right and wrong. How people deal with violence in the private sphere weakens the enforcement of the law and creates unpredictability and insecurity in the city. In Sibongile's and Fezila's experiences of violence, it is unclear when or whether the violence will stop, how long peace will last, and whether community mediation will work the next time round. Women have learned to expect little from the police, yet it is not unheard of to find a police officer who is sympathetic. In some cases, justice *is* served and the perpetrator is punished. While acting as important safety nets, community networks cannot always be relied upon. As a Burundian woman said, "I think people are tired of me crying all the time, they cannot help any more." Given the transient nature of life in Johannesburg, groups of people you have relied upon do not always stick around to help you out. Moreover, groups can also erode individuals' ability to survive. Just as the domestic sphere is a continual struggle to belong in a dislocated world, to be safe in an insecure city, to find freedom in a restricted city, so too is the city.

5

The Station, Camp, and Refugee: Xenophobic Violence and the City

It was midday when we arrived at Cleveland police station. The station is situated south of the city in an industrial area where light manufacturing industries and motor vehicle dealerships are interspersed with blue-collar residences. Two flags fluttered lightly in the winter breeze at the police station's unmanned gates: one South Africa's national flag, and the other the South African police flag. A single boom gate with a makeshift wooden guardhouse marked the station's entrance, which, like most South African Police Stations, was sprinkled with the standard brown brick architecture, a faded red tin roof with a blue gutter system skirting the buildings. Police stations always evoke an irrational sense of foreboding for me, so as we entered the police grounds, I was glad I was not alone. I was there with two other volunteers who worked for a human rights organization. At the very least, I thought to myself, if something happened to me at the police station, someone would know about it.

As we parked our car, we asked a passing policeman where the displaced people were, and he directed us to a courtyard at the back of the police station, between the police offices and holding cells and the barracks that provided police housing. A young man in red overalls and a helmet manned the gate into the courtyard. We realized that the security detail responsible for securing the fleeing migrants was the notorious "Red Ants." Many of those in the Cleveland courtyard had encountered the Red Ants, or heard of their raids in the inner city. Working together with the City of Joburg and the police, they are known for the military-style tactics with which they evacuate inner city residents from condemned buildings, resulting in homelessness, dispossession of property, and the arrest of "illegal aliens."[1]

The xenophobic violence had began a week earlier, on May 11, 2008, in Alexandra Johannesburg, a township in the northern parts of the city adjacent to Sandton, one of the city's wealthiest areas. For 15 days, foreign migrants and some South Africans were systematically attacked across various locations in the country, resulting in the killing of 62, displacement of thousands, and the loss of millions of Rand worth of property.[2] Attacks in Cleveland informal settlement began on May 18, 2008. Five people were burnt and beaten to death, 50 hospitalized , 15 shops were vandalized and looted, and 10 cars burned.[3] On the same day, about 300 people fled to the Cleveland police station to seek refuge from the violence.[4] Edward, a Kenyan man who lived in his shop a few blocks from the police station, had been asleep on the night the gangs broke into his electronic repair store. They stole the electronic equipment and tools and set the building alight. He managed to escape by begging for mercy and promising that he would leave the country. As we entered the courtyard, the irony of the situation was not lost to us. Foreign migrants, who ordinarily avoid the police, and have violent encounters with the Red Ants, were now dependent on them for protection. With no homes, and threats of death, their hope for survival from the violence on the streets was the one place they dreaded most, the police station.

Through three separate yet interrelated vignettes, I explore the practices of state agents, the camp as a place constructed within a particular juridical framework, and the figure of the refugee and their interactions with each other, as a microcosm of what is happening in the city. Using these three registers, this chapter provides texture to relationships between space, state, and refugee. First, it allows us to recast our understanding of the city's margins in relation to the center—highlighting the way actors often considered marginal to the city, co-produce urban practices that transform the very nature of the state. Second, it magnifies urban relationships, allowing us to see the nuances and contradictions of the interactions between the state and migrants. I argue that the crisis not only provides us an understanding of how an emergency context creates specific institutional practices, but it also amplifies our understanding of everyday relationships. Based on migrant experiences of the xenophobic violence in 2008, this chapter illustrates migrant's liminal lives in Johannesburg revealing how the violence has helped reinforce the ambiguity of life in the city.

Camps have been a site of scholarly interest as a means for understanding sovereignty and the nature of power in the modern state.[5]

From twentieth-century concentration camps to twenty-first-century refugee camps, the camp, Agamben argues, allows us to see the paradoxical nature of state power. Agamben advances two ideas that help us to examine the nature of the South African state and its relationship to foreign nationals. First, the camp exists within a "state of exception," where the juridical framework that governs society does not apply. Prisoners or refugees in camps are stripped fully of any rights and can exist only if the state suspended its own laws and acted outside of them. Second, refugees and prisoners in concentration camps, are reduced to "bare life," excluded from appealing for political claims and rights and the law from itself.[6]

Agamben's analysis is useful in as much as it draws attention to how states draw boundaries of inclusion and exclusion around particular populations. Unlike Agamben's camps, however, where the rights of those displaced were stripped to bare life, the xenophobic violence unwittingly resulted in the extension of migrant rights, allowing the displaced access to public assistance that many would ordinarily not qualify for, and providing amnesty for those illegally in the country. The extension of rights to displaced foreign nationals had the peculiar effect of highlighting the disjuncture between the law, and the attitudes of those responsible for implementing it. The tension between the values of the juridical framework and state agents, and oddly the almost arbitrary allocation of rights and their removal later, consolidated migrants' position as insider outsiders. Exploring the notion of the insider outsider, this chapter examines the mechanisms through which the state draws boundaries of inclusion and exclusion around foreign nationals. In examining the violence, we hold a spotlight on state actions and see how these reinforce migrant's legal limbo in South Africa. In previous chapters we encountered the differences between "street law" and the laws of the state. Here, this image becomes somewhat complicated by the tensions we see confronting state agents who are caught between enforcing the values and principles of the law and their own opinion of what is right. This highlights the schism that characterizes the country's legal framework and the attitudes of those responsible for enforcing it.[7] In this legal milieu and moral universe, the migrant becomes an ambivalent figure: on the one hand a victim in need of humanitarian aid, and on the other a "fearsome" other.

The xenophobic violence may be considered an extreme case for analyzing everyday migrant conditions and relationships. But the violence that broke out in May 2008 was not a single event, but the culmination of the dynamics of urban relationships that had been simmering under the surface.[8] For several years, advocacy groups and researchers had been predicting that the hostilities toward migrants would get out of hand if not addressed.[9] And nongovernmental organizations were not the only ones to see the warning signs. Indeed, government departments such as the Department of Social Development and Department of Home Affairs have admitted that the May 2008 violence was not surprising given the high degree of xenophobia in the country.[10] The violence and the *threat* of violence against those perceived as not belonging to South Africa is an extension of everyday life in the city. And this state of insecurity contributes to the city's liminal character. The police station and camp bring to light the nature of the relationship between migrants and the state in ways that extend the idea of Johannesburg's liminality. Migrants are caught in a legal no-man's-land, constructed as ambiguous figures with a lack of clarity about where they fit in South African society.

Vignette 1: Sergeant Khumalo's Dilemma—What About South Africans?

Three of us, two officials from a human rights organization and myself, were crammed in Sergeant Khumalo's office in Cleveland police station. We had requested a meeting with him because of concerns around safety in the camps for women and children. That morning, Fatuma, a Congolese woman had approached me, worried about the insecurity in the camp. Speaking in Kiswahili, she said that she wanted to move out of the police station as it was no longer safe. She explained that her 9-year-old daughter had gone to use the toilet at night, when two men tried to rape her. Her daughter's screams had woken people in the camp, and the men disappeared. "We came here for safety but we are not safe in this place. This place is not safe, outside is not safe, where can we go?" she asked distressed.

Our meeting with the superintendent was to discuss how security could be improved in the police station to protect those inside—particularly the women and children. As Superintendent Khumalo ushered us into his office, he said in isiZulu, "These people are always complaining, now they say their bread is stale and they want peanut butter. Most of us would want to have this bread. Next they will want jam, they didn't have these things before they came here. Does this mean we must give them a five-course meal?" The sergeant's comment that migrants were making excessive demands by asking for "luxuries" that they were not accustomed to, and getting goods and services that even South Africans did not have, was one that we would hear repeated often during this time. His ambivalence may have sounded cruel, given that the migrants had not voluntarily sought to be in the police station, and most of them had lost their homes and possessions, and some of them their lives. But as we sat in his office for the next hour, we began to understand the dilemma he faced. We may not have agreed with him, but we gained an understanding of some of the complexities that shape police relationships to foreign migrants.

To be fair, the police were landed a responsibility for which they were ill-prepared. The police station was not equipped to accommodate over 300 men, women, and children. And in a few hours of the refugees arriving, the toilets were blocked, the bathrooms a mess, and the grounds unrecognizable. They also had to coordinate the security, distribution of food, and other supplies for the displaced. And it was not just the new Cleveland police station residents that the police had to contend with. The sheer number of people from the press, people from NGOs, government officials, and high-level politicians who walked through the station everyday, disrupted day-to-day police activities. Sergeant Khumalo and the police had little support for the responsibility they had involuntarily assumed.

Besides the working conditions and logistical problems, Sergeant Khumalo was struggling internally with his own ambiguities. He found himself in a protective role that he was not prepared to play. Foreign migrants were people he saw as trouble makers who had no regard for the law, treated South Africans with disdain, and stole and mistreated South African women at will. As he recounted a long-standing battle between the police and a group of Nigerians on Cleveland street, he said to us, "You know, how can these people come to our Kraal and treat us with disrespect, as if we are nothing. It is difficult now to protect them. I am just being honest, maybe I don't think like that, but many of the boys, that is how they think." And Sergeant Khumalo was not the only one struggling with coming to terms with the contradiction of having to protect a population group he considered hostile and criminal. Sergeant Labuschagne, the police station's spokesperson, had lost her patience with the complaints coming from the refugees. On numerous occasions, she suggested that migrants were expecting a quality of life above what they were accustomed to. I overheard her remarking under her breath, "Now they are complaining about the poor living conditions, where were their kids staying before this?" The antiforeign sentiments held by the police are not limited to the two police officers mentioned here. A survey conducted by the Center for the Study of Violence and Reconciliation (CSVR) shows that 78.4 percent of police officers believe that foreigners, both legal and illegal, are criminals.[11] In an the interview with a female inspector, CSVR's report confirmed police prejudice toward foreign nationals:

> Police generally do not treat foreigners well and they call them by these derogatory names. They exploit them whenever they can because these people do not know their rights and they are illegally in this country. They can't generally open a case of abuse because that will not be investigated anyway.[12]

Although dominant attitudes toward foreigners are xenophobic and discriminatory, there are police officers who decry their colleagues' treatment of foreigners.[13] Moreover, some have forged close personal relationships with nonnationals, which have resulted in mutually beneficial relationships.[14] Nevertheless, the xenophobic violence and the processes that it ignited brought the police face-to-face with the contradiction between the country's juridical framework and their own prejudices and moralities, in ways that significantly tested South Africa's progressive constitution.

It was not simply that there was a disjuncture between the law, its mission to protect the displaced foreigners, and the policeman's personal feelings about South Africa's bogeymen (and women). The presence of the camp within the police station threatened the very core of police legitimacy. As our meeting drew to a close, Sergeant Khumalo got to the depth of what was troubling him:

> You must realize that when people see us here, protecting these foreigners, they will not trust us any more. We have come a long way as the police force. Under apartheid we were hated by our own people, now in this new dispensation we are trying to create trust within our communities. This situation can really take us back to those dark days. We have just regained the trust of our communities, this situation could destroy that.

The presence of refugees in the police station highlighted the conflicting nature of policing in postapartheid South Africa. Their legally mandated duty to protect those displaced put them at odds with their own feelings about foreigners, and raised fears that their legitimacy in the South African communities they worked with would be undermined. The dilemma facing Sergeant Khumalo is not isolated, nor is the ambivalence of police practices present only in relation to foreign migrants.[15] In her discussion of the prevalence of violence in everyday policing—a practice that the police publicly acknowledge is wrong, yet continue to enact "behind the scenes," Hornberger[16] suggests that the police operate in two dependent yet contradictory spheres of authority. An "official" practice that derives its authority from police's legally mandated functions, and an "informal" mode of policing that is not defined by the law, but by the polices' location as social actors embedded in a community with alternative moral registers of right and wrong.[17]

In many ways, the xenophobic violence brought the police face-to-face with the tension between the official and unofficial, the public and private, doing what is right according to the law and doing what is right "for South Africans." Under the scrutiny of the press, politicians, and those higher up in the state bureaucracy, the police had to project themselves as securing the lives of a group that they were often openly hostile toward. But behind the scenes was an undercurrent of discontent where their loyalty, legitimacy, and personal beliefs were being significantly tested.

The extension of protection and services to displaced populations presented a dilemma not only for the police, but also for South African policy makers in general. Humanitarian agencies, nongovernmental organizations, and well-wishers began to provide much-needed food, clothing, and basic supplies to the camps. Temporary clinics run by the *Medicines sans Frontiers* (MSF) were set up to provide primary health care. Even government departments began to visit the camps and provide emergency services. The Department of Education sent a team to visit the camps and provide free transport to school, Home Affairs set up temporary offices to register the displaced, while social workers from the Department of Social Development provided some supplies and services to those most vulnerable in the camps. But the extension of government services, and the flow of aid to the camps, only served to strain relationships between foreigners and South Africans further. Even as officials planned for the extension of services to those displaced, they did so reluctantly. In interviews and meetings held with police officials, government, and state institutions, I came across the same argument—that the state was giving "special treatment" to non-South Africans, when its own people struggled to get the same services. As a high-ranking official from a government institution who wished to remain anonymous admitted in an interview:

> Chapter 9 institutions [independent organizations set up by the South African constitution to protect human rights and the rights of vulnerable groups] were also ambivalent. Even institutionally based human rights activists did not want to defend migrants when South Africans were also suffering. They found it difficult to condemn the communities responsible for the violence, so they blamed the government. The messages became very confusing. On the one hand there was an outrage that the police were not doing enough to find the perpetrators. Then they would qualify their statement and say that all people do not have access to justice, conscious that South Africans themselves are also victims of crimes that often go unpunished.

The ambiguous response toward the violence, and toward foreign migrants helps us to better understand their dislocation in contemporary South Africa. They are not a strong political constituency in South Africa and with growing inequality, poverty, and unemployment, showing support for migrants, even if the "support" was merely acknowledging that an injustice had been committed, was politically difficult. Furthermore, against mounting populism, sympathy for displaced migrants was interpreted as being antagonistic toward South Africans, especially the poor. The reason for this is that the attacks against foreign nationals were explained partly as the result of the poor's frustration of growing poverty, relative deprivation, and poor service delivery.[18] In this context, expressing sympathy for displaced foreigners was interpreted as anti-poor, and against South Africans.

The responses of bureaucrats like Inspector Khumalo highlight the tension between the South African state's legal obligations, and those responsible for enforcing it. This tension reveals migrants' location in a postapartheid society. Sandwiched between an "official" and "unofficial" law, public responsibility and private attitudes, the migrant remains a liminal figure located between opposing sets of mores and values. However controversial, South Africa's humanitarian response, while showing commitment to human rights and the values that its constitution subscribes to, created at best an ambivalence toward migrants, and at worst entrenched "foreign-native" divisions even further. Migrants were reminded that they may live in South Africa, but they do not really belong in it.

Women's everyday lives in the city straddle these legal/illegal, formal/informal boundaries as they walk the streets, conduct their trade, and resolve domestic violence in their homes. They too live their lives weaving through these multiple spheres, creating a hybrid city where the distinctions between legal and illegal are no longer clearly discernible.

Vignette 2: The Camp

With the help of the United Nations High Commissioner for Refugees (UNHCR), the South African government set up ten refugee camps in the Gauteng area, the country's most populous province in which Johannesburg and Pretoria are located. Glenanda camp, (also known as Rifle Ridge camp because of its location on Rifle Ridge road in Johannesburg's southern suburbs) provided refuge for those in Cleveland police station. On June 1, 2008, four days after the provincial government declared the violence a provincial disaster, the temporary residents of Cleveland police station were relocated to Glenanda camp . Legislatively and administratively, the declaration of a provincial disaster was significant, as it provided the legal basis for state resources to be allocated to the victims of the violence who would otherwise not have qualified for state welfare.[19] By enacting the Provincial Disaster Act, the state temporarily defined the displaced as a population group that could legally receive emergency material assistance from the government. But declaring a disaster redefined the rights and entitlements of noncitizens, legal and illegal, in order to allow for the extension of state services and resources to populations (particularly those without any legal documentation) that may not have ordinarily qualified. Of course, in theory, foreign migrants, whether legal or not, have basic protection under the law. The presence of international actors, in particular the UNHCR who deployed their expertise and tents, also meant that the state was obliged to act within certain international legal codes. Although the camps were the responsibility of the South African government, there were concerns to ensure that "international standards" were applied and the camp seemed to be a merging of both local and international frameworks.[20]

Unlike the rest of the city, the police station and the camp provided amnesty for those staying illegally in the country, and those whose "papers" were not recognized on the city's streets, from harassment and deportation. Paradoxically, the police station, a symbol of immigration law enforcement, became a space of immunity. For a short space of time, the legal provisions that delineated legals from illegals, insiders from outsiders, were temporarily suspended. So too were the informal if corrupt practices, which used the lack of "proper documents" as the basis for the exchange of bribes. Pointing to this temporary reprieve, a woman from the Democratic Republic of the Congo said to me "at least until now they have not asked us to see our papers, for now we are safe." "We have many problems here in the police station" said another woman from Zimbabwe, "but nobody wants to see my paper...we have made a list of people from different countries and that is how they are giving us food. It is not about the visa here." While the camps represented a respite from predatory and discriminatory law enforcement, they were nevertheless spaces of uncertainty and fear. Migrants may have obtained the right to shelter, food, medical services, and other basic goods, but they nevertheless remained outsiders in the city, unable to return to their homes for fear of victimization. They found themselves suspended in the camps with few, if any, options to maneuver. Working in the camps, I heard these questions often "How long are we here?" "Where will we move to? Can we go back?" "Will we be relocated to a third country?" in the weeks following the violence. Nobody, not even government officials could answer these questions.

This insecurity resonates with the way migrants live in Johannesburg. For many new comers to its inner city, Johannesburg is a place of transition—a city where migrants' dreams are not to stay, but to accumulate wealth and return home, or move on to the suburbs or "greener" pastures in Europe and America. But with finding work and earning a decent living growing more and more difficult, migrants remain stuck, unable to actualize their goals. Their material insecurity, coupled with the hostility toward foreign migrants and their physical displacement, amplifies the uncertainty in peoples' lives that manifests itself in how they live: unwilling to root materially and psychologically in the city, yet not always succeeding to leave it. Migrants' lives in the city are fluid, indeterminate, and insecure—trapped in a space where they move neither forward nor backward.

Changing Tides◊ From Victim to Offender

In a space of just a few weeks, the status of refugee fleeing xenophobic violence has gone from victim to offender. The official line is that they are at best ungrateful and at worst criminals who have something to hide.[21]

The arbitrary way in which the South African government classified and reclassified the displaced further extended the sense of insecurity in the camps. While in the initial stages of the xenophobic violence the state's policy was to classify the displaced as victims in need of protection and services, this gradually changed as the "victims" began to make their own demands, challenging the authority of the state. What were initially set up as "temporary places of safety" became hotly contested sites over how migrant populations were classified, the obligations and entitlements of the different classification categories, and the authority of the South African state. In Glenanda camp, the Department of Home Affairs set up mobile offices to register and document those in the camp by issuing them a permit in terms of section 31(2) of the Immigration Act, which offered a six-month amnesty to them to stay in South Africa. On the day the department set up their tables to register refugees, there was much confusion in the camp. What did the six-month permit mean for those who had asylum-seeker, refugee, or other visas to be in South Africa? Wangūi, a Kenyan woman whom I regularly visited, had a life partner visa that allowed her to stay in South Africa for as long as she was with her South African partner. She was concerned that registering for a six-month visa would jeopardize her existing status. She said to me, "I told the officers about my situation, but they couldn't give me an answer. They told me they were there to register everyone and I could go to Home Affairs in six months about my case."

Although the six months provided those with no documentation immunity from deportation and an opportunity to regularize their stay, the registration did not make sense for those with existing documentation. By registering, would they be signing away their rights to be in South Africa after the six-month grace period? This uncertainty sparked a confrontation between the state and refugees, some of whom refused registration until they had clarity on their status beyond the six months that the state was offering. A government pamphlet circulating in the camp site threatened that "the failure to register would have negative consequences including the termination of assistance and protection by the government and may lead to your removal from the Republic of South Africa."[22] A provincial government official confirmed that in failing to register "we can take away their refugee status if they don't respect the laws of this country."[23] But human rights lawyers argued that there was no law that required those with existing documentation to register. Moreover, they argued that the rights of documented foreign nationals could not be taken away for failure to comply with a requirement that had no basis in the law. With the threats of deportation, and uncertainty about their legal status, the camp became a site of fear and anxiety for refugees. What began as a space where the South African state extended rights and protection to fleeing refugees, became a site where the rights of those who were bona fide refugees and legal residents were in fact under threat.

On July 23, Wangūi phoned to tell me that security officials had surrounded the camp. The Red Ants and the police who had for a brief moment protected the displaced, were now arresting them and taking them to Lindela—the deportation facility located a few kilometers north of Johannesburg. "I wanted to warn you not to come to the camp today," she said in a hushed voice, "nobody is being allowed in, they are arresting us and taking us to Lindela," she continued. Indeed, I later learned that NGOs, human rights lawyers and other humanitarian organizations were no longer allowed inside the camp. Over 400 refugees who had refused to register were put into trucks and sent to Lindela to await deportation. Two days later, the majority of them were released from the detention center because they had legal documentation allowing them to stay in South Africa, and their deportation would be illegal. They spent two days without any shelter or food on the R28 highway situated north of Johannesburg leading to Krugersdorp where Lindela is located.[24] Authorities threatened that they would arrest the displaced for obstructing traffic under the Traffic Act. On the night of July 28, six armored police vehicles removed the refugees peacefully. Over two hundred men were arrested for violation of the Traffic Act, and women and children were relocated to a place of safety in Krugersdorp.[25]

The camp, which had at one point provided the displaced relative safety from violent mobs, had now became a place of fear and insecurity. It symbolized the arbitrary and unpredictable nature of state power—magnanimous yet suspicious, humanitarian yet inhumane. The shift in rhetoric, attitude, and state action highlights its mercurial and arbitrary nature. Not long after the violence, prominent government leaders condemned the attacks publicly. In a televised statement, then president Thabo Mbeki stated that "never since the birth of our democracy have we witnessed such callousness."[26] The then deputy president, Phumzile Mlambo-Ngcuka, also spoke out against the violence.[27] Home Affairs Minister Mapisa-Nqakula, Security Minister Charles Nqakula, and Intelligence Minister Ronnie Kasrils made similar statements, all expressing shock and dismay at the violence against fellow Africans. When refugees began to make their own demands, the sympathy that they had garnered, at least in public, seemed to dissipate. And fed up with their demands, the state threatened to strip their rights by deporting and charging them with criminal offences.

The events at Glenanda camp provide a window into how the state constructs boundaries of inclusion and exclusion. By classifying those displaced as humanitarian victims, it used its Disaster Act to provide emergency services to people who would not ordinarily qualify for public funds and assistance. The Traffic Act provided the state an opportunity to reclassify some of the victims as perpetrators, and provided a mechanism for the arrest of over two hundred men. What happened in the police station and camps draws our attention to the state's practice of defining insiders and outsiders and to how these boundaries shift. Here, Agamben's work on the state of exception is useful because it allows us to see how practices of statehood continuously define and redefine welcome and unwelcome bodies in the polity.[28] The point is less who is included or excluded. The construction of the "other" is often based on arbitrary classifications of populations deemed at one point or another as dangerous to the state—such as classification based on nationality, ethnicity, health status, class, and so on.[29] It is rather the sovereign act of reconstituting certain individuals "as populations on whom new forms of regulation can be exercised."[30]

This shifting in boundaries points to what Das and Poole[31] call the illegibility of the state. Mbembe's point that the postcolonial state's arbitrary actions create an atmosphere of insecurity and uncertainty reinforce this idea of the state's illegibility.[32] The construction of the residents of Glenanda camp as victims, with certain rights and privileges, and then later as ungrateful law-breakers whose rights to be in South Africa could be stripped, highlights the way in which the practice of statehood, through the actions of the police, security, and camp managers defines the contours of acceptable bodies and unacceptable ones. The use of state power over bodies—biopolitics—to regulate urban territory allows us to see how the state exercises its authority and regulates urban space.

The displaced in Glenanda camp could be substituted for populations at the margins of our cities. As with those who found themselves in camps after the violence of 2008, the state is continually defining and redefining the urban bodies that are included and excluded within the city's legal framework. Whether it is illegal squatters, street traders, peri-urban dwellers without security of tenure, or simply the poor in gentrifying neighborhoods, urban practices of statehood involve the continual definition and redefinition of populations upon whom urban regulations are applied.

The idea of an arbitrary state, operating both inside and outside of the law, is evident in everyday urban life. Discussions of the state's role in informal trade in the city in chapter 2, for example, correspond with what we see in the camp. With illegal street trading, the city police continually define and redefine who can trade on the streets, and where and when they can sell their wares. But their ability to do this is dependent upon the dual roles they play in their "official" and "unofficial" capacities. To understand urban governance not just as a normative concept but as an actual practice, we need to come to terms with the state's own mechanisms for operating outside of its own laws and regulations. With the state straddling both the "official" and "unofficial" city, we no longer see informal spaces as the absence of the state, but as its presence in different and mutually reinforcing capacities. For example, when dealing with illegal trading, a policeman can choose to "suspend" the law and turn a "blind" eye to the traders in exchange for a bribe. In this sense, Agamben's "exception"—the ability of the state to suspend its laws and act outside of them—is not just confined to concentration camps or detention centers,[33] it is, as Das and Poole[34] argue, part of the everyday practice of statehood.

Vignette 3: The Refugee—Bare Human Life?

Though certain populations are pathologized through various kinds of power/knowledge practices, they do not submit to these conditions passively.[35]

I met Adele, an 18-year-old Congolese orphan, on my first visit to the Cleveland police station. She had been working for a South African family in exchange for a room. Her mother had died a few years before, leaving her, at the age of 16, without a home or anyone to take care of her. She had no relationship with her father or her family in the Congo. The exchange with the South African family seemed to work. Adele had a place to stay, and had even managed to take her matric exams in 2007. Things changed when the violence began in May. In the wake of the xenophobic violence, Adele had become a risk to the family, and she was asked to leave. She fled to Cleveland police station on the morning of the May 19. On my first visit, Adele asked us to help her get out of the police station. She felt alone and frightened. More than anything else, she wanted to continue her studies and go to the

University of Johannesburg. Within a week, one of the volunteers had found a home for Adele, but when we came back to tell her the news, she had changed her mind. Adele no longer wanted to leave the camp. There had been rumors going around that the South African government was in talks with the governments of Australia and Canada and that the displaced would be relocated to a third country for safety. Not wanting to give up what leverage she had in the camp, Adele was no longer interested in leaving the camp, convinced that she would be one of those chosen to go to Australia or Canada.

As the weeks in Glenanda camp passed, migrants began to position themselves as candidates for third country relocation. Histories of persecution in South Africa and at home were recounted and documented, as international networks were activated. Where women had welcomed any form of assistance and relocation immediately after the violence, they no longer did, as rumors of the possibility of getting to Canada, America, or Australia strengthened. In Glenanda camp, the registration of refugees began. While people made sure to get onto the Red Cross and the UNHCR's list, they were less keen on participating in the Home Affairs' registration campaign, believing that being on a list of an international body would provide better chances for overseas relocation. By now, Edward, who I had first met at Cleveland police station, had become a community leader. Bolstered by the media outrage, humanitarian response, and the high-level denunciation of the violence, the displaced found a political voice to mobilize, around the fearful conditions in which they lived in South Africa. Now that the world had witnessed the horrors of violence, the senseless purging of people who did not "belong" to South Africa, could they mobilize for resettlement? Together with a few self-elected leaders, they organized a boycott against registering with Home Affairs. The reasons were valid for those who had legal documents to be in South Africa. "It is like they are giving you something with one hand and taking it away with the other," Edward said to me. "Like me, I lost my business which I had here for many many years, they do not want to compensate me for what I have lost, and on top of that want to deny me my right to stay here. The only thing we will accept now is third country, South Africa is not safe anymore." For those without documentation however, Home Affairs was providing a reasonable alternative to being illegal—providing some time for those without permits to make their stay legal. For all migrants, however, there remained the question around whether the government would be able to guarantee their safety once they left the camp.

Migrants' concerns became greater as the government began gearing up for the closure of the camp, arguing that it had put in place measures for community integration. With the trauma of the violence still fresh in their minds, the reintegration program worried rather than reassured many of them. Indeed, experts argued that migrants' lives remained insecure and there was little evidence that the violence and hostility had subsided.[36] Aside from the real concerns for migrant's security was a conscious evaluation of their own leverage, and the power they had to highlight the insecurity in South Africa. Against this background, leaders' voices in camps became louder, demanding international intervention because the South African government had shown that it was unable to protect refugees. In camps in Cape Town, refugees went on a hunger strike threatening to drown themselves to draw international attention to their plight.[37] But as the refugee's voices grew, so too did the apathy toward them by government officials and the general public. Even sympathizers slowly lost steam, as a general ambivalence settled over their plight.

In recent years, the figure of the refugee, immigrant, or asylum seeker has come to evoke a multitude of emotions and reactions. For some, s/he summons people's fear, terror, hatred, or anger while for others s/he evokes sympathy, compassion, and kindness, yet for many the refugee is an ambivalent figure, conjuring contradictory and often conflicting emotions.[38] On the one hand, they are constructed as the "other," figures that threaten the social order, either because of their undecipherable cultural practices, their dependency on welfare, or their "tendency" to "steal" local women and jobs. On the other hand, humanitarian discourses focus on the refugee's vulnerability and desperation. Although the construction of displaced populations as needing assistance and sympathy is important, the focus of their vulnerability has tended to represent them as vulnerable, disempowered, and desperate.[39] As Malkki[40] says, refugees' apparent helplessness and silence calls for the actions of others more powerful.

The events in Glenanda camp allow us to see the character of the refugee as more than just "bare life." Although Agamben's insight into the nature of sovereignty—and the arbitrary way in which boundaries of inclusion and exclusion are constructed—is significant, there remain shortcomings in his treatise of the refugee. Presenting refugees as bare life and lacking agency obscures our ability to see the forms of power and resistance embodied in marginal populations. In Glenanda, those seeking refuge from violence began to draw on international and local legal frameworks to claim their rights. They moved into police stations for safety, sites that are often associated with the threat of violence and the unpredictability of state power, invoking their rights to state protection. By refusing to be enumerated by the state, and using their bodies as weapons of resistance (for example, refusing to move from the R28 highway, and in another camp, going on a hunger strike) those displaced made evident their agency. At the point of resistance, the "bare life" margins become instrumental in coproducing the center. Refugee's reactions to enumeration precipitated a response by the state to declare the boycott illegal, sending the displaced to Lindela deportation camp even though many had documentation to be in the country. This not only highlights how the state authority continually shifts boundaries of legality and illegality. But more importantly, also that populations in the margins are implicated in shaping state actions. Claiming that populations at the margins have agency is not to ignore the challenges they face in the struggle for everyday survival. Rather, it draws attention to the active ways in which populations that are often ignored as peripheral are subjected to, yet also reconfigure, state power.

Conclusion

The camp is a microcosm of life in the city, amplifying the actions of state agents, institutions, and migrant populations in ways that highlight the nature of urban relationships and ways of being in the city. The camp represents the geographic and psychological liminal state, a place where not only are people's lives suspended, but also where the legal frameworks that regulate urban life are in flux. In this liminal space, migrants are both insiders and outsiders—at once asserting their rights to state protection and a livelihood in the city, but at the same time their right to exclusion and to claim third country relocation. For displaced migrants in Glenanda camp, two distinct and seemingly contradictory arguments developed that highlight the continual interaction between being an insider and an outsider in the liminal city. The first argument was that migrants are part and parcel of the new South Africa, contributing to its economy, culture, and diversity. With this assertion, the displaced sought inclusion in South Africa's legal framework, in particular rights for greater protection of their lives, property, and the right to live and work in the country. The second argument was that migrants are forced by state and street laws to be outsiders—as a result they are marginalized and at times violently threatened in South Africa. Given this, displaced migrants argued that they should be removed from South Africa to a location that was safer and allowed them to earn a living to support their families. The use of both the insider and outsider arguments was tactical, its strength drawn from the ability to claim both identities at once. This is the liminal city, where notions of belonging and dislocation occur simultaneously and where the disadvantages of dislocation can be turned into advantages.

It is not just migrants who use their location as insiders and outsiders. The camp points to how the state operates both inside and outside of its own laws. In the camp, as in the liminal city, state regulatory frameworks are fluid, highlighting the unpredictable ways in which boundaries of who belongs and who does not are drawn. Not unlike the city roadblocks, or the regulation of street trading, the camp is an unpredictable fluid space where laws and regulations are made and unmade. The interactions between state actors and migrant populations reveal the insecurity and uncertainty of urban life. Urban dwellers' everyday lives are centered around negotiating these insecurities—developing an agility in their social bonds. They claim a rootedness to the city as a mechanism for accessing its material resources, yet their social and material investments remain outside it. Never fully claiming one over the other, they develop an agility to maximize their locations. In this liminal space, urban life becomes a continual play on the notion of being an insider and an outsider, both for urban dwellers, and for the officers they come into contact with.

6

Conclusion: Ways of Seeing—Migrant Women in the Liminal City

This book is about the city's in-between spaces, exploring the nexus of gender, migration, and urbanization in the contemporary African context. It seeks to understand how women from the rest of the African continent experience migration to Johannesburg in postapartheid South Africa by interrogating their subjective interpretations of their lives, suspended between a past "back home" and a future elsewhere. These experiences are set against the background of changing sociopolitical and economic contexts in their own countries, South Africa's democratization, and growing postapartheid nationalist discourses. By investigating the ways in which cross-border women negotiate, navigate, and shape the multiple sociocultural and economic spaces they encounter in Johannesburg, their lives expand our understanding of mobility and how it impacts the sociopolitical and spatial structures of the city. Women's journeys to Johannesburg, notions of home and belonging, economic activities, self-representations, and everyday practices reconfigure urban space and, in doing so, transform our understanding of the nature of urban regulation, state power, and modes of belonging in the city. Through their lives in the margins, this book holds open the space in the city's interstices long enough to understand the relationships that constitute it. From this location, we explore how a newly democratized society is addressing broader questions on nationhood, deepening poverty, and notions of inclusion and exclusion.

And what do we see? What does looking at the city through women's personal experiences tell us about the nature of urban life in Johannesburg? Answering these questions requires more than just describing the experiences of women, their victimization, or their stories of strength and resistance. Going beyond these discourses of victims and victors—beyond simply reviewing women's narratives and experiences—their daily practices take us to places that disrupt our habitual ways of seeing the city. Women's everyday lives and relationships are revealed in ways that have implications not only for them, but also for the city as a whole. By focusing on the lives of a population group that is often hidden from view, this book presents a novel way of seeing the city from a viewpoint that is not easily discernible from more formal and "objective" inquiries into urban life. These women may seem marginal to the city, but their everyday practices show how they produce new modes of urban regulation, creating moral economies and circuits of exchange that transform our view of urban governance and relationships. Indeed, women allow us to recast our understanding of the margins in relation to the center—seeing them not as marginal, but as critical to shaping the city.

Cross-border women live paradoxical lives. They are invisible officially, but visible in discourses of the other. They live in Johannesburg but remain dislocated. They move to Johannesburg for its promise of wealth and safety but face poverty and violence there. The city is about these contradictions, often lived simultaneously—even at times seamlessly—in everyday life. Women's lives call into question common assumptions about how we think about urban space, marginality, and governance. What does being "legal" mean in a city where those with valid visas or refugee permits are considered illegal on the streets? What is "official" when police officers collude to turn a blind eye on "unofficial" street trading? What is "urban governance" in a context where multiple regulating authorities exist with differing values and moral economies? How do we conceptualize urban development in a place where few see themselves as part of the city's future? And how should we characterize women who, despite their displacement and marginality, resist being the victims of their circumstances?

Women's experiences scramble our learned ways of organizing the city's socio-spatial form and preconceptions of those living in its margins in ways that significantly alter our understanding of processes of urbanization in Johannesburg and, more generally, in African cities. Their narratives take us out of our comfort zones—rendering our existing maps and registers of the city incapable of navigating its complexities. In a city where, understandably, much of the recent scholarly literature has focused on the role of the state in transforming apartheid's historical racial and economic divides, we need to shift our gaze and look at how ordinary urban dwellers are, in their everyday lives, transforming the postapartheid metropolis.

Reading the Liminal City

But how do we capture the interstitial spaces that women occupy? How do we get out of our habitual ways of seeing the city and still make sense of the complexities of everyday life? To better understand urban processes, we need to approach the city as a space that is the outcome of a dynamic interrelationship between structural forces and migrant women's actions (or inactions) toward these. As foreign women negotiate the city's economic and institutional structures, they create urban spaces that remain unexplained by theories that focus solely on its institutional and governance models. The interrelationship between migrant women's urban practices and structural forces produce complex renderings of the city, making visible more textured lives, relationships, and spaces. Cross-border women's unique gendered, national, ethnic, and class locations create an alternative knowledge of the city. Through relationships with their families in sending countries, and social networks in Johannesburg, the South African state, and the labor market, they reveal the temporal yet enduring nature of urban relationships, the tactical nature of urban interactions, and the paradoxical yearning to belong and at the same time detach from social networks and familial ties.

Exploring women's locations in the liminal city therefore requires an approach that moves beyond their material locations in relation to poverty and crime, levels of service delivery, institutional arrangements, and legal frameworks. These tools of "modern statecraft" that organize urban space into readable administrative registers[1] may be useful to state institutions and donor organizations in making urban space legible, but they represent a partial reading of the city. The city is not only an ensemble of policy regimes and the modes of control drawn upon by planners, policy makers, and city officials to manage the city. It is also comprised of urban dwellers' own systems of knowing and understanding their experiences—the codes and symbols *they* use to interpret their experiences, the tactics they employ to navigate it, the vocabularies they use do describe it, and the images they see in their imaginings of it. Donald argues that "the city is the way we moderns live and act, as much as where."[2] Seeing the city in this way lays the foundation for understanding urbanization as a subjective experience without discounting the materiality of cities. Processes of urbanization cannot be under-stood simply through the material/objective existence of cities, but also in how these realities interact with urban dwellers' own ideas, meanings, and interpretations of urban space. Thus, the city exists in its physical realm and in the way people talk about, concep-tualize, and imagine it. It exists in discursive practices, in visual signs, and as thought. Importantly, it lies not only in what people say, but also in their silences; not only in their images, but also in those images that cannot be seen. To understand a city requires an approach that examines both urban dwellers' subjectivities and the environment in which they are produced. In doing so, it reveals how urban residents react to, and interact with their environment, creat-ing new knowledges of the city.

To read the city in this way requires an approach that analyzes dom-inant regimes of knowledge and, at the same time, interrogates how urban dwellers in the interstices engage and make sense of their urban lives. It is an approach that not only unpacks the logics of global capi-talism, state institutions and laws, planning, and policy systems, but also analyzes how marginalized populations produce new logics and systems of knowledge within these structures. De Certeau makes the point that urban dwellers' actions are not merely background activities that mirror dominant institutional or cultural patterns. Rather, they produce local practices that subvert and manipulate dominant cul-tural practices "in order to adapt it to their own interests and rules."[3] Although migrant women's actions are not always oppositional, they employ tactics to engage with the city's economic, social, and political structures that allow them to escape "official regulations" without rendering formal rules redundant.

Revealing these nuances requires giving voice to migrant women's world-views, the meanings they attribute to their experiences, and analyzing how these are shaped, and how they in turn shape the nature of the city. This book has shown how structural conditions shape migrant women's perceptions and schemas (the ways they orga-nize, interpret, and infuse meanings in events in their everyday life). It also reveals how women operating within these structural grids find agency or remain constrained by their circumstances. Their actions (or inaction) within their contexts generate new discourses, symbols, and practices that manipulate, or "talk back" at dominant systems of knowledge, and at other times, reinforce these systems. This approach to the city is underscored by the idea that migrant women's margin-ality and socioeconomic locations create subjectivities that are not necessarily subsumed in dominant knowledge and power regimes but that, in fact, produce ways of knowing that counter existing dominant discourses. Approaching the city as the dynamic interface between structure and agency provides insights that help us better understand contemporary processes of urbanization.

Visuality—Reading the City through Women's Images

To access the space between structure and agency, I used women's words and images as vehicles for telling the story of a city where many come in search of a better life. Although I use conventional academic sources of information, I have let their words and images take the lead, following their characters as they move through the streets and their homes, encountering the institutions, people, and communities that shape urban life. To understand their lives, to really "see" the city the way they do, I moved beyond the interview format, complimenting interviews and ethnographic methods with images taken by the women themselves. The visual techniques worked both as mnemonics, prompting conversation and interaction between us, and as sources of evidence in their own right.

The use of visual methodologies in social science research is fast becoming accepted as a viable and credible means of better understanding populations that are politically, socially, and economically marginalized. But the use of images in the academic world is not new. Historians use photographs to gain insight into the past.[4] Visual anthropologists argue that photography constructs "ethnographic authority."[5] For others, photographs taken in people's socio-cultural contexts provide insights into ordinary people's everyday lives that words alone do not expose.[6] While Johannesburg has seen a growing collection of photographic work over the last decade,[7] there has been little attention given to the use of photography as a method of analysis and theorization of the city. Moreover, few of the published images are taken by the "research subjects" themselves, giving us an opportunity to see the city through the eyes of ordinary urban dwellers. Terry Kurgan's recently published *Hotel Yeoville* is an exception.[8] This approach of using research participants' own images is viewed as empowering and has led to its frequent use amongst marginalized groups—becoming an important channel for understanding social experiences "in their own terms."[9] Similarly,

Goldstein suggests that visual methodologies in urban contexts give research subjects control over the medium of representation, allowing them the latitude for "identity-building"—constructing the way in which they would like to be perceived by the researcher and society at large.[10]

Women's images not only provided avenues for seeing the city through migrant women's eyes, it also offered a means for reading "resistance" at the city's margins. As Hall points out, oral and visual languages are not produced in a vacuum.[11] Women's images of the city are not simply reflective mirrors into their worlds, but rather representations of what they want to reveal of their lives. It is not only that their gender, class, and specific histories influence how they narrate their stories, or what images they take. It is also that their *intentions* shape the content of the interviews and pictures. No matter how "marginalized" or "dispossessed," women *show* agency in their words and images not only by selecting what to reveal and what to conceal, but also by determining *how* and when they choose to do so. Migrant women's words and images are infused with their values, politics, and aspirations. Their representations of the city are knowingly or unknowingly political, disrupting the essentializing imagery of a population group often shown as victims, poor and disempowered in iconic photography.[12]

Indeed, the images moved beyond providing visual evidence of women's material conditions in the city, providing an important platform for "seeing" the city through its margins. Migrant women's words and images explore the tensions between what we know—our learned tropes for describing the city—and their everyday lives. Bringing these disparities to the surface, we are able to rethink some of the ways in which we conceptualize and know the city. Experiencing the city through their eyes and words allows us to explore how they navigate relationships with the state, host and sending communities, and their own ethnic and national groups in Johannesburg. How they negotiate these boundaries—maneuvering around, manipulating and, at times, surrendering to them—configures the city and its spaces.

Yet, notwithstanding the camera's empowering quality, I was acutely aware of its use as an *incriminating* tool. While conducting research, I was often confronted with the dilemma of making migrant women's lives visible, yet alert to the possibility that particular modes of visibility could increase their vulnerability. On the one hand, I wanted to use their narratives and images to humanize and break down the stereotypical ways in which they are constructed in public discourse. On the other, I understood the dangers of visibility amongst a group that sometimes needed to remain invisible, particularly with respect to the state. Although I received consent to use women's images, and involved them in the selection processes for publication, the tension between visibility and invisibility continued to be one that concerned me. As Sontag succinctly argues:

> Photographs furnish evidence. Something we hear about, but doubt seems proven when we're shown a photograph of it. In one version of its utility, the camera record incriminates . . . Photographs became a useful tool of modern states in the surveillance and control of their increasingly mobile populations.[13]

Because of its power to produce *"visual facts,"*[14] the camera has become an important tool for making populations legible. The proliferation of closed-circuit cameras on city streets, at border control points, in public and private buildings, as both a surveillance and bio-data collection tool serve to both control individual behavior, and make populations "visible" to the state. In this sense, the camera is a central tool in Foucault's "society of panopticism" where the gaze of the state is less about effecting justice, than regulating, through disciplinary power, individual behavior.[15]

Theoretically, the use of images raises questions about what can be captured by the camera, and the spaces that remain hidden and beyond its reach. Ultimately, the snapshot is a signification of the political, social, and economic realities women face in their everyday experiences. Seeing the city through women's images allows us to reflect upon the complexities of living in the city. And it is precisely the tension that the camera surfaces between visibility and invisibility, empowerment and disempowerment that brings home the nature of life in the city's margins. Short[16] writes that "the simple dichotomy between resistances and subordination, the official strategies and the everyday tactics, soon breaks down when we consider real people and everyday events." The liminal city is a place of shifting boundaries. The constant tension between structure and agency generates a city in which identities are continuously made and remade. Where relationships are on the one hand tactical and instrumental, while on the other enduring and unshakeable. The liminal city scrambles our familiar urban registers, forcing us to find new moors, all the while recognizing that these too are changing.

Of Victims and Heroines?

The focus on the feminization of migration has made an important contribution in drawing attention to women's movement, directing academics and practitioners' attention to a broad range of women's migration experiences. Yet despite breaking the silence on women's migrations, the focus of this literature has been disappointingly narrow, typically highlighting women's vulnerability to trafficking, prostitution, and coerced and exploitative labor.[17] Not unrelated to this body of literature is the humanitarian discourse that tends to depict refugee women as victims in need of assistance. Humanitarian reports often highlight women's lack of documentation, their vulnerability to rape, xenophobia, violence, and the theft of their property.[18] While these observations are real, what they are silent on is how women negotiate these otherwise dangerous spaces, the strategies they use protect themselves and their families, and the "deals" they make to survive. These actions may not always guarantee women's safety or legality, but they demonstrate human agency. As Agustin points out:

> In the majority of press accounts, migrant women are presented as selling sex in the street, while in public forums and academic writing they are constructed as "victims of trafficking." The obsession with "trafficking" obliterates not only all the human agency necessary to undertake migrations but the experiences of migrants who do not engage in sex work. Many thousands of women who more or less chose to sell sex as well as all women working in domestic or caring services are "disappeared" when moralistic and often sensationalistic topics are the only ones discussed.[19]

When academic and humanitarian discourses highlight women's vulnerability, women's actions and means of survival are erased, obscuring a comprehensive understanding of the ways in which they steer through these otherwise difficult circumstances. Yet, depicting women as heroines who have overcome significant structural obstacles to move is not the answer. Discourses of women's heroism or victimization tend to dehumanize them, creating images of two-dimensional cardboard characters. By looking closely at women's everyday lives, it is clear that these categories are disconnected from their experiences, and unhelpful in explaining lived experiences. Women's daily lives are too complex to fit neatly into binary categories of "victims" or "victors." They have agency in the migration process; they actively participate in making decisions to move and forge relationships that have strategic benefit. Nevertheless, they continue to live under oppressive social conditions of various kinds. Being foreign, they are constructed as the "other," excluding them from participating in South Africa's formal economy and marking them as targets for exploitative practices by police, smugglers, and others. Yet, at times they also strategically use victimhood and their position as the "other" to get what they want—a strategy that Utas[20] calls "victimcy," and that is described elsewhere by De Kock[21] as "subversive subservience." My interaction with Sibongile, a Zimbabwean woman points to the ways in which women resist these simple categories.

Sibongile worked at a restaurant in the northern suburbs of Johannesburg. She was a member of a group a colleague and I convened, of 11 migrant women who met every fortnight to discuss pictures they had taken of their everyday lives in Johannesburg. At the first group workshop I was struck by the repetition of the narrative of despair amongst the women. When I compared it with subsequent workshops, where women shared more of their experiences of triumph, and how they had overcome difficult situations, I wondered what had changed over the few months we had been meeting, and why there seemed to be a more even distribution of discussions of success and hopelessness. In a conversation with Sibongile at her workplace a few months later, I asked her whether things had improved over the few months we had been meeting, because there seemed to be a shift in her testimonies. She was quiet for a moment and then she said to me:

> When we first met, we did not know what the project was or what we could get out of it. I thought that maybe you could help with getting us jobs or papers. So I was saying my situation was bad in case you guys offered us something . . . It's not that it is not bad; what I said was true, you know it's true. After a while we just took you as friends, just people who we meet and laugh and share together with . . . and you know I also wanted to show people I am not stupid, and I can make my own life even with difficulties.

Perceiving that my colleague and I may be in a position to help her, Sibongile told us what she thought might help improve her situation. Her problems with Home Affairs, keeping up with her ever-growing responsibilities toward her extended family in Johannesburg and Zimbabwe, and her anxiety over being HIV positive were not untrue, but she admits to highlighting these to our attention in case we could intervene and help. If I was to rely solely on the first interview, I could easily have misread Sibongile as disheartened and broken by her experiences. Yet, she was conscious that while pulling at our heartstrings could get her some form of assistance, she did not want the group to think of her solely as a victim.

We see some of this agency in the police station and refugee camps in Johannesburg, where those displaced by the xenophobic violence in 2008 actively used the violence as a means for increasing their leverage for third country relocation. By portraying themselves as victims of senseless violence in an increasingly hostile South Africa, many hoped to find passage to countries like the United States, Canada, and Australia. To say this is not to deny that the violence occurred, or that its victims feared for their lives. Rather, it is to argue that migrants knew what was at stake, and for the short while that the international media had a spotlight on their plight, they used it to push for an outcome that they wanted. All too often however, we are reminded of the limits of such displays of resistance. As it turned out, the mass relocation to third countries did not happen. Some, like Edward, a Kenyan man who had become a leader at Glenanda camp, were deported for inciting violence, while the majority returned to their lives in South Africa, rebuilding what had been torn down, with no compensation for their losses. Even though they did not get the mass relocations they sought, migrants' voices raised international awareness of their plight, bringing to light some of the inimical modes of the exclusion of minorities in postapartheid South Africa.

Even where women act against discrimination in the labor market or violence at home, their actions are framed as much by economic, legal, and political forces as by other nonmaterial systems of regulation. It is in these social aspirations—respectability, dignity, pride—that we see how community sanction and regulation has far-reaching consequences on women's actions and lives. Unpacking these complexities allows us to emerge with a more textured understanding of women who move, and the communities and institutions that they encounter as they do so. Migrant women's own voices and images illustrate that they cannot be placed in static categories. Doing this not only misrepresents who they are, but also limits our understanding of the nature of migration and urbanization on the continent.

Although migrant women's experiences are specific, they share much with marginal populations. Their nationality may produce particular experiences in Johannesburg; their exclusion from the formal labor market, the precariousness of their livelihoods, and the lack of an effective political voice resonates with other urban dwellers living in the margins of the city. Indeed, they share certain class, gendered, and "outsider" characteristics with others, including categories of women of South African origin. For example, many of the issues around safety, domestic violence and the insensitivity of the police to domestic abuse resonate with South African women's own experiences of the city.[22] Similarly, South Africans moving to the city from rural areas also experience processes of social and ethnic discrimination and various modes exclusion from urban resources.[23] So, while the reasons for their exclusion may differ, the effects are the similar to those experienced by foreign migrants. Looking at the situated experiences of other urban populations in the city's margins and investigating the tactics and strategies they use to survive in the city can therefore add to our understanding of urbanization.

Such an analysis is important not only for scholarship, but also for developing appropriate policy responses. By moving beyond discourses that marginalized groups are powerless, disenfranchised, and have no voice in contemporary urban politics, we are able to see the instances where they *do* have influence, and the spaces where they *can* negotiate a livelihood in the city. With knowledge of their strengths and weaknesses, policy interventions can provide more targeted support in ways that build on the strengths and do not undermine people's attempts to survive in the city.

Rethinking Governance, Belonging and Development in the Liminal City

Urban governance has a tendency to construct African cities as problematic spaces in which inequality, poverty, poor service delivery, crime, and weak institutions result in difficult living conditions for residents.[24] While these analyses are important, they tend to understand cities through institutional frameworks and the agendas of states, international organizations, and NGOs. The interpretations, schemas, and desires of city dwellers remain absent as those of planners and policy makers define the normative visions for the city. Even though community participation and inclusive decision making have become *de rigueur* in governance discourses in practice, scholars have questioned the extent to which such processes really deliver on community needs and desires.[25] Yet, it is not only that the practical application of community decision making is difficult to realize, it is also that the nature of the "conversation" and the character of the engagement is determined by how state institutions "listen" and engage with citizenry. While this is important from an institutional point of view, participation processes often do not seek to understand people's actions, relationships, and their own understanding of the city. Friedman writes that "rather than seeing participation as a process in which governments create forums to include citizens in decisions, we need to view it as one in which citizens, on their own terms, use their capacity to organize and mobilize to claim a say in how they are governed."[26] Governance approaches to the city emphasize institutional ways of seeing, listening, and engaging with urban dwellers, their efforts aimed at getting urban dwellers to participate in platforms that have been defined by government institutions. Little emphasis is placed on understanding the multiple ways in which urban dwellers organize in the city and access urban resources, or even whether they see the city as part of their future. This book brings to life a view "from below," drawing on scholars like Simone,[27] and reinforcing Demissie's[28] argument that we need to understand how urban dwellers navigate the city, access urban resources, and relate to the state and others. In other words, we need to turn the urban question on its head and ask not how the state and its institutions regulate urban space, but how urban dwellers' actions regulate the city.

The experiences of migrant women, who are considered marginal in the city by politicians and policy makers, makes this a worthwhile pursuit, if only because it highlights that they may not be as marginal as we think. The gendered analysis aims not only at drawing attention to the experiences of migrant women in cities, but also at challenging the way in which scholars, policy makers, and urban planners have characteristically seen the city. In other words, it seeks to understand the city not only through women's material locations in relation to poverty, crime, levels of service delivery, institutional arrangements, and the city's legal frameworks. For, while important, these indicators do not necessarily reflect how women understand their own locations in the city, nor do they necessarily represent the registers that they use to make sense of it. Rather, *this book approaches the city through migrant women's voices and eyes—using their own vocabularies and ways of making sense of their worlds.* Their ways of seeing and understanding expand our knowledge of the city, forcing us to question the extent to which urban spaces can be "known" through governance frameworks that tend to view the city "from above."

Migrant women's narratives reveal how the actions of state agents, migrants, and others reconfigure authority, which results in irregular, if corrupt, practices that echo those elsewhere on the continent.[29] They also complicate analyses that attribute weakness in governance to a "lack of capacity," a "lack of political will," or "the absence of the state."[30] While these factors no doubt contribute to a failure in governance, they are nevertheless blinded to the ways in which the state *is present* and wittingly or unwittingly *active* in producing new configurations of authority and power. The liminal city is generative, producing hybrid forms of regulation, evolving values, and new identities. In the liminal city, what we define as formal and informal, official and unofficial, legal and illegal are no longer recognizable if we retain strict boundaries between them. Moving through the city, migrant women show how the official and unofficial realms meld with each other through people's actions and behavior. At police border posts, in homes and on street corners, they expose the multiple spheres of authority that regulate urban practices, highlighting how these shape the nature of street trading, cross-border migration, and domestic violence. Focusing on the actors involved in these subeconomies reveals that the state itself produces the unofficial, illegible, and illegal city. When city police accept bribes to allow migrants to trade in a prohibited area, they act outside of the law. Ironically, they are able to do so precisely because of the power vested in them by the state. Put differently, their "official" position strengthens their status in the "unofficial" economy. They operate within the legal and illegal realms, positioned both inside and outside of the state. The study of women at the margins and displaced migrants at police stations and refugee camps thus allows us to see how marginal spaces reconstitute state power. It is from these liminal spaces "that such agents, functioning both within and outside the state, can establish, consolidate, and advance their exercise of power."[31]

This has significant implications on how we conceptualize urban governance in Johannesburg and other African cities. Perhaps it is not so much that there is an absence of a "strong" local government, or a lack of state capacity to regulate and direct urban economies and territories. The state after all is a strong and significant presence in women's daily lives. Indeed, how they move through the streets is determined in part by where police roadblocks are, where Home Affairs and refugee offices are located, and where and when police raids will occur. Arguing for stronger state regulation in cities fails to take into consideration that state power does exist in these seemingly unregulated spaces, but it exists paradoxically because of the ability of state agents to be both within and outside of the law. Yet if we flip our perspective, we see how the actions of state agents are influenced, in part, by those at the margins. The presence of foreign migrants shapes how state agents interact in their relationships with them. This is not to say that bribery or relationships of exchange do not exist between South Africans and the state; these kinds of relationships and subeconomies are universal. The point here is that policy makers and humanitarian and political discourses tend to portray marginal populations as lacking influence, but looking closer, we see how the margins too can influence the nature of state practice. These liminal spaces in the city play an integral role in reconstituting the nature of the state.

In writing this book, I run the risk of confirming stereotypes of migrants generally, and women in particular as corrupt people with questionable morals and social values. Their stories about illegal street trading, bribery, illegally subletting rooms or obtaining refugee or immigration papers point to the kind of underground economy and corruption that "good governance" and anti corruption stings are supposed to eradicate. While women acknowledge that they participate in activities that are illegal, they actively condemn corruption, recognizing that practices that drive them underground make the possibility of living legally even more difficult. Yet they find themselves in a strange relationship to state rules and regulations, given that these give them few choices for surviving without breaking one law or another. Moreover, many of the transactions occur with the complicity of state agents, and these overt and tacit reciprocal agreements redefine what is considered acceptable and unacceptable behavior. Urban relationships are so intertwined with everyday politics of survival that a "moral" person can break the law, as long as the reasons are justified and the means used are acceptable. The definition of acceptable can change from one person to another, but there is often a collective understanding of what it means to be good, and do right. Consider a Ugandan woman Stella's response to the question of how she reconciles bribing state officials with her strong Christian values.

> You are pushed against a wall and your options are running out. I ask myself, should I stay still and starve and go down? If it is about survival, preventing my own death, God wouldn't judge me because he sees I am pushed against a wall and I have no choices. If I just stay with the status quo I will die. First of all God gave me a brain to survive. Doing things under the table, getting papers, trying to earn an honest

living, I am not killing anybody. In any case, God owns everywhere, and I am a citizen of any place where he is. I am hungry, how should I survive, through prostitution? That is the real crime. This [getting illegal papers] is the lesser of two evils.

For Stella, bribing a state official is acceptable if this means regularizing her status in the country and avoiding starvation. In fact, using God-given abilities to outwit the state system in order to survive is considered as a virtue. Besides, God's rules, and the rules laid down by the state occupy different levels of importance. God has the higher moral ground, and as such breaking a law considered illegal by the state is acceptable in this moral universe. This is not to say that there is no boundary between good and evil. Where she would bribe an official to get immigration documents, she considers prostitution and killing unacceptable and immoral. These complex moral universes that define what is right and wrong, where and to whom obligations lie in the city underscore the existence of multiple authorities and regulatory frameworks that shape urban behavior and relationships. Writing about the underground economy in Chicago's housing projects, Venkatesh outlines the coexistence of regulatory authorities: "Though technically illegal, underground exchange still has a rich and evolving, moral pulse which regulates recognized codes of conduct, expectations of appropriate behavior and patterns of conflict mediation."[32]

The city then is not a space with a coherent set of rules and regulations that are applied evenly across space. Women's lives reveal that there is not one system of rule and governance, but rather multiple interacting spheres of values that are mediated through a milieu of social ties—kinship, ethnic, religious, national. Migrant women's experiences of the city reveal the presence of *their own regimes* of accountability, responsiveness, and participation in the city, based on forms of identity and solidarity that are not necessarily mediated by the "state" or configured as "civil society." Gendered, national, and ethnic identities are important, but they remain fragile forms of solidarity in the city.

Women's multiple regimes of accountability and forms of participation in the city invite us to rethink how we understand notions of citizenship, community, and urban development. Their practices work against local government strategies to build strong democratic citizenship and communities. These concepts make assumptions that people can or want to be considered part of a community and are invested in the future of the territory that they occupy. And with community members invested in the place, they are likely to become active in local issues—schools, infrastructure, leadership, and other social concerns in their neighborhood. But with people whose lives are not place-bound, with few social and physical investments in the place they live in, these basic foundations for urban development fall away. Community participation in planning processes makes little sense when you do not expect to occupy the space you are in, in five or ten years. For actors who live in "legal limbo," and whose "outsider" status results in real and sometimes violent exclusions from the South African polity, the notion of creating a "democratic citizenship," even one that expands the notion of citizenship to include "all those who live in South Africa," is questionable. Their ambiguous legal status obviously restricts their engagement with the state and the city, compelling them to actively disengage, remain invisible, and build, even if it is in their imagination, a life elsewhere. As a result, women adopt a more tactical relationship to the city. They will live in the city for as long as it takes to get what they want out of it, but they do not necessarily wish to forge a lasting relationship with it. Their investments and futures seem set elsewhere, either "back home," or outside the continent.

Women's "social investments"—their relationships—also reveal their resistance to ties to community. In the inner city, we do not see the kind of social capital that Putnam[33] predicts, or the self-identification with or identifiable "ghetto culture" present in the ethnic ghettos that the Chicago school describes.[32] The language of marginalization and belonging does not adequately capture the diversity of experiences of people who remain in-between and do not see themselves as becoming a part of a place-bound community. Migrant women work against belonging in ethnic enclaves, using these ties when they need to but also actively resisting being drawn into them. Because few expect to stay in the inner city (and, eventually, Johannesburg), communal ties are characterized by a tension between autonomy and membership. Between needing a social network in times of difficulty, but also choosing to be excluded from the social obligations and responsibility that come with belonging. Although migrant women may be unique because of their ambiguous legal status, the nature and character of their relationship with the city is not necessarily confined to foreign nationals. Indeed, other authors also show how nationals employ similar tactics, choosing when to engage with the state and when to become invisible to it, when to claim to be part of a specific community, and when to disengage from it.[33] This way of being in the city calls for a shift in the way we understand urban development. If the matrices of development success are linked to a specific territory, to the idea of planning for the future and the notion of a community with a common purpose, then the liminal city acts against these developmental foundations. Migrant women's lives resist long-standing relationships to community or place. While they may dream of a stable domestic existence, they are often unable and unwilling to invest in their long-term stability in Johannesburg. Efforts to build community or encourage community participation as we understand it miss these vital aspects of life in the interstices.

The liminal city is a gateway, not a ghetto. No one expects to stay or root there, their aspirations are shaped by moving toward something else, toward a new suburb, city, or another part of the world. But unlike the global "gateway" cities, where people, goods, and capital flow through unfettered, the liminal city is a gateway in which many are trapped. Unlike Turner's initiates, whose liminal existence had an ending, maturation in the liminal city remains elusive and often unattainable. And while the experiences described here have been drawn from cross-border women's lives, the inner city has a significant population in transience and transition without a fixed end point.[34] Like a revolving door, those in this space remain in its vortex, unable to go back or move forward. The liminal city is, to borrow from Gotz and Simone,[35] always in the state of "becoming." Drawn by its promise, migrant women remain stuck in the liminal whirlwind, not only because of the structural obstacles they face, but also because of the moral universes they occupy. These universes determine how success is measured, what being a good woman means, and the parameters of their relationships to others. The result is a productive city that is co-constructed by formal and informal rules. Its actors develop multiple forms of urban regulation based on multiple value systems; their ways of belonging in the city bring fresh insight to more conventional understandings of the nature of community reciprocity and bonds; ideas of success and "doing well" shift as their opportunities diminish and obligations expand; their relationships to the city challenge us to rethink place-bound development and urban planning; and they call to question discourses of women's victimhood showing how they are not always victims or heroines in their everyday lives.

African cities defy easy characterization. Cities are at once spaces of opportunity and abject poverty; connected to global circuits of people, goods, and ideas, yet simultaneously contain spaces of marginalization; cities are places of hope and creativity and at the same time of despair and despondency; they are the harbingers of democracy yet sites where some of the most violent abuses of human rights have taken place. Urban life in Africa often means straddling multiple worlds—the global and local, modern and "traditional," urban and rural, and even having roots in numerous countries. Women migrants' lives exemplify these complexities and tensions. Not only are they caught between global and local circuits, but are also, through their movement and ambition, continuously renegotiating patriarchy, livelihoods, moral and cultural norms, and ways of belonging. Women's ways of belonging in the city describe not just how they "root" in a place, but also how they actively position themselves as outsiders, not bound to the territory that they occupy. Understanding these urban dynamics thus requires multiple approaches to the city that acknowledge not only the structural forces that shape urban life, but also the ways urban dwellers' navigate and fine-tune them. Urbanizing Africans see cities as sites of opportunity, growth, and social and economic mobility. While there are risks and frustrations in these cities—as there are in cities throughout the world—those who choose to live here do so in the hope of fulfilling their ambitions of personal development, escaping patriarchy, and accessing global networks. The challenge for African urban scholars is to use these experiences to develop more appropriate theoretical and policy models. By grounding urban analyses in everyday lives, we come closer to understanding what the city means in people's lives, and how urban actors in the margins and the center contribute to its creation.

Notes

Preface

1. Kikuyu word for grandmother.
2. Ann Oakley, "Interviewing Women: A Contradiction in Terms," in *Doing Feminist Research*, ed. Helen Roberts, new ed. (London: Routledge, 1981), 30–61.
3. Karen Jacobsen and Loren B. Landau, "The Dual Imperative in Refugee Research: Some Methodological and Ethical Considerations in Social Science Research on Forced Migration," *Disasters* 27, no. 3 (2003): 185–206.
4. Ingrid Palmary, "Situating Women in War and Displacement: Intersections of 'Race,' Nationalism and Gender in the Context of Forced Migration and Humanitarian Assistance" (PhD diss., Manchester: Metropolitan Manchester University, 2005).

1   Introduction: Welcome to Hillbrow, You Will Find Your People Here

1. Norman Ohler, Ponte City (Cape Town: David Philip Publishers, 2003), 63.
2. Philip Bonner and Lauren Segal, *Soweto: A History* (Cape Town: Maskew Miller Longman, 1998).
3. Statistics South Africa, *Census 2011: The South Africa I Know, the Home I Understand* (Pretoria: Statistics South Africa, 2012).
4. Bonner and Segal, *Soweto*.
5. Gauteng City-Region Observatory, "May 2012 Population Density," GCRO Map of the Month (Gauteng: Gauteng City-Region Observatory, May 2012), http://www.gcro.ac.za/maps-gis/map-of-the-month.
6. Charles Van Onselen, *Studies in the Social and Economic History of the Witwatersrand 116–1914: New Nineveh* (Essex: Longman Group United Kingdom, 1982); Keith Sidney Orrock Beavon, *Johannesburg: The Making and Shaping of the City*, 1st ed. (Pretoria: University of South Africa Press, 2004); Philip Bonner, Peter Delius, and Deborah Posel, *Apartheid's Genesis, 1935–1962*, illustrated edition (Johannesburg: Ravan Press, 1994); Philip L. Bonner and Noor Nieftagodien, *Alexandra: A History* (Johannesburg: Wits University Press, 2008).

7. Mark Swilling, *Governing Africa's Cities* (Johannesburg: Witwatersrand University Press, 1997).

8. Bonner, Delius, and Posel, *Apartheid's Genesis, 1935–1962*.

9. Beavon, *Johannesburg*.

10. Neil Fraser, "Hip, Hip Hotels," *Citichat*, May 10, 2010, http://www.joburg. org.za/index.php?option=com_content&view=article&id=5163:hip-hip-hotels&catid=201:citichat-2010&Itemid=335.

11. Peter Gibbon and Adebayo Olukoshi, eds., *Structural Adjustment and Socio-Economic Change in Sub-Saharan Africa: Some Conceptual, Methodological and Research Issues* (Uppsala: Nordiska Afrikainstitutet, 1996).

12. Lawrence Schlemmer, *Immigrants in Johannesburg: Estimating Numbers and Assessing Impacts*, CDE In Depth 9 (Johannesburg, South Africa: Center for Development and Enterprise, 2008).

13. Statistics South Africa, *Census 2011*.

14. These are 2007 estimates, Schlemmer, *Immigrants in Johannesburg*.

15. Gauteng City-Region Observatory, "May 2012 Population Density."

16. Norman Ohler, *Ponte City* (Cape Town: David Philip Publishers, 2003).

17. Alan Morris, *Bleakness and Light: Inner City Transition in Hillbrow, Johannesburg* (Witwatersrand University Press, 1999), 327.

18. Wits, Tufts, and IFAS, "Migration and the New African City" (Johannesburg: Forced Migration Studies Program, University of the Witwatersrand, 2006).

19. Ibid.

20. Nthabiseng Motsemme, "The Mute Always Speak: On Women's Silences at the Truth and Reconciliation Commission," *Current Sociology* 52, no. 5 (September 1, 2004): 909–932, doi:10.1177/0011392104045377; Naomi R. White, "Marking Absences: Holocaust Testimony and History," in *The Oral History Reader*, ed. Robert Perks and Thomson Alistair (London: Psychology Press, 1998), 172–182.

21. Tamara Giles-Vernick, "Lives, Histories and Sites of Recollection," in *African Words, African Voices: Critical Practices in Oral History*, ed. Luise S. White, Stephan F. Miescher, and David William Cohen (Bloomington: Indiana University Press, 2001), 194–213.

22. Motsemme, "The Mute Always Speak"; Nomboniso Gasa, "Introduction: Basus'iimbokodo, Bawel'imilambo, New Freedoms and New Challenges, a Continuing Dialogue," in *Women in South African History: Basus'iimbokodo, Bawel'imilambo / They Remove Boulders and Cross Rivers*, ed. Nomboniso Gasa (Pretoria: Human Sciences Research Council, 2007), xiii–xxxvii; Joan Sangster, "Telling Our Stories: Feminist Debates and the Use of Oral History," in *The Oral History Reader*, ed. Robert Perks and Alistair Thomson (London: Psychology Press, 1998), 87–100; White, "Marking Absences."

23. For a longer discussion of the visual methods used in this research see: Caroline Wanjiku Kihato, "Gender and Migration: Feminist Interventions," in *Now You See Me Now You Don't: Methodologies and Methods of the Interstices*, ed. Ingrid Palmary et al. (London: Zed Books, 2010), 141–162.

24. Jessica Evans and Professor Stuart Hall, *Visual Culture: The Reader*, 1st ed. (London: Sage Publications, 1999).

25. John Berger, *Ways of Seeing*, 1st ed. (London: Penguin [Non-Classics], 1990), 7.

26. Evans and Hall, *Visual Culture*.

27. Lisa H. Malkki, "Speechless Emissaries: Refugees, Humanitarianism, and Dehistoricization," *Cultural Anthropology* 11, no. 3 (1996): 377.

28. Marianne Hirsch, "Introduction: Familial Looking," in *The Familial Gaze*, ed. Marianne Hirsch, 1st ed. (Sudbury: Dartmouth, 1999), x–xxv.

29. AbdouMaliq Simone and Abdelghani Abouhani, *Urban Africa: Changing Contours of Survival in the City* (Pretoria: Unisa Press, 2005), 1.

30. Fran Tonkiss, *Space, the City and Social Theory: Social Relations and Urban Forms* (Cambridge: Polity Press, 2005), 113.

31. See Patrick Bond, *Cities of Gold, Townships of Coal: Essays on South Africa's New Urban Crisis* (Trenton: Africa World Press, 2000); Rodney Davenport, "Historical Background of the Apartheid City to 1948," in *Apartheid City in Transition*, ed. Mark Swilling, Richard Humphries, and Khehla Shubane (Cape Town: Oxford University Press, 1991), 1–18; Deborah Posel, "Curbing African Urbanisation in the 1950s and 1960s," in *Apartheid City in Transition*, ed. Mark Swilling, Richard Humphries, and Khehla Shubane (Cape Town: Oxford University Press, 1991), 19–32.

32. Mark Swilling "Building Democratic Local Urban Governance in Southern Africa," in *Governing Africa's Cities*, ed. Mark Swilling (Johannesburg: Witwatersrand University Press, 1997), 211–274; Susan Parnell et al., *Democratising Local Government: The South African Experiment* (Cape Town: University of Cape Town Press, 2002); Jo Beall, Owen Crankshaw, and Susan Parnell, *Uniting a Divided City: Governance and Social Exclusion in Johannesburg* (London: Routledge, 2002); Philip Harrison, Marie Huchzermeyer, and Mzwanele Mayekiso, *Confronting Fragmentation: Housing and Urban Development in a Democratising Society* (Cape Town: University of Cape Town Press, 2003).

33. Udesh Pillay, Richard Tomlinson, and Jacques du Toit, *Democracy and Delivery: Urban Policy in South Africa* (Cape Town: Human Sciences Research Council, 2006); Harrison, Huchzermeyer, and Mayekiso, *Confronting Fragmentation*; Marie Huchzermeyer and Aly Karam, eds., *Informal Settlements: A Perpetual Challenge?*, 1st ed. (Cape Town: University of Cape Town Press, 2006); Van Donk, Mirjam, *Local Government and Gender: A Reality Check. Survey of Selected Municipalities in the Western Cape* (Cape Town: Gender Advocacy Program, 1998).

34. Thomas Kuhn, *The Structure of Scientific Revolutions*, First Edition, Second Impression. (Chicago: University of Chicago Press, 1962).

35. Ed Soja, "Six Discourses on the Postmetropolis," in *Imagining Cities: Scripts, Signs and Memories*, ed. Sallie Westwood and John Williams (New York: Routledge, 1996), 21.

36. John R Short, *Urban Theory: A Critical Assessment* (Basingstoke, UK: Palgrave Macmillan, 2006), 226.

37. AbdouMaliq Simone, *For the City Yet to Come: Changing African Life in Four Cities* (Durham, NC: Duke University Press Books, 2004).

38. Ibid.; Dominique Malaquais, "Douala/Johannesburg/New York: Cityscapes Imagined," in *Cities in Contemporary Africa*, ed. Martin J Murray and Garth Andrew Myers, 1st ed. (New York: Palgrave Macmillian, 2007), 31–52; Marie-Françoise Plissart and Filip De Boeck, *Kinshasa: Tales of the Invisible City* (Antwerpen: Ludion, 2005).

39. John Urry, *Sociology Beyond Societies: Mobilities for the Twenty-First Century*, 1st ed. (London: Routledge, 2000), 26.

40 John Law, *After Method: Mess in Social Science Research*, annotated edition (London: Routledge, 2004), 2.

41. Saskia Sassen, *Cities in a World Economy*, 3rd ed. (Thousand Oaks, CA: Pine Forge Press, 2006); Saskia Sassen, *Globalization and Its Discontents: Essays on the New Mobility of People and Money*, First Edition (New York: New Press, 1999); Saskia Sassen, *The Global City: New York, London, Tokyo.*, 2nd ed. (Princeton, NJ: Princeton University Press, 2001); S. Sassen, "Local Actors in Global Politics," *Current Sociology 52*, no. 4 (2004): 649; Manuel Castells, *The Rise of the Network Society (The Information Age: Economy, Society and Culture, Volume 1)*, 2nd ed. (Wiley-Blackwell, 2000); Anthony Giddens, *The Consequences of Modernity*, 1st ed. (Stanford: Stanford University Press, 1991); David Harvey, *The Condition of Postmodernity: An Enquiry into the Origins of Cultural Change* (Cambridge, MA: Blackwell, 1990); David Held and Anthony McGrew, eds., *The Global Transformations Reader*, 1st ed. (Cambridge, UK: Polity, 2000).

42. Victor Turner, *The Ritual Process: Structure and Anti-Structure*, 2nd Edition (Ithaca New York: Cornell University Press, 1977), 94.

43. Turner, *The Ritual Process*.

44. Janet Wolff, "The Invisible Flâneuse. Women and the Literature of Modernity," *Theory, Culture & Society* 2, no. 3 (1985): 37 –46, doi:10.1177/02632764 85002003005; Kristine B. Miranne and Alma H. Young, "Introduction," in *Gendering the City: Women, Boundaries, and Visions of Urban Life*, ed. Kristine B Miranne and Alma H Young (Lanham, MD: Rowman & Littlefield, 2000), 1–16; Bridge, Gary and Watson, Sophie, "Introduction: Reading Division and Difference," in *The Blackwell City Reader*, ed. Gary Bridge and Sophie Watson (Oxford: Wiley-Blackwell, 2002), 237–243.

45. Kathleen E Sheldon, ed., *Courtyards, Markets, City Streets: Urban Women in Africa* (Boulder, CO: Westview Press, 1996) makes this point.

46. See for example, Ibid.; Luise White, *The Comforts of Home: Prostitution in Colonial Nairobi*, 1st ed. (Chicago: University of Chicago Press, 1990); Christine Obbo, *African Women: Their Struggle for Economic Independence* (London: Zed Books, 1980); For Johannesburg see: Belinda Bozzoli and Mmantho Nkotsoe, *Women of Phokeng: Consciousness, Life Strategy and Migrancy in South Africa, 1900–83* (Johannesburg: Raven Press, 1991); Ellen Hellmann, *Rooiyard: a Sociological Survey of an Urban Native Slum Yard* (London: Oxford University Press., 1948); Philip Bonner, "Desireable or Undesireable Basotho Women: Liquor, Prostitution and the Migration of Basotho Women to the Rand, *1920–1945*," in *Women and Gender in Southern*

Africa to 1945, ed. Cherryl Walker (Claremont: David Philip Publishers, 1990), 221–250; Walker, Cherryl, "Gender and the Development of the Migrant Labour System C. 1850–1930," in *Women and Gender in Southern Africa to 1945*, ed. Cherryl Walker (Claremont: David Philip Publishers, 1990), 168–196; And more recently, Kate Lefko-Everett, *Voices from the Margins: Migrant Women's Experiences in Southern Africa* (Cape Town: Southern African Migration Project, 2007), http://dspace.cigilibrary.org/jspui/handle/123456789/30713.

47. Walter Benjamin, *Charles Baudelaire: A Lyric Poet in the Era of High Capitalism*, trans. Harry Zohn (Brooklyn: Verso Books, 1997); Walter Benjamin, *The Arcades Project*, ed. Rolf Tiedemann, trans. Howard Eiland and Kevin McLaughlin (Cambridge: Belknap Press of Harvard University Press, 2002).

48. bell hooks, *Feminist Theory: From Margin to Center*, 2nd ed. (Cambridge, MA: South End Press, 2000).

49. Ellen Hellmann, *Rooiyard: a Sociological Survey of an Urban Native Slum Yard* (London: Oxford University Press., 1949).

50. Luise White, *The Comforts of Home: Prostitution in Colonial Nairobi*, 1st ed. (Chicago: University of Chicago Press, 1990).

51. Philip Bonner, "Desireable or Undesireable Basotho Women: Liquor, Prostitution and the Migration of Basotho Women to the Rand, 1920–1945," in *Women and Gender in Southern Africa to 1945*, ed. Cherryl Walker (Claremont: David Philip Publishers, 1990), 221–250; Cherryl Walker, *Women and Gender in Southern Africa to 1945* (Claremont: David Philip Publishers, 1990).

52. Hellmann, *Rooiyard*.

53. Miranne and Young, "Introduction."

54. Patricia Hill Collins, *Black Feminist Thought: Knowledge, Consciousness, and the Politics of Empowerment*, Revised, 10th Anniv., 2nd (New York: Routledge, 2000), 13.

55. Christina Hughes, *Key Concepts in Feminist Theory and Research*, 1st ed. (London: Sage Publications, 2002).

56. Veena Das and Deborah Poole, "State and Its Margins: Comparative Ethnographies," in *Anthropology in the Margins of the State*, ed. Veena Das and Deborah Poole, 1st ed., School of American Research Advanced Seminar Series (Santa Fe, NM: School of American Research Press, 2004), 19.

57. Edward W. Said, *Out of Place. A Memoir* (New York: Vintage Books, 1999), 186.

2   The Notice: Rethinking Urban Governance in the Age of Mobility

* An earlier version of this chapter appeared as *"The city from its margins: Rethinking urban governance through the everyday lives of migrant women in Johannesburg" Social Dynamics* 37 no.3 (September 2011): 349–362.

1. Richard E Stren and Rodney R White, eds., *African Cities in Crisis: Managing Rapid Urban Growth,* African Modernization and Development Series v. 5 (Boulder, CO: Westview Press, 1989); Mohamed Halfani, "The Challenge of Urban Governance in East Africa: Responding to an Unrelenting Crisis," in *Cities and Governance: New Directions in Latin America, Asia and Africa,* ed. Patricia L McCarney (Toronto: University of Toronto Press, 1996), 183–203; Patricia L. McCarney, Mohamed Halfani, and Alfredo Rodriguez, "Toward an Understanding of Governance: The Emergence of an Idea and Its Implications for Urban Research in Developing Countries," in *Urban Research in the Developing World, Volume 4: Perspectives on the City,* eds. Richard Stren and Judith K Bell, 1st ed. (Toronto: University of Toronto, 1995); Patricia L. McCarney, "Considerations of the Notion of 'Governance'—New Directions for Cities in the Developing World" in *Cities and Governance: New Directions in Latin America, Asia and Africa,* ed. Patricia L McCarney (Toronto: University of Toronto Press, 1996); Mark Swilling, "Building Democratic Local Urban Governance in Southern Africa," in *Governing Africa's Cities,* ed. Mark Swilling. (Johannesburg: Witwatersrand University Press, 1997), 211–274.

2. Patricia L McCarney, "Considerations of the Notion of 'Governance'." 4.

3. Mark Swilling, "Building Democratic Local Urban Governance in Southern Africa," in *Governing Africa's Cities,* ed. Mark Swilling (Johannesburg: Witwatersrand University Press, 1997), 211–274; Susan Parnell et al., *Democratising Local Government: The South African Experiment* (Cape Town: University of Cape Town Press, 2002); Jo Beall, Owen Crankshaw, and Susan Parnell, *Uniting a Divided City: Governance and Social Exclusion in Johannesburg* (London: Routledge, 2002).

4. Steven Friedman, "A Quest for Control: High Modernism and Its Discontents in Johannesburg, South Africa," in *Urban Governance Around the World,* ed. Ruble A. Blair, et al. (Washington, DC: Woodrow Wilson Int. Ctr for Scholars, 2005), 31–68; Steven Friedman, "A Voice Is Heard in the City: Inclusive Cities and Citizen Voice," in *Urban Diversity: Space, Culture, and Inclusive Pluralism in Cities Worldwide,* ed. Caroline Wanjiku Kihato et al., 1st ed. (Baltimore: The Johns Hopkins University Press, 2010), 341–360.

5. Tom Lodge, "The South African Local Government Elections of December 2000," *Politikon: South African Journal of Political Studies* 28, no. 1 (May 2001): 21–46, doi:10.1080/02589340120058085.

6. Philip Harrison, "Integrated Development Plans and Third Way Politics," in *Democracy and Delivery: Urban Policy in South Africa,* ed. Udesh Pillay, Richard Tomlinson, and Jacques du Toit (Cape Town: Human Sciences Research Council, 2006), 186–207; Philip Harrison, "The Genealogy of South Africa's Integrated Development Plan," *Third World Planning Review* 23, no. 2 (2001): 175–193.

7. Ministry for Provincial Affairs and Constitutional Development, *The White Paper on Local Government* (Pretoria: CTP Book Printers, 1998); Ivor Chipkin, "A Developmental Role for Local Government," in *Democratising Local Government: The South African Experiment,* ed. Susan Parnell et al. (Cape Town: University of Cape Town Press, 2002), 57–78; Susan Parnell

et al., *Democratising Local Government: The South African Experiment* (Cape Town: University of Cape Town Press, 2002); Philip Harrison, Marie Huchzermeyer, and Mzwanele Mayekiso, *Confronting Fragmentation: Housing and Urban Development in a Democratising Society* (Cape Town: University of Cape Town Press, 2003).

8. Ilda Lindell, "The Multiple Sites of Urban Governance: Insights from an African City," *Urban Studies* 45, no. 9 (August 2008): 1882, doi:10.1177/0042098008093382.

9. Edgar Pieterse, *City Futures: Confronting the Crisis of Urban Development* (London: Zed Books, 2008); F. Demissie, "Imperial Legacies and Postcolonial Predicaments: An Introduction," *African Identities* 5, no. 2 (2007): 155–165; AbdouMaliq Simone, "The Dilemmas of Informality for African Governance," in *Democratising Local Government: The South African Experiment*, ed. Susan Parnell et al. (Cape Town: University of Cape Town Press, 2002), 294–304; AbdouMaliq Simone, "Urban Circulation and the Everyday Politics of African Urban Youth: The Case of Douala, Cameroon.," *International Journal of Urban & Regional Research* 29, no. 3 (2005): 516–532, doi:10.1111/j.1468–2427.2005.00603.x.

10. Parnell et al., *Democratising Local Government*; Beall, Crankshaw, and Parnell, *Uniting a Divided City*; Philip Harrison, Marie Huchzermeyer, and Mzwanele Mayekiso, *Confronting Fragmentation*.Susan Parnell et al., *Democratising Local Government*.

11. Ministry for Provincial Affairs and Constitutional Development, *The White Paper on Local Government*.

12. Chipkin, "A Developmental Role for Local Government."

13. Patrick Bond, *Cities of Gold, Townships of Coal: Essays on South Africa's New Urban Crisis* (Trenton: Africa World Press, 2000).

14. Susan Parnell, "Constructing a Developmental Nation—the Challenge of Including the Poor in the Post-apartheid City," *Transformation: Critical Perspectives on Southern Africa* 58, no. 1 (2005): 20–44.

15. Title borrowed from a paper by Caroline Kihato and Loren B. Landau, *The Uncaptured Urbanite: Migration and State Power in Johannesburg* (Johannesburg: University of the Witwatersrand, Forced Migration Studies Programme [Forced Migration Working Paper Series], 2006).

16. Yakoob Makda, "From Slum to (financial) Sustainability: Johannesburg's Better Building Program," *Development Update* 5, no. 1 (2004): 180/1.

17. See City of Johannesburg Metropolitan Municipality, "Street Trading By-laws No.179" (City of Johannesburg, 2004), http://www.joburg.org.za/bylaws/streettrading_by-laws.pdf.

18. See Erica Emdon, "The Limits of Law: Social Rights and Urban Development," in *Emerging Johannesburg*, ed. Richard Tomlinson et al., 1st ed. (London: Routledge, 2003), 215–230.

19. Kihato and Landau, *The Uncaptured Urbanite*.

20. Göran Hydén, *Beyond Ujamaa in Tanzania: Underdevelopment and an Uncaptured Peasantry* (Berkeley: University of California Press, 1980).

21. Roni Amit et al., "National Survey of the Refugee Reception and Status Determination System in South Africa" (Johannesburg: Migrant Rights

Monitoring Project Research Report, 2009); Integrated Regional Information Networks (IRIN), "South Africa: Rethinking Asylum," *IRIN news*, August 15, 2008, http://www.irinnews.org/report.aspx?reportid=79850; CORMSA, *Protecting Refugees, Asylum Seekers and Immigrants in South Africa* (Johannesburg: CORMSA, 2008).

22. CORMSA, *Protecting Refugees.*

23. DHA, "Turnaround Strategy," in *Document Presented to a Briefing of the Joint Committee of Parliament* (Cape Town: Department of Home Affairs, 2004).

24. DHA, "Building a New Home Affairs: An Update on the Transformation Program," in *Presentation to the Select Committee on Social Services* (Cape Town: Department of Home Affairs, 2008).

25. Saskia Sassen, "Globalization or Denationalization?" *Review of International Political Economy* 10, no. 1 (February 2001): 1–22, doi:10.1080/0969229 032000048853; Saskia Sassen, *Globalization and Its Discontents: Essays on the New Mobility of People and Money*, First Edition (New York: New Press, 1999); Zygmunt Bauman, *Globalization: The Human Consequences* (New York: Columbia University Press, 1998).

26. AbdouMaliq Simone, *For the City Yet to Come: Changing African Life in Four Cities* (Durham NC: Duke University Press Books, 2004), 118.

27. Bauman, *Globalization*, 78.

28. CORMSA, *Protecting Refugees*; Loren B. Landau and Tamlyn Monson, "Immigration and Subterranean Sovereignty in South African Cities," in *Ungoverned Spaces: Alternatives to State Authority in an Era of Softened Sovereignty*, ed. Anne Clunan and Harold Trinkunas (Stanford, CA: Stanford Security Studies, 2010), 153–174.

29. Loren B. Landau, "Inclusion in Shifting Sands: Rethinking Mobility and Belonging in African Cities," in *Urban Diversity: Space, Culture, and Inclusive Pluralism in Cities Worldwide,* ed. Caroline Wanjiku Kihato et al., 1st ed. (Baltimore: The Johns Hopkins University Press, 2010), 169–186.

30. John R Short, *Urban Theory: A Critical Assessment* (Basingstoke, UK: Palgrave Macmillan, 2006).

31. James C Scott, *Seeing Like a State: How Certain Schemes to Improve the Human Condition Have Failed*, Yale Agrarian Studies (New Haven, CT: Yale University Press, 1998), 3.

32. See also, Michel Foucault, *Power: The Essential Works of Michel Foucault 1954–1984 (Essential Works of Foucault 3)*, ed. James D. Faubion (London: Penguin Books Ltd, 1994); Andrew Barry, Thomas Osborne, and Nikolas S. Rose, *Foucault and Political Reason: Liberalism, Neoliberalism, and Rationalities of Government* (Chicago: University of Chicago Press, 1996); Graham Burchell, Colin Gordon, and Peter Miller, *The Foucault Effect: Studies in Governmentality*, 1st ed. (Chicago: University of Chicago Press, 1991).

33. Foucault, *Power*; Burchell, Gordon, and Miller, *The Foucault Effect.*

34. Bauman, *Globalization*, 30.

35. Faranaaz Parker, "Jo'burg Sends in Red Ants in Defiance of ConCourt," *The M&G Online*, 2012, http://mg.co.za/article/2012–01–18-joburg-sends-in-red-ants-defiance-of-concourt/; Richard Bullard, "Illegal Immigrants

Deserve What's Coming to Them," *Sunday Times*, October 19, 2003, 1st ed.; Eric Pelser, "Operation Crackdown: The New Police Strategy," *Nedbank ISS Crime Index* 4, no. 2 (2000), http://www.iss.co.za/PUBS/CRIMEINDEX/00VOL402/OperatCrackdown.html; Thomas Thale, "Drama as Police Swoop on Inner City Buildings," *City of Joburg*, September 25, 2003, http://www.joburg.org.za/2003/spet/sept25_hillbrowswoop.stm.

36. James C. Scott, "Afterword to 'Moral Economies, State Spaces, and Categorical Violence'," *American Anthropologist* 107, no. 3 (September 1, 2005): 399, doi:10.1525/aa.2005.107.3.395.

37. Veena Das and Deborah Poole, "State and Its Margins: Comparative Ethnographies," in *Anthropology in the Margins of the State*, ed. Veena Das and Deborah Poole, 1st ed., School of American Research Advanced Seminar Series (Santa Fe, NM: School of American Research Press, 2004), 3–34.

38. For more on the method used for the study, see Caroline Wanjiku Kihato, "Gender and Migration: Feminist Interventions," in *Now You See Me Now You Don't: Methodologies and Methods of the Interstices*, ed. Ingrid Palmary et al. (London: Zed Books, 2010), 141–162.

39. Pradeep Jeganathan, "Checkpoint: Anthropology, Identity, and the State," in *Anthropology in the Margins of the State*, ed. Veena Das and Deborah Poole, 1st ed., School of American Research Advanced Seminar Series (Santa Fe, NM: School of American Research Press, 2004), 194.

40. Victoria Sanford, "Contesting Displacement in Columbia: Citizenship and State Sovereignty at the Margins," in *Anthropology in the Margins of the State*, ed. Veena Das and Deborah Poole, 1st ed., School of American Research Advanced Seminar Series (Santa Fe, NM: School of American Research Press, 2004), 253–277; Jeganathan, "Checkpoint"; Daniel Jordan Smith, *A Culture of Corruption: Everyday Deception and Popular Discontent in Nigeria* (Princeton: Princeton University Press, 2008).

41. Sanford, "Contesting Displacement," 259.

42. Anne L Clunan and Harold A Trinkunas, eds., *Ungoverned Spaces: Alternatives to State Authority in An Era of Softened Sovereignty* (Stanford, CA: Stanford Security Studies, 2010), 8.

43. Scott, *Seeing Like a State*.

44. Foucault, *Power*; Michel Foucault, *Power/Knowledge: Selected Interviews and Other Writings, 1972–1977*, ed. Colin Gordon (London: Pearson Education, 1980); Andrew Barry, Thomas Osborne, and Nikolas S. Rose, *Foucault and Political Reason: Liberalism, Neo-liberalism, and Rationalities of Government* (Chicago: University of Chicago Press, 1996); Burchell, Gordon, and Miller, *The Foucault Effect*.

45. Bauman, *Globalization*.

46. Michel Foucault, *Discipline and Punish: The Birth of the Prison* (New York: Pantheon Books, 1977); Foucault, *Power*.

47. Loren B Landau, "Recognition, Community and the Power of Mobility in Africa's New Urban Estuaries," in *Mobility and the State in Africa*, ed. Darshan Vigneswaran and Joel Quirk (Philadelphia: University of Pennsylvania Press, Forthcoming), 32.

48. Smith, *A Culture of Corruption*, 72.

49. Ibid.
50. Sudhir Alladi Venkatesh, *Off the Books: The Underground Economy of the Urban Poor* (Cambridge, MA: Harvard University Press, 2009), 218.
51. Smith, *A Culture of Corruption.*
52. Ciaran Cronin, "Bourdieu and Foucault on Power and Modernity," *Philosophy & Social Criticism* 22, no. 6 (November 1, 1996): 56, doi:10.1177/019145379602200603.
53. Anne Clunan, "Ungoverned Spaces? The Need for Reevaluation," in *Ungoverned Spaces: Alternatives to State Authority in An Era of Softened Sovereignty*, ed. Anne L Clunan and Harold A Trinkunas (Stanford, CA: Stanford Security Studies, 2010), 6.
54. Marie Huchzermeyer, "Housing for the Poor? Negotiated Housing Policy in South Africa," *Habitat International* 25, no. 3 (2001): 303–331; Tanya Zack and Sarah Charlton, "Better Off, but . . . Beneficiaries' Perceptions of the Government's Housing Subsidy Scheme" (Unpublished paper prepared for the Department of Housing, Pretoria, 2003).
55. See Martin J. Murray, *Taming the Disorderly City: The Spatial Landscape of Johannesburg After Apartheid*, 2nd ed. (Ithaca: Cornell University Press, 2008); Simone, *For the City Yet to Come.*

3   Between Pharaoh's Army and the Red Sea: Social Mobility and Social Death in the Context of Women's Migration

1. Adam Smith, c.f. Amartya Kumar Sen, *Social Exclusion: Concept, Application, and Scrutiny*, Development Papers No. 1 (Manila: Asian Development Bank, 2000), 4.
2. Patterson Orlando, *Slavery And Social Death: A Comparative Study* (Cambridge, MA: Harvard University Press, 1982).
3. Ibid.; Claudia Card, "Genocide and Social Death," *Hypatia* 18 (2003): 63–79, doi:10.1353/hyp.2003.0006.
4. Robin Cohen, *Endgame in South Africa?* (Suffolk: James Currey, 1986); Jonathan Crush, Alan Jeeves, and David Yudelman, *South Africa's Labor Empire: A History of Black Migrancy to the Gold Mines* (Boulder, CO: Westview Press [Short Disc], 1991).
5. Monica Boyd and Elizabeth Grieco, "Women and Migration: Incorporating Gender into International Migration Theory," *The Migration Information Source*, 2003, http://www.migrationinformation.org/feature/display.cfm?id=106; Josef Gugler and Gudrun Ludwar-Ene, "Gender and Migration in Africa South of the Sahara," in *The Migration Experience in Africa*, ed. Jonathan Baker and Tade Akin Aina (Uppsala: Nordiska Afrikainstitutet, 1995), 257–268.
6. Hania Zlotnik, "Women as Migrants and Workers in Developing Countries," *International Journal of Contemporary Sociology* 30, no. 1 (1993): 39–62; Susan Hanson and Geraldine Pratt, *Gender, Work and Space*, 1st ed.

(London: Routledge, 1995); Sylvia Chant and Sarah A. Radcliffe, "Migration and Development: The Importance of Gender," in *Gender and Migration in Developing Countries*, ed. Sylvia Chant (London and New York: Belhaven Press, 1992), 1–29; Sara R. Curran and Abigail C. Saguy, "Migration and Cultural Change: A Role for Gender and Social Networks," *Journal of International Women's Studies* 2, no. 3 (2001): 54–77; P. R. Pessar and S. J. Mahler, "Transnational Migration: Bringing Gender In," *International Migration Review* 37, no. 3 (2003): 812–846; Boyd and Grieco, "Women and Migration."

7. Monica Kiwanuka, "For Love or Survival: Migrant Women's Narratives of Survival and Intimate Partner Violence in Johannesburg," in *Gender and Migration: Feminist Intervention*, ed. Ingrid Palmary et al. (London: Zed Books, 2010), 163–179; Kate Lefko-Everett, *Voices from the Margins: Migrant Women's Experiences in Southern Africa* (Cape Town: Southern African Migration Project, 2007), http://dspace.cigilibrary.org/jspui/handle/123456789/30713; Victor Muzvidziwa, "Zimbabwe's Cross-Border Women Traders: Multiple Identities and Responses to New Challenges," *Journal of Contemporary African Studies* 19, no. 1 (January 2001): 67–80, doi:10.1080/02589000120028175; Belinda Dodson, "Women on the Move: Gender and Cross-Border Migration to South Africa from Lesotho, Mozambique and Zimbabwe," in *On Borders: Perspectives on International Migration in Southern Africa*, ed. David Alexander McDonald (Ontario: Southern African Migration Project, 2000), 119–150; Belinda Dodson, *Women on the Move: Gender and Cross-border Migration to South Africa* (Pretoria: Idasa, 1998), 9; Theresa Ulicki and Jonathan Crush, "Gender, Farmwork, and Women's Migration from Lesotho to the New South Africa," *Canadian Journal of African Studies* (2000): 64–79; Julie Middleton, "Barriers to Protection: Gender-Related Persecution and Asylum in South Africa," in *Gender and Migration: Feminist Intervention*, ed. Ingrid Palmary et al. (London: Zed Books, 2010), 67–85.

8. Jane I. Guyer, "Household and Community in African Studies," *African Studies Review* 24, no. 2/3 (1981): 87–137.

9. Belinda Bozzoli and Mmantho Nkotsoe, *Women of Phokeng: Consciousness, Life Strategy, and Migrancy in South Africa, 1900–1983* (Johannesburg: Ravan Press, 1991); Christine Obbo, *African Women: Their Struggle for Economic Independence* (London: Zed Books, 1981); Luise White, *The Comforts of Home: Prostitution in Colonial Nairobi*, 1st ed. (Chicago: University of Chicago Press, 1990).

10. Peter Bukasa Kankonde, "Transnational Family Ties, Remittance Motives, and Social Death Among Congolese Migrants: A Socio-Anthropological Analysis.," *Journal of Comparative Family Studies* 41, no. 2 (Spring 2010): 225–243; Dominique Vidal, "Living in, out of, and between Two Cities: Migrants from Maputo in Johannesburg.," *Urban Forum* 21, no. 1 (February 2010): 55–68, doi:10.1007/s12132-010-9080-y.

11. Hania Zlotnik, "The Global Dimensions of Female Migration," *Migration Information Source*, 2003, http://www.migrationinformation.org/Feature/display.cfm?ID=109.

12. Cerstin Sander and Samuel Maimbo, "Migrant Labor Remittances in Africa: Reducing Obstacles to Developmental Contributions," *Africa Regional Working Paper Series* 1 (2005): 80–93.
13. Kankonde, "Transnational Family Ties, Remittance Motives, and Social Death Among Congolese Migrants."
14. Dilip Ratha and William Shaw, *Economic Implications of Remittances and Migration* (Washington, DC: World Bank, 2006)
15. Ibid.
16. George J. Borjas, "Economic Theory and International Migration," *International Migration Review* (1989): 457–485; Michael P. Todaro, *Economics for a Developing World*, 2nd ed. (Essex: Longman, 1982); ibid.
17. Borjas, "Economic Theory and International Migration," 461.
18. Todaro, *Economics for a Developing World*, 213.
19. Anna Lindley, *The Early Morning Phonecall: Remittances from a Refugee Diaspora Perspective*, Working Paper No. 47 (Oxford: Center on Migration, Policy and Society, 2007).
20. See Curran and Saguy, "Migration and Cultural Change." Their work illustrates how gender influences remittance patterns.
21. Stephen Castles and Mark J. Miller, *The Age of Migration, Third Edition: International Population Movements in the Modern World* (New York: The Guilford Press, 2003).
22. Sen, *Social Exclusion*; Amartya Sen, *Development as Freedom*, Reprint (New York: Anchor, 1999).
23. Sen, *Development as Freedom*.
24. Ibid.
25. Martha C. Nussbaum, "Poverty and Human Functioning: Capabilities as Fundamental Entitlements," in *Poverty and Inequality*, ed. David Grusky and Ravi Kanbur, annotated edition (Palo Alto: Stanford University Press, 2006), 47–75.
26. Sen, *Development as Freedom*, 3.
27. Curran and Saguy, "Migration and Cultural Change."
28. Curran and Saguy, "Migration and Cultural Change."
29. Mark Granovetter, "Economic Action and Social Structure: The Problem of Embeddedness," *American Journal of Sociology* 91, no. 3 (November 1, 1985): 481–510.
30. Ibid.
31. Martha C. Nussbaum, *Creating Capabilities: The Human Development Approach* (Cambridge, MA: Belknap Press of Harvard University Press, 2011).
32. Nussbaum, "Poverty and Human Functioning."
33. Ibid., 48.
34. William Julius Wilson, *The Truly Disadvantaged: The Inner City, the Underclass, and Public Policy* (Chicago: University of Chicago Press, 1990).
35. Sen, *Social Exclusion*.
36. Wits, Tufts, and IFAS, "Migration and the New African City" (Johannesburg: Forced Migration Studies Programme, University of the Witwatersrand, 2006).

37. Dodson, *Women on the Move.*

38. Bozzoli and Nkotsoe, *Women of Phokeng.*

39. White, *The Comforts of Home.*

40. Dodson, *Women on the Move.*

41. Z. Jinnah, "Making Home in a Hostile Land: Understanding Somali Identity, Integration, Livelihood and Risks in Johannesburg," *Journal of Sociology and Anthropology* 1, no. 1 (2010): 91–99.

42. Jeanne Batalova and Michael Fix, *Uneven Progress: The Employment Pathways of Skilled Immigrants in the United States* (Washington, DC: Migration Policy Institute, 2008).

43. Marie Wentzel, Johan Viljoen, and Pieter Kok, "Contemporary South African Migration Patterns and Intentions," in *Migration in South and Southern Africa: Dynamics and Determinants*, ed. Pieter Kok, Derik Gelderblom, and John Oucho (Pretoria: HSRC Press, 2006), 171–204.

44. Kankonde, "Transnational Family Ties, Remittance Motives, and Social Death Among Congolese Migrants"; Désiré wa Kabwe and Aurelia wa Kabwe Segatti, "Paradoxical Expressions of a Return to the Homeland: Music and Literature Among the Congolese (Zairean) Diaspora," in *New African Diasporas*, ed. Khalid Koser (London: Routledge, 2003), 124–139; Didier Gondola, *The History of Congo*, annotated edition (Westport: Greenwood, 2002).

45. Todaro, *Economics for a Developing World.*

46. Kankonde, "Transnational Family Ties, Remittance Motives, and Social Death Among Congolese Migrants."

47. Didier C. Gondola, "Dream and Drama: The Search for Elegance Among Congolese Youth," *African Studies Review* 42, no. 1 (1999): 23–48.

48. Rousseau C et al., "Between Myth and Madness: The Premigration Dream of Leaving Among Young Somali Refugees" Text, accessed September 9, 2011, http://www.ingentaconnect.com/content/klu/medi/1998/00000022/00000004/00192801.

49. Gloria Anzaldúa, *Borderlands / La Frontera: The New Mestiza, Third Edition*, 3rd ed. (San Francisco: Aunt Lute Books, 2007), 19.

50. Victor Turner, *The Ritual Process: Structure and Anti-Structure*, 2nd ed. (Ithaca, NY: Cornell University Press, 1977), 97.

51. Kankonde, "Transnational Family Ties, Remittance Motives, and Social Death Among Congolese Migrants."

4 Turning the Home Inside-Out—Private Space and Everyday Politics

1. Claudia Jones, *An End to the Neglect of the Problems of the Negro Woman!* (New York: National Women's Commission, C. P. U.S.A., 1949).

2. Carol Hanisch, "The Personal Is Political," *Notes from the Second Year: Women's Liberation* (1970): 76–78, http://www.carolhanisch.org/CHwritings/PersonalisPol.pdf.

3. Charles Mills W, *The Sociological Imagination* (Oxford: Oxford University Press, 1959).

4. Manuel Castells, *Urban Question: A Marxist Approach* (London: Edward Arnold, 1977); David Harvey, *Social Justice and the City*. (London: Edward Arnold, 1973); David Harvey, "The Urban Process Under Capitalism: A Framework for Analysis," in *The Blackwell City Reader*, ed. Gary Bridge and Sophie Watson (Oxford: Wiley-Blackwell, 2002), 116–124.

5. Ernest W. Burgess, "The Growth of the City," in *The Blackwell City Reader*, ed. Gary Bridge and Sophie Watson (Oxford: Wiley-Blackwell, 2002), 244–250.

6. Tamara K. Hareven, "The History of the Family as an Interdisciplinary Field," *The Journal of Interdisciplinary History* 2, no. 2 (1971): 399–414; Elizabeth H. Pleck, "Two Worlds in One: Work and Family," *Journal of Social History* 10, no. 2 (1976): 178–195; John Modell and Tamara K. Hareven, "Urbanization and the Malleable Household: An Examination of Boarding and Lodging in American Families," *Journal of Marriage and Family* 35, no. 3 (1973): 467–479.

7. Leonore Davidoff, "Regarding Some 'Old Husbands' Tales': Public and Private in Feminist History," in *Feminism, the Public and the Private*, ed. Joan B. Landes (Oxford: Oxford University Press, USA, 1998), 164–194.

8. Modell and Hareven, "Urbanization and the Malleable Household."

9. See Miriam Grant, "Strangers in Our Home: Spatiality and Locale of Monomatapa Township, Gwelo, Rhodesia (1953–1979)," *Canadian Journal of African Studies* (1998): 32–64.

10. See Aderanti Adepoju, *Family, Population and Development in Africa* (London: Zed Books, 1997); Sally E. Findley, "Migration and Family Interactions in Africa," in *Family, Population and Development in Africa*, ed. Aderanti Adepoju (London: Zed Books, 1997), 109–138.

11. Laura Longmore, *The Dispossessed: A Study of the Sex-life of Bantu Women in Urban Areas in and Around Johannesburg* (Cape Town: J. Cape, 1959); Ellen Hellmann, *Rooiyard: a Sociological Survey of an Urban Native Slum Yard* (London: Oxford University Press., 1949); Christine Obbo, *African Women: Their Struggle for Economic Independence* (London: Zed Books, 1981); Luise White, *The Comforts of Home: Prostitution in Colonial Nairobi*, 1st ed. (Chicago: University of Chicago Press, 1990); Philip Bonner, "Desireable or Undesireable Basotho Women: Liquor, Prostitution and the Migration of Basotho Women to the Rand, 1920–1945," in *Women and Gender in Southern Africa to 1945*, ed. Cherryl Walker (Claremont: David Philip Publishers, 1990), 221–250; Walker, Cherryl, "Gender and the Development of the Migrant Labour System c. 1850–1930," in *Women and Gender in Southern Africa to 1945*, ed. Cherryl Walker (Claremont: David Philip Publishers, 1990), 168–196.

12. M. Huchzermeyer, "Housing for the Poor? Negotiated Housing Policy in South Africa," *Habitat International* 25, no. 3 (2001): 303–331; J. Hills, "Inclusion or Exclusion? The Role of Housing Subsidies and Benefits," *Urban Studies* 38, no. 11 (2001): 1887–1902; Tanya Zack and Sarah Charlton, "Better Off, but . . . Beneficiaries' Perceptions of the Government's Housing Subsidy Scheme" (Unpublished paper prepared for the Department of Housing, Pretoria, 2003).

13. Alison Todes, "Housing Integrated Urban Development and the Compact City Debate," in *Confronting Fragmentation: Housing and Urban Development*

in a Democratising Society, ed. Philip Harrison, Marie Huchzermeyer, and Mzwanele Mayekiso (Cape Town: University of Cape Town Press, 2003), 109–139.

14. Yakoob Makda, "From Slum to (Financial) Sustainability: Johannesburg's Better Building Programme," *Development Update* 5, no. 1 (2004): 177–186.

15. Richard Tomlinson, "HIV/AIDS and Urban Disintegration in Johannesburg," in *Confronting Fragmentation: Housing and Urban Development in a Democratising Society*, ed. Philip Harrison, Marie Huchzermeyer, and Mzwanele Mayekiso (Cape Town: University of Cape Town Press, 2003), 76–87.

16. Claire Benit-Gbaffou, Sophie Didier, and Marianne Morange, "Communities, the Private Sector, and the State Contested Forms of Security Governance in Cape Town and Johannesburg," *Urban Affairs Review* 43, no. 5 (2008): 691–717.

17. Beatrice Hibou, "From Privatising the Economy to Privatising the State: An Analysis of the Continual Formation of the State," in *Privatising the State* (London: C. Hurst, 2004), 1–47.

18. Sarah Deutsch, *Women and the City: Gender, Space, and Power in Boston, 1870–1940* (Oxford: Oxford University Press, 2000), 13.

19. Navnita Chadha Behera, *Gender, Conflict and Migration* (New Delhi: Sage Publications, 2006), 37.

20. Saba Gul Khattak, "Violence and Home: Afghan Women's Experience of Displacement," in *Gender, Conflict and Migration*, ed. Navnita Chadha Behera (New Delhi: Sage Publications, 2006), 116–136.

21. Ibid.

22. Caroline Wanjiku Kihato, "A Picture Speaks a Thousand Words," *Scrutiny2* 15, no. 1 (May 2010): 33–54, doi:10.1080/18125441.2010.500457.

23. Marianne Hirsch, "Introduction: Familial Looking," in *The Familial Gaze*, ed. Marianne Hirsch, 1st ed. (Sudbury: Dartmouth, 1999), x–xxv; Deborah Willis, *Picturing Us: African American Identity in Photography* (New York: New Press, 1994); bell hooks, "In Our Glory: Photography and Black Life," in *Picturing Us: African American Identity in Photography*, ed. Deborah Willis (New York: New Press, 1994), 43–54.

24. bell hooks, "In Our Glory," 46.

25. Charlotte Perkins Gilman, *Women and Economics: A Study of the Economic Relation Between Women and Men* (New York: Prometheus Books, 1994); Betty Friedan, *The Feminine Mystique*, Reprint (New York: W. W. Norton, 2001).

26. Modell and Hareven, "Urbanization and the Malleable Household."

27. Chandra Talpade Mohanty, *Feminism Without Borders: Decolonizing Theory, Practicing Solidarity* (Durham: Duke University Press Books, 2003).

28. Sarah Pink, *Home Truths: Gender, Domestic Objects and Everyday Life*, English ed. (Oxford: Berg, 2004).

29. Ibid., 91.

30. Grant, "Strangers in Our Home." makes the same argument of urbanizing Africans in post–Second World War Rhodesia.

31. Lisa Vetten, "Addressing Domestic Violence in South Africa: Reflections on Strategy and Practice" (New York: UN Division for the Advancement of Women, 2005).

32. Monica Kiwanuka, "For Love or Survival: Migrant Women's Narratives of Survival and Intimate Partner Violence in Johannesburg," in *Gender and Migration: Feminist Intervention*, ed. Ingrid Palmary et al. (London: Zed Books, 2010), 163–179.

33. CORMSA, *Protecting Refugees, Asylum Seekers and Immigrants in South Africa* (Johannesburg: CORMSA, 2008); Kiwanuka, "For Love or Survival"; Anita Raj and Jay Silverman, "Violence Against Immigrant Women," *Violence Against Women* 8, no. 3 (March 1, 2002): 367–398, doi:10.1177/10778010222183107.

34. R. Jewkes et al., "Preventing Rape and Violence in South Africa: Call for Leadership in a New Agenda for Action," *MRC Policy Brief* (2009), http://www.mrc.ac.za/gender/prev_rapedd041209.pdf.

35. Lisa Vetten, "Addressing Domestic Violence in South Africa."

36. Joanna Vearey, "Hidden Spaces and Urban Health: Exploring the Tactics of Rural Migrants Navigating the City of Gold.," *Urban Forum* 21, no. 1 (February 2010): 37–53, doi:10.1007/s12132-010-9079-4.

37. Jewkes et al., "Preventing Rape and Violence in South Africa."

38. Kiwanuka, "For Love or Survival."

39. Sangeetha Madhavan and Loren B. Landau, "Bridges to Nowhere: Hosts, Migrants and the Chimera of Social Capital in Three African Cities," *Population and Development Review* 37, no. 3 (2011): 473–497.

40. Graeme Gotz and AbdouMaliq Simone, "On Belonging and Becoming in African Cities," in *Emerging Johannesburg*, ed. Richard Tomlinson et al., 1st ed. (London: Routledge, 2003), 123–147.

41. Georg Simmel, "Metropolis and Mental Life," in *Understanding Everyday Life*, ed. Tony Bennett and Diane Watson, 1st ed. (Oxford: Wiley-Blackwell, 2002), 124–126.

42. Nick Devas, *Urban Governance Voice and Poverty in the Developing World* (Oxford: EarthScan, 2004), 63.

43. Louis Wirth, "Urbanism as a Way of Life," *American Journal of Sociology* (1938): 12.

44. AbdouMaliq Simone, "The Ambivalence of the Arbitrary.," *Theory, Culture & Society* 28, no. 1 (January 2011): 129–137, doi:10.1177/0263276410387624.

45. Theresa A. Martinez, "Making Oppositional Culture, Making Standpoint: A Journey into Gloria Anzald'ua's Borderlands," *Sociological Spectrum* 25, no. 5 (2005): 539–570.

5   The Station, Camp, and Refugee: Xenophobic Violence and the City

1. Richard Bullard, "Illegal Immigrants Deserve What's Coming to Them," *Sunday Times* (Johannesburg, October 19, 2003), 1st edition; Thomas

Thale, "Drama as Police Swoop on Inner City Buildings," *City of Joburg*, September 25, 2003, http://www.joburg.org.za/2003/spet/sept25 _hillbrowswoop.stm; Faranaaz Parker, "Jo'burg Sends in Red Ants in Defiance of ConCourt," *The M&G Online*, 2012, http://mg.co.za /article/2012–01–18-joburg-sends-in-red-ants-defiance-of-concourt/.

2. Jean-Pierre Misago et al., "May 2008 Violence Against Foreign Nationals in South Africa: Understanding Causes and Evaluating Responses" (Johannesburg: Forced Migration Studies Programme, 2010).

3. Ibid.

4. Ibid.

5. Giorgio Agamben, *Homo Sacer: Sovereign Power and Bare Life*, 1st ed. (Palo Alto: Stanford University Press, 1998); Hannah Arendt, *Essays in Understanding*, ed. Jerome Kohn, 1st ed. (New York: Houghton Mifflin Harcourt, 1994).

6. Agamben, *Homo Sacer.*

7. Tamlyn Monson, *Report on the SAHRC Investigation into Issues of Rule of Law, Justice and Impunity Arising Out of the 2008 Public Violence Against Non-nationals* (Johannesburg: South African Human Rights Commission, 2010); Julia Hornberger, *Policing and Human Rights: The Meaning of Violence and Justice in the Everyday Policing of Johannesburg*, 1st ed. (London: Routledge, 2011); Darshan Vigneswaran and Julia Hornberger, *Beyond Good Cop / Bad Cop: Understanding Informality and Police Corruption in South Africa* (Johannesburg, South Africa: African Center for Migration in Society, 2009).

8 Monson, *Report on the SAHRC Investigation.*

9. Francis B. Nyamnjoh, *Insiders and Outsiders: Citizenship and Xenophobia in Contemporary Southern Africa* (London: Zed Books, 2006); Jonathan Crush, Vincent Williams, and Kate Lefko-Everett, *The Perfect Storm: Xenophobia in Contemporary South Africa*, 50 (Cape Town: Southern African Migration Project, 2008); Michael Neocosmos, *From "Foreign Natives" to "Native Foreigners": Explaining Xenophobia in Post-apartheid South Africa, Citizenship and Nationalism, Identity and Politics*, 2nd ed. (Dakar, Senegal: CODESRIA, 2010).

10. See Monson, *Report on the SAHRC Investigation.*

11. Gareth Newham, Themba Masuku, and Jabu Dlamini, *Diversity and Transformation in the South African Police Service: A Study of Police Perspectives on Race, Gender and the Community in the Johannesburg Policing Area* (Johannesburg: Centre for the Study of Violence and Reconciliation, 2006).

12. Cf. Ibid., 44.

13. Newham, Masuku, and Dlamini, *Diversity and Transformation in the South African Police Service.*

14. Julia Hornberger, "'My Police—your Police': The Informal Privatisation of the Police in the Inner City of Johannesburg," *African Studies* 63, no. 2 (2004): 213–230; Hornberger, *Policing and Human Rights.*

15. See for example Jonny Steinberg, *Thin Blue: The Unwritten Rules of South African Policing* (Jeppestown: Jonathan Ball Publishing, 2009).

16. Hornberger, *Policing and Human Rights.*

17. Ibid.; Vigneswaran and Hornberger, *Beyond Good Cop / Bad Cop.*

18   Devan Pillay, "Relative Deprivation, Social Instability and Cultures of Entitlement," in *Go Home or Die Here: Violence, Xenophobia and the Reinvention of Difference in South Africa*, ed. Tawana Kupe, Eric Worby, and Shireen Hassim (Johannesburg: Witwatersrand University Press, 2008), 93–103; Stephen Gelb, "Behind Xenophobia in South Africa—Poverty or Inequality?," in *Go Home or Die Here: Violence, Xenophobia and the Reinvention of Difference in South Africa*, ed. Tawana Kupe, Eric Worby, and Shireen Hassim (Johannesburg: Witwatersrand University Press, 2008), 79–91; Melinda Silverman and Tanya Zack, "Housing Delivery, the Urban Crisis and Xenophobia," in *Go Home or Die Here: Violence, Xenophobia and the Reinvention of Difference in South Africa*, ed. Tawana Kupe, Eric Worby, and Shireen Hassim (Johannesburg: Witwatersrand University Press, 2008), 147–159.

19.   Monson, *Report on the SAHRC Investigation.*

20.   Celia W. Dugger and Alan Cowell, "South Africa Weighs Plan to Shelter Refugees," *The New York Times*, May 29, 2008, sec. International / Africa, http://www.nytimes.com/2008/05/29/world/africa/29safrica.html.

21.   Nicole Johnston, "Out in the Cold (Once Again)," *Mail & Guardian* (Johannesburg, July 28, 2008), http://mg.co.za/article/2008–07–28-out-in-the-cold-once-again.

22.   Amnesty International, "'Talk for Us Please': Limited Options Acing Individual Displaced by Xenophobic Violence." (Amnesty International, September 2008).

23.   Johnston, "Out in the Cold (Once Again)."

24.   Judith Hayem, "May 2008 as a Revelator? National Identity, Human Rights and the Nature of Politics" (presented at the 3rd European Conference on African Studies 4–7 June, Leipzig, 2009).

25.   Shaun Smillie and Kanina Foss, "Peaceful Refugee Removal Next to Highway," *IOL News* (Johannesburg, July 29, 2008), http://www.iol.co.za/news/south-africa/peaceful-refugee-removal-next-to-highway-1.410178#.UE2-ekTdlJM.

26.   Thabo Mbeki, "Radio and Television Address to the Nation by the President of South Africa, Thabo Mbeki, on the Occasion of Africa Day" (South African Government Information, May 25, 2008), http://www.info.gov.za/speeches.

27.   Phumzile Mlambo-Ngcuka , "Deputy President Phumzile Mlambo-Ngcuka Speaks Out Against the Violent Attacks on Foreigners and Calls for Calm" (South African Government Information, May 23, 2008), http://www/info.gov.za/speeches.

28.   Giorgio Agamben, "We Refugees," *Symposium* 49, no. 2 (1995): 114–119; Veena Das and Deborah Poole, "State and Its Margins: Comparative Ethnographies," in *Anthropology in the Margins of the State*, ed. Veena Das and Deborah Poole, 1st ed., School of American Research Advanced Seminar Series (Santa Fe, NM: School of American Research Press, 2004), 3–34.

29.   Michel Foucault, *Discipline and Punish: The Birth of the Prison* (New York: Pantheon Books, 1977); Agamben, "We Refugees."

30. Das and Poole, "State and Its Margins," 13.
31. Das and Poole, "State and Its Margins."
32. Achille Mbembe, *On the Postcolony*, 1st ed. (Berkeley: University of California Press, 2001).
33. Giorgio Agamben, *State of Exception*, 1st ed. (Chicago: University of Chicago Press, 2005).
34. Das and Poole, "State and Its Margins."
35. Ibid., 19.
36. Loren B. Landau, ed., *Exorcising the Demons Within: Xenophobia, Violence and Statecraft in Contemporary South Africa* (Johannesburg: Wits University Press, 2011); Monson, *Report on the SAHRC Investigation*; Misago et al., "May 2008 Violence Against Foregin Nationals in South Africa."
37. Andrea Hart and Jean Yung, "Refugees in Mass Suicide Scare," *IOL News* (June 9, 2008), Online edition, http://www.iol.co.za/news/south-africa/refugees-in-mass-suicide-scare-1.403665#.UFmhahjdlJM.
38. Michalinos Zembylas, "Agamben's Theory of Biopower and Immigrants/Refugees / Asylum Seekers: Discourses of Citizenship and the Implications for Curriculum Theorizing," *Journal of Curriculum Theorizing* 26, no. 2 (September 12, 2010), http://journal.jctonline.org/index.php/jct/article/viewArticle/195.
39. Lisa H. Malkki, "Speechless Emissaries: Refugees, Humanitarianism, and Dehistoricization," *Cultural Anthropology* 11, no. 3 (1996): 377–404.
40. Ibid.

6 Conclusion: Ways of Seeing—Migrant Women in the Liminal City

1. James C Scott, *Seeing Like a State: How Certain Schemes to Improve the Human Condition Have Failed*, (New Haven, CT: Yale University Press, 1998); Michel Foucault, *Power: The Essential Works of Michel Foucault 1954–1984 (Essential Works of Foucault 3)*, ed. James D. Faubion (London: Penguin Books, 1994).
2. James Donald, *Imagining The Modern City*, 1st ed. (Minneapolis: University of Minnesota Press, 1999), 13.
3. Michel De Certeau, *The Practice of Everyday Life* (Berkeley: University of California Press, 1984), xiii.
4. Jeff Guy, *The View Across the River: Harriette Colenso and the Zulu Struggle Against Imperialism* (Claremont: David Philip Publishers, 2001).
5. Barbara Wolbert, "The Anthropologist as Photographer: The Visual Construction of Ethnographic Authority," *Visual Anthropology* 13, no. 4 (2000): 321–343.
6. Susan Sontag, *On Photography* (New York: Picador, 1977); Jay Ruby, "Seeing Through Pictures: The Anthropology of Photography" 1, no. 4 (1981): 3–16.

7. See for example, Guy Tillim, *Jo'burg* (Johannesburg: STE Publishers, 2005); Terry Kurgan and Jo Ractliffe, *Johannesburg Circa Now: Photography and the City* (Johannesburg: T. Kurgan and J. Ractliffe, 2005).

8. Terry Kurgan's *Hotel Yeoville* (Johannesburg: Fourthwall Books, 2013) provides a rich archive of images and short films shot by Yeoville residents.

9. See for example, Lorraine Young and Hazel Barrett, "Adapting Visual Methods: Action Research with Kampala Street Children," *Area* 33, no. 2 (2002): 144; bell hooks, "In Our Glory: Photography and Black Life," in *Picturing Us: African American Identity in Photography*, ed. Deborah Willis (New York: New Press, 1994), 43–54.

10. Daniel M. Goldstein, "Desconfianza and Problems of Representation in Urban Ethnography," *Anthropological Quarterly* 75, no. 3 (2002): 485–517.

11. Stuart Hall, "The Work of Representation," in *Representation: Cultural Representations and Signifying Practices*, ed. Stuart Hall, 1st ed. (London: Sage Publications & Open University, 1997), 13–64; Jessica Evans and Professor Stuart Hall, *Visual Culture: The Reader,* 1st ed. (London: Sage Publications, 1999).

12. See Sebastiao Salgado, "Migrations: Humanity in Transition. Interview with Nandy Madlin," 2005, http://pdngallery.com/legends/legends10/migration.pdf.

13. Sontag, *On Photography*, 5.

14. Peter Hamilton, "Representing the Social: France and Frenchness in Post-war Humanist Photography," in *Representation: Cultural Representations and Signifying Practices*, ed. Stuart Hall, 1st ed. (London: Sage Publications & Open University, 1997), 81.

15. Foucault, *Power*.

16. John R. Short, *Urban Theory: A Critical Assessment* (Basingstoke, UK: Palgrave Macmillan, 2006), 40.

17. See Nicola Piper, "Feminization of Labor Migration as Violence Against Women International, Regional, and Local Nongovernmental Organization Responses in Asia," *Violence Against Women* 9, no. 6 (2003): 723–745; Gloria Chammartin, "The Feminization of International Migration," *International Migration Programme: International Labour Organization* (2001): 37–40.

18. See Jina Krause-Vilmar and Josh Chaffin, *No Place to Go but up: Urban Refugees in Johannesburg, South Africa* (New York: Women's Refugee Commission, 2011).

19. Laura M. Agustin, "A Migrant World of Services," *Social Politics: International Studies in Gender, State & Society* 10, no. 3 (2003): 378.

20. Mats Utas, "Victimcy, Girlfriending, Soldiering: Tactic Agency in a Young Woman's Social Navigation of the Liberian War Zone," *Anthropological Quarterly* 78, no. 2 (2005): 403–430.

21. Leone De Kock, *Civilising Barbarians: Missionary Narrative and African Textual Response in Nineteenth-Century South Africa* (Johannesburg: Witwatersrand University Press, 1996).

22. See Lisa Vetten, "Addressing Domestic Violence in South Africa: Reflections on Strategy and Practice" (New York: UN Division for the Advancement of Women, 2005).

23. Joanna Vearey, "Hidden Spaces and Urban Health: Exploring the Tactics of Rural Migrants Navigating the City of Gold," *Urban Forum* 21, no. 1 (February 2010): 37–53, doi:10.1007/s12132–010–9079–4.

24. Arne Tostensen, Inge Tvedten, and Mariken Vaa, *Associational Life in African Cities: Popular Responses to the Urban Crisis* (Uppsala: Nordic Africa Institute, 2001); Patsy Healey and Stuart Cameron, *Managing Cities: The New Urban Context*, ed. Simin Davoudi, Stephen Graham, and Ali Madani-Pour (San Francisco: J. Wiley, 1995), http://en.scientificcommons.org/22435110; Richard E Stren and Rodney R White, eds., *African Cities in Crisis: Managing Rapid Urban Growth*, African Modernization and Development Series v. 5 (Boulder: Westview Press, 1989).

25. Patrick Heller, "Reclaiming Democratic Spaces: Civics and Politics in Posttransition Johannesburg," in *Emerging Johannesburg*, ed. Richard Tomlinson et al., 1st ed. (London: Routledge, 2003), 155–184; Jo Beall, Owen Crankshaw, and Susan Parnell, *Uniting a Divided City: Governance and Social Exclusion in Johannesburg* (London: Routledge, 2002).

26. Steven Friedman, "A Voice Is Heard in the City: Inclusive Cities and Citizen Voice," in *Urban Diversity: Space, Culture, and Inclusive Pluralism in Cities Worldwide*, ed. Caroline Wanjiku Kihato et al., 1st ed. (Baltimore: The Johns Hopkins University Press, 2010), 355.

27. AbdouMaliq Simone, "The Dilemmas of Informality for African Governance," in *Democratising Local Government: The South African Experiment*, ed. Susan Parnell et al. (Cape Town: University of Cape Town Press, 2002), 294–304; AbdouMaliq Simone, "Urban Circulation and the Everyday Politics of African Urban Youth: The Case of Douala, Cameroon.," *International Journal of Urban & Regional Research* 29, no. 3 (2005): 516–532, doi:10.1111/j.1468–2427.2005.00603.x.

28. Fassil Demissie, "Imperial Legacies and Postcolonial Predicaments: An Introduction," *African Identities* 5, no. 2 (2007): 155–165.

29. Jean-François Bayart and International African Institute, *The Criminalization of the State in Africa*, African Issues (Oxford: International African Institute in association with J. Currey, 1999).

30. Anne Clunan, "Ungoverned Spaces? The Need for Reevaluation," in *Ungoverned Spaces: Alternatives to State Authority in An Era of Softened Sovereignty*, ed. Anne L Clunan and Harold A Trinkunas (Stanford, CA: Stanford Security Studies, 2010), 3–16.

31. Victoria Sanford, "Contesting Displacement in Columbia: Citizenship and State Sovereignty at the Margins," in *Anthropology in the Margins of the State*, ed. Veena Das and Deborah Poole, 1st ed., School of American Research Advanced Seminar Series (Santa Fe, NM: School of American Research Press, 2004), 259.

32. Sudhir Alladi Venkatesh, *Off the Books: The Underground Economy of the Urban Poor* (Cambridge: Harvard University Press, 2009), 218.

33. William Julius Wilson, *The Truly Disadvantaged: The Inner City, the Underclass, and Public Policy* (Chicago: University of Chicago Press, 1990); Sudhir Alladi Venkatesh, *American Project: The Rise and Fall of a Modern Ghetto* (Cambridge, MA: Harvard University Press, 2002).
34. Graeme Gotz and Simone AbdouMaliq, "On Belonging and Becoming in African Cities," in *Emerging Johannesburg*, ed. Richard Tomlinson et al., 1st ed. (London: Routledge, 2003), 123–147; AbdouMaliq Simone, *For the City Yet to Come: Changing African Life in Four Cities* (Durham, NC: Duke University Press Books, 2004); F. Le Marcis, "The Suffering Body of the City," *Public Culture* 16, no. 3 (2004): 453–477.
35. Wits, Tufts, and IFAS, "Migration and the New African City,"Johannesburg: Forced Migration Studies Programme, University of the Witwatersrand, 2006; Loren B. Landau and Veronique Gindrey, "Gauteng 2055: Trend Paper: Population and Migration" (Report compiled for the Gauteng Department of Economic Development, 2008); Sangeetha Madhavan and Loren B. Landau, "Bridges to Nowhere: Hosts, Migrants and the Chimera of Social Capital in Three African Cities," *Population and Development Review* 37, no. 3 (2011): 473–497.
36. Gotz and AbdouMaliq, "On Belonging and Becoming in African Cities."

Bibliography

Adepoju, Aderanti. *Family, Population and Development in Africa*. London: Zed Books, 1997.

Agamben, Giorgio. *Homo Sacer: Sovereign Power and Bare Life*. 1st edition. Palo Alto: Stanford University Press, 1998.

———. *State of Exception*. 1st edition. Chicago: University of Chicago Press, 2005.

———. "We Refugees." *Symposium* 49, no. 2 (1995): 114–119.

Agustin, Laura M. "A Migrant World of Services." *Social Politics: International Studies in Gender, State & Society* 10, no. 3 (2003): 377–396.

Amit, Roni, Darshan Vigneswaran, George M. Wachira, and Tamlyn Monson. "National Survey of the Refugee Reception and Status Determination System in South Africa" (Johannesburg: Migrant Rights Monitoring Project Research Report, 2009).

Amnesty International. "'Talk for Us Please': Limited Options Facing Individuals Displaced by Xeonophobic Violence." Amnesty International, September 2008.

Anzaldúa, Gloria. *Borderlands / La Frontera: The New Mestiza, Third Edition*. San Francisco: Aunt Lute Books, 2007.

Arendt, Hannah. *Essays in Understanding*. Edited by Jerome Kohn. 1st edition. New York: Houghton Mifflin Harcourt, 1994.

Barry, Andrew, Thomas Osborne, and Nikolas S. Rose. *Foucault and Political Reason: Liberalism, Neo-liberalism, and Rationalities of Government*. Chicago: University of Chicago Press, 1996.

Batalova, Jeanne, and Michael Fix. *Uneven Progress: The Employment Pathways of Skilled Immigrants in the United States*. Washington, DC: Migration Policy Institute, 2008.

Bauman, Zygmunt. *Globalization: The Human Consequences*. New York: Columbia University Press, 1998.

Bayart, Jean-François and International African Institute. *The Criminalization of the State in Africa*. African Issues. Oxford: International African Institute in association with J. Currey, 1999.

Beall, Jo, Owen Crankshaw, and Susan Parnell. *Uniting a Divided City: Governance and Social Exclusion in Johannesburg*. London: Routledge, 2002.

Beavon, Keith Sidney Orrock. *Johannesburg: The Making and Shaping of the City*. 1st edition. Pretoria: University of South Africa Press, 2004.

Behera, Navnita Chadha. *Gender, Conflict and Migration*. New Delhi: Sage Publications, 2006.

Benit-Gbaffou, Claire, Sophie Didier, and Marianne Morange. "Communities, the Private Sector, and the State Contested Forms of Security Governance in Cape Town and Johannesburg." *Urban Affairs Review* 43, no. 5 (2008): 691–717.

Benjamin, Walter. *Charles Baudelaire: A Lyric Poet in the Era of High Capitalism*. Translated by Harry Zohn. Brooklyn: Verso Books, 1997.

———. *The Arcades Project*. Edited by Rolf Tiedemann. Translated by Howard Eiland and Kevin McLaughlin. Cambridge, MA: Belknap Press of Harvard University Press, 2002.

Berger, John. *Ways of Seeing*. 1st edition. London: Penguin (Non-Classics), 1990.

Bond, Patrick. *Cities of Gold, Townships of Coal: Essays on South Africa's New Urban Crisis*. Trenton: Africa World Press, 2000.

Bonner, Philip. "Desireable or Undesireable Basotho Women: Liquor, Prostitution and the Migration of Basotho Women to the Rand, 1920–1945." In *Women and Gender in Southern Africa to 1945*. Edited by Cherryl Walker. Claremont: David Philip Publishers, 1990, 221–250.

Bonner, Philip, Peter Delius, and Deborah Posel. *Apartheid's Genesis, 1935–1962*. Illustrated edition. Johannesburg: Ravan Press, 1994.

Bonner, Philip, and Lauren Segal. *Soweto: A History*. Cape Town: Maskew Miller Longman, 1998.

Bonner, Philip L. and Noor Nieftagodien. *Alexandra: A History*. Johannesburg: Wits University Press, 2008.

Borjas, George J. "Economic Theory and International Migration." *International Migration Review* (1989): 457–485.

Boyd, Monica and Elizabeth Grieco. "Women and Migration: Incorporating Gender into International Migration Theory." *The Migration Information Source*, 2003. http://www.migrationinformation.org/feature/display.cfm?id=106.

Bozzoli, Belinda and Mmantho Nkotsoe. *Women of Phokeng: Consciousness, Life Strategy, and Migrancy in South Africa, 1900–1983*. Johannesburg: Ravan Press, 1991.

Bridge, Gary and Watson, Sophie. "Introduction: Reading Division and Difference." In *The Blackwell City Reader*. Edited by Gary Bridge and Sophie Watson. Oxford: Wiley-Blackwell, 2002, 237–243.

Bullard, Richard. "Illegal Immigrants Deserve What's Coming to Them." *Sunday Times*. Johannesburg, October 19, 2003, 1st edition.

Burchell, Graham, Colin Gordon, and Peter Miller. *The Foucault Effect: Studies in Governmentality*. 1st edition. Chicago: University of Chicago Press, 1991.

Burgess, Ernest W. "The Growth of the City." In *The Blackwell City Reader*. Edited by Gary Bridge and Sophie Watson. Oxford: Wiley-Blackwell, 2002, 244–250.

Card, Claudia. "Genocide and Social Death." *Hypatia* 18 (2003): 63–79. doi:10.1353/hyp.2003.0006.

Castells, Manuel. *The Rise of the Network Society (The Information Age: Economy, Society and Culture, Volume 1)*. 2nd edition. Oxford: Wiley-Blackwell, 2000.

———. *Urban Question: A Marxist Approach*. London: Edward Arnold, 1977.

Castles, Stephen and Mark J. Miller. *The Age of Migration, Third Edition: International Population Movements in the Modern World*. New York: The Guilford Press, 2003.

Certeau, Michel De. *The Practice of Everyday Life*. Berkeley: University of California Press, 1984.

Chammartin, Gloria. "The Feminization of International Migration." *International Migration Programme: International Labour Organization* (2001): 37–40.

Chant, Sylvia and Sarah A. Radcliffe. "Migration and Development: The Importance of Gender." In *Gender and Migration in Developing Countries*. Edited by Sylvia Chant. London and New York: Belhaven Press, 1992, 1–29.

Chipkin, Ivor. "A Developmental Role for Local Government." In *Democratising Local Government: The South African Experiment*. edited by Susan Parnell, Edgar Pieterse, Mark Swilling, and Dominique Wooldridge. Cape Town: University of Cape Town Press, 2002, 57–78.

City of Johannesburg Metropolitan Municipality. "Street Trading By-laws No.179." City of Johannesburg, 2004. http://www.joburg.org.za/bylaws/streettrading_by-laws.pdf.

Clunan, Anne. "Ungoverned Spaces? The Need for Reevaluation." In *Ungoverned Spaces: Alternatives to State Authority in An Era of Softened Sovereignty*. Edited by Anne L Clunan and Harold A Trinkunas. Stanford, CA: Stanford Security Studies, 2010, 3–16.

Clunan, Anne L and Harold A Trinkunas, eds. *Ungoverned Spaces: Alternatives to State Authority in An Era of Softened Sovereignty*. Stanford, CA: Stanford Security Studies, 2010.

Cohen, Robin. *Endgame in South Africa?* Suffolk: James Currey, 1986.

Collins, Patricia Hill. *Black Feminist Thought: Knowledge, Consciousness, and the Politics of Empowerment*. Revised, 10th Anniv., 2nd edition. New York: Routledge, 2000.

CORMSA. *Protecting Refugees, Asylum Seekers and Immigrants in South Africa*. Johannesburg: CORMSA, 2008.

Cronin, Ciaran. "Bourdieu and Foucault on Power and Modernity." *Philosophy & Social Criticism* 22, no. 6 (November 1, 1996): 55–85. doi:10.1177/019145379602200603.

Crush, Jonathan, Alan Jeeves, and David Yudelman. *South Africa's Labor Empire: A History of Black Migrancy to the Gold Mines*. Boulder, CO: Westview Press (Short Disc), 1991.

Crush, Jonathan, Vincent Williams, and Kate Lefko-Everett. *The Perfect Storm: Xenophobia in Contemporary South Africa*. 50. Cape Town: Southern African Migration Project, 2008.

Curran, Sara R. and Abigail C. Saguy. "Migration and Cultural Change: A Role for Gender and Social Networks." *Journal of International Women's Studies* 2, no. 3 (2001): 54–77.

Das, Veena and Deborah Poole. "State and Its Margins: Comparative Ethnographies." In *Anthropology in the Margins of the State*. Edited by Veena Das and Deborah Poole. 1st edition. School of American Research Advanced Seminar Series. Santa Fe, NM: School of American Research Press, 2004, 3–34.

Davenport, Rodney. "Historical Background of the Apartheid City to 1948." In *Apartheid City in Transition*. Edited by Mark Swilling, Richard Humphries, and Khehla Shubane. Cape Town: Oxford University Press, 1991, 1–18.

Davidoff, Leonore. "Regarding Some 'Old Husbands' Tales': Public and Private in Feminist History." In *Feminism, the Public and the Private*. Edited by Joan B. Landes. Oxford: Oxford University Press, 1998, 164–194.

De Kock, Leone. *Civilising Barbarians: Missionary Narrative and African Textual Response in Nineteenth-Century South Africa*. Johannesburg: Witwatersrand University Press, 1996. http://www.getcited.org/pub/100279974.

Demissie, F. "Imperial Legacies and Postcolonial Predicaments: An Introduction." *African Identities 5*, no. 2 (2007): 155–165.

Department of Home Affairs (DHA). "Building a New Home Affairs: An Update on the Transformation Programme." In *Presentation to the Select Committee on Social Services*. Cape Town: Department of Home Affairs, 2008.

Department of Home Affairs (DHA). "Turnaround Strategy." In *Document Presented to a Briefing of the Joint Committee of Parliament*. Cape Town: Department of Home Affairs, 2004.

Deutsch, Sarah. *Women and the City: Gender, Space, and Power in Boston, 1870–1940*. Oxford: Oxford University Press, 2000.

Devas, Nick. *Urban Governance Voice and Poverty in the Developing World*. Oxford: EarthScan, 2004.

Dodson, Belinda. *Women on the Move: Gender and Cross-Border Migration to South Africa*. Pretoria: Idasa, 1998

———. "Women on the Move: Gender and Cross-Border Migration to South Africa from Lesotho, Mozambique and Zimbabwe." In *On Borders: Perspectives on International Migration in Southern Africa*. Edited by David Alexander McDonald. Ontario: Southern African Migration Project, 2000, 119–150.

Donald, James. *Imagining The Modern City*. 1st edition. Minneapolis: University of Minnesota Press, 1999.

Dugger, Celia W. and Alan Cowell. "South Africa Weighs Plan to Shelter Refugees." *The New York Times*, May 29, 2008, sec. International / Africa. http://www.nytimes.com/2008/05/29/world/africa/29safrica.html.

Emdon, Erica. "The Limits of Law: Social Rights and Urban Development." In *Emerging Johannesburg*. Edited by Richard Tomlinson, Robert Beauregard, Lindsay Bremmer, and Xolela Mangcu. 1st edition. London: Routledge, 2003, 215–230.

Evans, Jessica, and Professor Stuart Hall. *Visual Culture: The Reader*. 1st edition. London: Sage Publications, 1999.

Findley, Sally E. "Migration and Family Interactions in Africa." In *Family, Population and Development in Africa*. Edited by Aderanti Adepoju. London: Zed Books, 1997, 109–138.

Foucault, Michel. *Discipline and Punish: The Birth of the Prison.* New York: Pantheon Books, 1977.

Foucault, Michel. *Power/Knowledge: Selected Interviews and Other Writings, 1972-1977.* Edited by Colin Gordon. London: Pearson Education, 1980.

———. *Power: The Essential Works of Michel Foucault 1954–1984 (Essential Works of Foucault 3).* Edited by James D. Faubion. London: Penguin Books, 1994.

Fraser, Neil. "Hip, Hip Hotels." *Citichat,* May 10, 2010. http://www.joburg.org.za/index.php?option=com_content&view=article&id=5163:hip-hip-hotels&catid=201:citichat-2010&Itemid=335.

Friedan, Betty. *The Feminine Mystique.* Reprint. New York: W. W. Norton, 2001.

Friedman, Steven. "A Quest for Control: High Modernism and Its Discontents in Johannesburg, South Africa." In *Urban Governance Around the World.* Edited by Blair A. Ruble, Richard E. Stren, Joseph S. Tulchin, and Diana H. Varat, 31–68. Washington, DC: Woodrow Wilson Int. Ctr. for Scholars, 2005.

Friedman, Steven. "A Voice Is Heard in the City: Inclusive Cities and Citizen Voice." In *Urban Diversity: Space, Culture, and Inclusive Pluralism in Cities Worldwide.* Edited by Caroline Wanjiku Kihato, Mejgan Massoumi, Blair A. Ruble, Pep Subirós, and Allison M. Garland. 1st edition. Baltimore: The Johns Hopkins University Press, 2010, 341–360.

Gasa, Nomboniso. "Introduction: Basus'iimbokodo, Bawel'imilambo, New Freedoms and New Challenges, a Continuing Dialogue." In *Women in South African History: Basus'iimbokodo, Bawel'imilambo / They Remove Boulders and Cross Rivers.* Edited by Nomboniso Gasa. Pretoria: Human Sciences Research Council, 2007, xiii–xxxvii.

Gauteng City-Region Observatory. "May 2012 Population Density." GCRO Map of the Month. Gauteng: Gauteng City-Region Observatory, May 2012. http://www.gcro.ac.za/maps-gis/map-of-the-month.

Gelb, Stephen. "Behind Xenophobia in South Africa—Poverty or Inequality?" In *Go Home or Die Here: Violence, Xenophobia and the Reinvention of Difference in South Africa.* Edited by Tawana Kupe, Eric Worby, and Shireen Hassim. Johannesburg: Witwatersrand University Press, 2008, 79–91.

Gibbon, Peter and Adebayo Olukoshi, eds. *Structural Adjustment and Socio-Economic Change in Sub-Saharan Africa: Some Conceptual, Methodological and Research Issues.* Uppsala: Nordiska Afrikainstitutet, 1996.

Giddens, Anthony. *The Consequences of Modernity.* 1st edition. Stanford, CA: Stanford University Press, 1991.

Giles-Vernick, Tamara. "Lives, Histories and Sites of Recollection." In *African Words, African Voices: Critical Practices in Oral History.* Edited by Luise S. White, Stephan F. Miescher, and David William Cohen. Bloomington: Indiana University Press, 2001, 194–213.

Gilman, Charlotte Perkins. *Women and Economics: A Study of the Economic Relation Between Women and Men.* New York: Prometheus Books, 1994.

Goldstein, Daniel M. "Desconfianza and Problems of Representation in Urban Ethnography." *Anthropological Quarterly* 75, no. 3 (2002): 485–517.

Gondola, Didier. *The History of Congo*. Annotated edition. Westport: Greenwood, 2002.

Gondola, Didier C. "Dream and Drama: The Search for Elegance Among Congolese Youth." *African Studies Review* 42, no. 1 (1999): 23–48.

Gotz, Graeme, and Simone AbdouMaliq. "On Belonging and Becoming in African Cities." In *Emerging Johannesburg*. Edited by Richard Tomlinson, Robert Beauregard, Lindsay Bremmer, and Xolela Mangcu. 1st edition. London: Routledge, 2003, 123–147.

Granovetter, Mark. "Economic Action and Social Structure: The Problem of Embeddedness." *American Journal of Sociology* 91, no. 3 (November 1, 1985): 481–510.

Grant, Miriam. "Strangers in Our Home: Spatiality and Locale of Monomatapa Township, Gwelo, Rhodesia (1953–1979)." *Canadian Journal of African Studies* (1998): 32–64.

Gugler, Josef, and Gudrun Ludwar-Ene. "Gender and Migration in Africa South of the Sahara." In *The Migration Experience in Africa*. Edited by Jonathan Baker and Tade Akin Aina. Uppsala: Nordiska Afrikainstitutet, 1995, 257–268.

Guy, Jeff. *The View Across the River: Harriette Colenso and the Zulu Struggle Against Imperialism*. Claremont: David Philip Publishers, 2001.

Guyer, Jane I. "Household and Community in African Studies." *African Studies Review* 24, no. 2/3 (1981): 87–137.

Hall, Stuart. "The Work of Representation." In *Representation: Cultural Representations and Signifying Practices*. Edited by Stuart Hall. 1st edition. London: Sage Publications and Open University, 1997, 13–64.

Halfani, Mohamed. "The Challenge of Urban Governance in East Africa: Responding to an Unrelenting Crisis." In *Cities and Governance: New Directions in Latin America, Asia and Africa*. Edited by Patricia L. McCarney, 183–203. Toronto: University of Toronto Press, 1996.

Hamilton, Peter. "Representing the Social: France and Frenchness in Post-war Humanist Photography." In *Representation: Cultural Representations and Signifying Practices*. Edited by Stuart Hall. 1st edition. London: Sage Publications and Open University, 1997, 75–150.

Hanisch, Carol. "The Personal Is Political." *Notes from the Second Year: Women's Liberation* (1970): 76–78. http://www.carolhanisch.org/CHwritings/PersonalisPol.pdf.

Hanson, Susan and Geraldine Pratt. *Gender, Work and Space*. 1st edition. London: Routledge, 1995.

Hareven, Tamara K. "The History of the Family as an Interdisciplinary Field." *The Journal of Interdisciplinary History* 2, no. 2 (1971): 399–414.

Harrison, Philip, Marie Huchzermeyer, and Mzwanele Mayekiso. *Confronting Fragmentation: Housing and Urban Development in a Democratising Society*. Cape Town: University of Cape Town Press, 2003.

Harrison, Philip. "Integrated Development Plans and Third Way Politics." In *Democracy and Delivery: Urban Policy in South Africa*. Edited by Udesh Pillay, Richard Tomlinson, and Jacques du Toit. Cape Town: Human Sciences Research Council, 2006, 186–207.

———. "The Genealogy of South Africa's Integrated Development Plan." *Third World Planning Review* 23, no. 2 (2001): 175–193.

Hart, Andrea, and Jean Yung. "Refugees in Mass Suicide Scare." *IOL News.* June 9, 2008, Online edition. http://www.iol.co.za/news/south-africa/refugees-in-mass-suicide-scare-1.403665#.UFmhahjdlJM.

Harvey, David. *Social Justice and the City.* London: Edward Arnold, 1973.

———. *The Condition of Postmodernity: An Enquiry into the Origins of Cultural Change.* Cambridge MA: Blackwell, 1990.

———. "The Urban Process Under Capitalism: A Framework for Analysis." In *The Blackwell City Reader.* Edited by Gary Bridge and Sophie Watson. Oxford: Wiley-Blackwell, 2002, 116–124.

Hayem, Judith. "May 2008 as a Revelator? National Identity, Human Rights and the Nature of Politics." Presented at the 3rd European Conference on African Studies 4–7 June, Leipzig, 2009.

Healey, Patsy. and Cameron Stuart. *Managing Cities: The New Urban Context.* Edited by Simin Davoudi, Stephen Graham, and Ali Madani-Pour. San Francisco: J. Wiley, 1995. http://en.scientificcommons.org/22435110.

Held, David and Anthony McGrew, eds. *The Global Transformations Reader.* 1st edition. Cambridge, UK: Polity, 2000.

Heller, Patrick. "Reclaiming Democratic Spaces: Civics and Politics in Posttransition Johannesburg." In *Emerging Johannesburg.* Edited by Richard Tomlinson, Robert Beauregard, Lindsay Bremmer, and Xolela Mangcu. 1st edition. London: Routledge, 2003, 155–184.

Hellmann, Ellen. *Rooiyard: a Sociological Survey of an Urban Native Slum Yard.* London: Oxford University Press, 1949.

Hibou, Beatrice. "From Privatising the Economy to Privatising the State: An Analysis of the Continual Formation of the State." In *Privatising the State.* London: C. Hurst, 2004, 1–47.

Hills, J. "Inclusion or Exclusion? The Role of Housing Subsidies and Benefits." *Urban Studies* 38, no. 11 (2001): 1887–1902.

Hirsch, Marianne. "Introduction: Familial Looking." In *The Familial Gaze.* Edited by Marianne Hirsch. 1st edition. Sudbury: Dartmouth, 1999, x–xxv.

hooks, bell. "In Our Glory: Photography and Black Life." In *Picturing Us: African American Identity in Photography.* Edited by Deborah Willis. New York: New Press, 1994, 43–54.

hooks, bell. *Feminist Theory: From Margin to Center.* 2nd edition. Cambridge, MA: South End Press, 2000.

Hornberger, Julia. "'My Police—Your Police': The Informal Privatisation of the Police in the Inner City of Johannesburg." *African Studies* 63, no. 2 (2004): 213–230.

———. *Policing and Human Rights: The Meaning of Violence and Justice in the Everyday Policing of Johannesburg.* 1st edition. London: Routledge, 2011.

Huchzermeyer, Marie. "Housing for the Poor? Negotiated Housing Policy in South Africa." *Habitat International* 25, no. 3 (2001): 303–331.

Huchzermeyer, Marie and Aly Karam, eds. *Informal Settlements: A Perpetual Challenge?* 1st edition. Cape Town: University of Cape Town Press, 2006.

Hughes, Christina. *Key Concepts in Feminist Theory and Research.* 1st edition. London: Sage Publications Ltd, 2002.

Hydén, Göran. *Beyond Ujamaa in Tanzania: Underdevelopment and an Uncaptured Peasantry.* Berkeley: University of California Press, 1980.

Jacobsen, Karen and Loren B. Landau. "The Dual Imperative in Refugee Research: Some Methodological and Ethical Considerations in Social Science Research on Forced Migration." *Disasters* 27, no. 3 (2003): 185–206.

Jeganathan, Pradeep. "Checkpoint: Anthropology, Identity, and the State." In *Anthropology in the Margins of the State.* Edited by Veena Das and Deborah Poole. 1st ed. School of American Research Advanced Seminar Series. Santa Fe, NM: School of American Research Press, 2004, 67–80.

Jewkes, R., N. Abrahams, S. Mathews, M. Seedat, and A. Van Niekerk. "Preventing Rape and Violence in South Africa: Call for Leadership in a New Agenda for Action." *MRC Policy Brief* (2009). http://www.mrc.ac.za/gender/prev_rapedd041209.pdf.

Jinnah, Z. "Making Home in a Hostile Land: Understanding Somali Identity, Integration, Livelihood and Risks in Johannesburg." *Journal of Sociology and Anthropology* 1, no. 1 (2010): 91–99.

Johnston, Nicole. "Out in the Cold (Once Again)." *Mail & Guardian.* July 28, 2008. http://mg.co.za/article/2008–07–28-out-in-the-cold-once-again.

Jones, Claudia. *An End to the Neglect of the Problems of the Negro Woman!* New York: National Women's Commission, C. P. U.S.A, 1949.

Kankonde, Peter Bukasa. "Transnational Family Ties, Remittance Motives, and Social Death Among Congolese Migrants: A Socio-Anthropological Analysis." *Journal of Comparative Family Studies* 41, no. 2 (Spring 2010): 225–243.

Khattak, Saba Gul. "Violence and Home: Afghan Women's Experience of Displacement." In *Gender, Conflict and Migration.* Edited by Navnita Chadha Behera. New Delhi: Sage Publications, 2006, 116–136.

Kihato, Caroline, and Loren B. Landau. *The Uncaptured Urbanite: Migration and State Power in Johannesburg.* Johannesburg: University of the Witwatersrand, Forced Migration Studies Programme (Forced Migration Working Paper Series), 2006.

Kihato, Caroline Wanjiku. "A Picture Speaks a Thousand Words." *Scrutiny2* 15, no. 1 (May 2010): 33–54. doi:10.1080/18125441.2010.500457.

———. "Gender and Migration: Feminist Interventions." In *Now You See Me Now You Don't: Methodologies and Methods of the Interstices.* Edited by Ingrid Palmary, Erica Burman, Khatidja Chantler, and Peace Kiguwa. London: Zed Books, 2010, 141–162.

Kiwanuka, Monica. "For Love or Survival: Migrant Women's Narratives of Survival and Intimate Partner Violence in Johannesburg." In *Gender and Migration: Feminist Intervention.* Edited by Ingrid Palmary, Erica Burman, Khatidja Chantler, and Peace Kiguwa. London: Zed Books, 2010, 163–179.

Krause-Vilmar, Jina, and Josh Chaffin. *No Place to Go but up: Urban Refugees in Johannesburg, South Africa.* New York: Women's Refugee Commission, 2011.

Kuhn, Thomas. *The Structure of Scientific Revolutions*. 1st edition. 2nd Impression. Chicago: University of Chicago Press, 1962.

Kurgan, Terry. *Hotel Yeoville*. Johannesburg: Fourthwall Books, 2013.

Kurgan, Terry and Jo Ractliffe. *Johannesburg Circa Now: Photography and the City*. Johannesburg: T. Kurgan and J. Ractliffe, 2005.

Landau, Loren B. "Recognition, Community and the Power of Mobility in Africa's New Urban Estuaries." In *Mobility and the State in Africa*. Edited by Darshan Vigneswaran and Joel Quirk. Philadelphia: University of Pennsylvania Press, Forthcoming.

Landau, Loren B., ed. *Exorcising the Demons Within: Xenophobia, Violence and Statecraft in Contemporary South Africa*. Wits University Press, 2011.

———. "Inclusion in Shifting Sands: Rethinking Mobility and Belonging in African Cities." In *Urban Diversity: Space, Culture, and Inclusive Pluralism in Cities Worldwide*. Edited by Caroline Wanjiku Kihato, Mejgan Massoumi, Blair A. Ruble, Pep Subirós, and Allison M. Garland. 1st edition. Baltimore: The Johns Hopkins University Press, 2010, 169–186.

Landau, Loren B. and Tamlyn Monson. "Immigration and Subterranean Sovereignty in South African Cities." In *Ungoverned Spaces: Alternatives to State Authority in an Era of Softened Sovereignty*. Edited by Anne Clunan and Harold Trinkunas. Stanford, CA: Stanford Security Studies, 2010, 153–174.

Landau, Loren B., and Veronique Gindrey. *Gauteng 2055 Trend Paper: Population and Migration*. Johannesburg: Report compiled for the Gauteng Department of Economic Development, 2009.

Law, John. *After Method: Mess in Social Science Research*. Annotated edition. London: Routledge, 2004.

Lefko-Everett, Kate. *Voices from the Margins: Migrant Women's Experiences in Southern Africa*. Cape Town: Southern African Migration Project, 2007. http://dspace.cigilibrary.org/jspui/handle/123456789/30713.

Le Marcis, F. "The Suffering Body of the City." *Public Culture* 16, no. 3 (2004): 453–477.

Lindell, Ilda. "The Multiple Sites of Urban Governance: Insights from an African City." *Urban Studies* 45, no. 9 (August 2008): 1879–1901. doi:10.1177/0042098008093382.

Lindley, Anna. *The Early Morning Phonecall: Remittances from a Refugee Diaspora Perspective*. Working Paper No. 47. Oxford: Centre on Migration, Policy and Society, 2007.

Lodge, Tom. "The South African Local Government Elections of December 2000." *Politikon: South African Journal of Political Studies* 28, no. 1 (May 2001): 21–46. doi:10.1080/02589340120058085.

Longmore, Laura. *The Dispossessed: A Study of the Sex-life of Bantu Women in Urban Areas in and Around Johannesburg*. Cape Town: J. Cape, 1959.

Madhavan, Sangeetha and Loren B. Landau. "Bridges to Nowhere: Hosts, Migrants and the Chimera of Social Capital in Three African Cities." *Population and Development Review* 37, no. 3 (2011): 473–497.

Makda, Yakoob. "From Slum to (Financial) Sustainability: Johannesburg's Better Building Programme." *Development Update* 5, no. 1 (2004): 177–186.

Malaquais, Dominique. "Douala/Johannesburg/New York: Cityscapes Imagined." In *Cities in Contemporary Africa*. Edited by Martin J Murray and Garth Andrew Myers. 1st edition. New York: Palgrave Macmillian, 2007, 31–52.

Malkki, Lisa H. "Speechless Emissaries: Refugees, Humanitarianism, and Dehistoricization." *Cultural Anthropology* 11, no. 3 (1996): 377–404.

Martinez, Theresa A. "Making Oppositional Culture, Making Standpoint: A Journey into Gloria Anzald'ua's Borderlands." *Sociological Spectrum* 25, no. 5 (2005): 539–570.

Mbeki, Thabo. "Radio and Television Address to the Nation by the President of South Africa, Thabo Mbeki, on the Occassion of Africa Day." South African Government Information, May 25, 2008. http://www.info.gov.za/speeches.

Mbembe, Achille. *On the Postcolony*. 1st edition. Berkeley: University of California Press, 2001.

McCarney, Patricia L. *Cities and Governance: New Directions in Latin America, Asia and Africa*. Toronto: University of Toronto Press, 1996.

McCarney, Patricia L. "Considerations of the Notion of 'Governance'—New Directions for Cities in the Developing World." In *Cities and Governance: New Directions in Latin America, Asia and Africa*. Edited by Patricia L McCarney, 3–22. Toronto: University of Toronto Press, 1996.

McCarney, Patricia L, Mohamed Halfani, and Rodriguez, Alfredo. "Toward an Understanding of Governance: The Emergence of an Idea and Its Implications for Urban Research in Developing Countries." In *Urban Research in the Developing World, Volume 4: Perspectives on the City*. Edited by Richard Stren and Judith K Bell. 1st edition. Toronto: University of Toronto, 1995.

Middleton, Julie. "Barriers to Protection: Gender-Related Persecution and Asylum in South Africa." In *Gender and Migration: Feminist Intervention*. Edited by Ingrid Palmary, Erica Burman, Khatidja Chantler, and Peace Kiguwa. London: Zed Books, 2010, 67–85.

Mills, Charles, W. *The Sociological Imagination*. Oxford: Oxford University Press, 1959.

Ministry for Provincial Affairs and Constitutional Development. *The White Paper on Local Government*. Pretoria: CTP Book Printers, 1998.

Miranne, Kristine B. and Alma H. Young. "Introduction." In *Gendering the City: Women, Boundaries, and Visions of Urban Life*. Edited by Kristine B Miranne and Alma H Young. Lanham, MD: Rowman & Littlefield, 2000, 1–16.

Misago, Jean-Pierre, Tamlyn Monson, Tara Polzer, and Loren B. Landau. "May 2008 Violence Against Foreign Nationals in South Africa: Understanding Causes and Evaluating Responses." Johannesburg: Forced Migration Studies Programme, 2010.

Mlambo, Ngcuka. "Deputy President Phumzile Mlambo-Ngcuka Speaks Out Against the Violent Attacks on Foreigners and Calls for Calm." South African Government Information, May 23, 2008. http://www/info.gov.za/speeches.

Modell, John, and Tamara K. Hareven. "Urbanization and the Malleable Household: An Examination of Boarding and Lodging in American Families." *Journal of Marriage and Family* 35, no. 3 (1973): 467–479.

Mohanty, Chandra Talpade. *Feminism Without Borders: Decolonizing Theory, Practicing Solidarity*. Durham: Duke University Press Books, 2003.

Monson, Tamlyn. *Report on the SAHRC Investigation into Issues of Rule of Law, Justice and Impunity Arising Out of the 2008 Public Violence Against Non-nationals*. Johannesburg: South African Human Rights Commission, 2010.

Morris, Alan. *Bleakness and Light: Inner City Transition in Hillbrow*. Johannesburg: Witwatersrand University Press, 1999.

Motsemme, Nthabiseng. "The Mute Always Speak: On Women's Silences at the Truth and Reconciliation Commission." *Current Sociology* 52, no. 5 (September 1, 2004): 909–932. doi:10.1177/0011392104045377.

Murray, Martin J. *Taming the Disorderly City: The Spatial Landscape of Johannesburg After Apartheid*. 2nd edition. Ithaca: Cornell University Press, 2008.

Muzvidziwa, Victor. "Zimbabwe's Cross-Border Women Traders: Multiple Identities and Responses to New Challenges." *Journal of Contemporary African Studies* 19, no. 1 (January 2001): 67–80. doi:10.1080/02589000120028175.

Neocosmos, Michael. *From "Foreign Natives" to "Native Foreigners": Explaining Xenophobia in Post-apartheid South Africa, Citizenship and Nationalism, Identity and Politics*. 2nd edition. Dakar, Senegal: CODESRIA, 2010.

Newham, Gareth, Themba Masuku, and Jabu Dlamini. *Diversity and Transformation in the South African Police Service: A Study of Police Perspectives on Race, Gender and the Community in the Johannesburg Policing Area*. Johannesburg: Centre for the Study of Violence and Reconciliation, 2006.

Nussbaum, Martha C. *Creating Capabilities: The Human Development Approach*. Cambridge, MA: Belknap Press of Harvard University Press, 2011.

———. "Poverty and Human Functioning: Capabilities as Fundamental Entitlements." In *Poverty and Inequality*. Edited by David Grusky and Ravi Kanbur. Annotated edition. Palo Alto: Stanford University Press, 2006, 47–75.

Nyamnjoh, Francis B. *Insiders and Outsiders: Citizenship and Xenophobia in Contemporary Southern Africa*. London: Zed Books, 2006.

Oakley, Ann. "Interviewing Women: A Contradiction in Terms." In *Doing Feminist Research*. Edited by Helen Roberts. New edition. London: Routledge, 1981, 30–61.

Obbo, Christine. *African Women: Their Struggle for Economic Independence*. London: Zed Books, 1981.

Ohler, Norman. *Ponte City*. Cape Town: David Philip Publishers, 2003.

Onselen, Charles Van. *Studies in the Social and Economic History of the Witwatersrand 116–1914: New Nineveh*. Essex: Longman Group United Kingdom, 1982.

Palmary, Ingrid. "Situating Women in War and Displacement: Intersections of 'Race,' Nationalism and Gender in the Context of Forced Migration and Humanitarian Assistance." PhD dissertation, Metropolitan Manchester University, 2005.

Parker, Faranaaz. "Jo'burg Sends in Red Ants in Defiance of ConCourt." *The M&G Online*, 2012. http://mg.co.za/article/2012–01–18-joburg-sends-in-reds-ants-defiance-of-concourt/.

Parnell, Susan. "Constructing a Developmental Nation—the Challenge of Including the Poor in the Post-apartheid City." *Transformation: Critical Perspectives on Southern Africa* 58, no. 1 (2005): 20–44.

Parnell, Susan, Edgar Pieterse, Mark Swilling, and Dominique Wooldridge. *Democratising Local Government: The South African Experiment.* Cape Town: University of Cape Town Press, 2002.

Patterson Orlando. *Slavery And Social Death: A Comparative Study.* Cambridge, MA: Harvard University Press, 1982.

Pelser, Eric. "Operation Crackdown: The New Police Strategy." *Nedbank ISS Crime Index* 4, no. 2 (2000). http://www.iss.co.za/PUBS/CRIMEINDEX / 00VOL402/OperatCrackdown.html.

Pessar, P. R. and S. J. Mahler. "Transnational Migration: Bringing Gender In." *International Migration Review* 37, no. 3 (2003): 812–846.

Pieterse, Edgar. *City Futures: Confronting the Crisis of Urban Development.* London: Zed Books, 2008.

Pillay, Devan. "Relative Deprivation, Social Instability and Cultures of Entitlement." In *Go Home or Die Here: Violence, Xenophobia and the Reinvention of Difference in South Africa.* Edited by Tawana Kupe, Eric Worby, and Shireen Hassim. Johannesburg: Witwatersrand University Press, 2008, 93–103.

Pillay, Udesh, Richard Tomlinson, and Jacques du Toit. *Democracy and Delivery: Urban Policy in South Africa.* Cape Town: Human Sciences Research Council, 2006.

Pink, Sarah. *Home Truths: Gender, Domestic Objects and Everyday Life.* English edition. Oxford: Berg, 2004.

Piper, Nicola. "Feminization of Labor Migration as Violence Against Women International, Regional, and Local Nongovernmental Organization Responses in Asia." *Violence Against Women* 9, no. 6 (2003): 723–745.

Pleck, Elizabeth H. "Two Worlds in One: Work and Family." *Journal of Social History* 10, no. 2 (1976): 178–195.

Plissart, Marie-Françoise and Filip De Boeck. *Kinshasa: Tales of the Invisible City.* Antwerpen: Ludion, 2005.

Posel, Deborah. "Curbing African Urbanisation in the 1950s and 1960s." In *Apartheid City in Transition.* Edited by Mark Swilling, Richard Humphries, and Khehla Shubane. Cape Town: Oxford University Press, 1991, 19–32.

Putnam, Robert D. *Making Democracy Work: Civic Traditions in Modern Italy.* Princeton, NJ: Princeton University Press, 1994.

Raj, Anita and Jay Silverman. "Violence Against Immigrant Women." *Violence Against Women* 8, no. 3 (March 1, 2002): 367–398. doi:10.1177 /10778010222183107.

Ratha, Dilip and William Shaw. *Economic Implications of Remittances and Migration.* Washington, DC: World Bank, 2006. http://siteresources.worldbank. org/INTTOPCONF3/Resources/1588024–1163704792404/S2_P1_RATHA.pdf.

Rousseau C., Said T. M, Gagne M-J, and Bibeau G. "Between Myth and Madness: The Premigration Dream of Leaving Among Young Somali Refugees." Text. Accessed September 9, 2011. http://www.ingentaconnect.com/content/klu /medi/1998/00000022/00000004/00192801.

Ruby, Jay. "Seeing Through Pictures: The Anthropology of Photography" *Critical Arts* 1, no. 4 (1981): 3–16.

Said, Edward W. *Out of Place. A Memoir.* New York: Vintage Books, 1999.

Salgado, Sebastiao. "Migrations: Humanity in Transition. Interview with Nandy Madlin," 2005. http://pdngallery.com/legends/legends10/migration.pdf.

Sander, Cerstin, and Samuel Maimbo. "Migrant Labor Remittances in Africa: Reducing Obstacles to Developmental Contributions." *Africa Regional Working Paper Series* 1 (2005): 80–93.

Sanford, Victoria. "Contesting Displacement in Columbia: Citizenship and State Sovereignty at the Margins." In *Anthropology in the Margins of the State.* Edited by Veena Das and Deborah Poole. 1st edition. School of American Research Advanced Seminar Series. Santa Fe, NM: School of American Research Press, 2004, 253–277.

Sangster, Joan. "Telling Our Stories: Feminist Debates and the Use of Oral History." In *The Oral History Reader.* Edited by Robert Perks and Alistair Thomson. London: Psychology Press, 1998, 87–100.

Sassen, S. "Local Actors in Global Politics." *Current Sociology* 52, no. 4 (2004): 649.

Sassen, Saskia. *Cities in a World Economy.* 3rd edition. Thousand Oaks, CA: Pine Forge Press, 2006.

———. *Globalization and Its Discontents: Essays on the New Mobility of People and Money.* 1st edition. New York: New Press, 1999.

———. "Globalization or Denationalization?" *Review of International Political Economy* 10, no. 1 (February 2001): 1–22. doi:10.1080/096922903200004 8853.

———. *The Global City: New York, London, Tokyo.* 2nd edition. Princeton, NJ: Princeton University Press, 2001.

Schlemmer, Lawrence. *Immigrants in Johannesburg: Estimating Numbers and Assessing Impacts.* CDE In Depth 9. Johannesburg: Centre for Development and Enterprise, 2008.

Scott, James C. *Seeing Like a State: How Certain Schemes to Improve the Human Condition Have Failed.* Yale Agrarian Studies. New Haven, CT: Yale University Press, 1998.

———. "Afterword to 'Moral Economies, State Spaces, and Categorical Violence'." *American Anthropologist* 107, no. 3 (September 1, 2005): 395–402. doi:10.1525/aa.2005.107.3.395.

Sen, Amartya. *Development as Freedom.* Reprint. New York: Anchor, 1999.

Sen, Amartya Kumar. *Social Exclusion: Concept, Application, and Scrutiny.* Development Papers No. 1. Manila: Asian Development Bank, 2000.

Sheldon, Kathleen E., ed. *Courtyards, Markets, City Streets: Urban Women in Africa.* Boulder, CO: WestviewPress, 1996.

Short, John R. *Urban Theory: A Critical Assessment.* Basingstoke, UK: Palgrave Macmillan, 2006.

Silverman, Melinda, and Tanya Zack. "Housing Delivery, the Urban Crisis and Xenophobia." In *Go Home or Die Here: Violence, Xenophobia and the Reinvention of Difference in South Africa.* Edited by Tawana Kupe, Eric Worby, and Shireen Hassim. Johannesburg: Witwatersrand University Press, 2008, 147–159.

Simmel, Georg. "Metropolis and Mental Life." In *Understanding Everyday Life*. Edited by Tony Bennett and Diane Watson. 1st edition. Oxford: Wiley-Blackwell, 2002, 124–126.

Simone, AbdouMaliq and Abdelghani Abouhani. *Urban Africa: Changing Contours of Survival in the City*. London: Zed Press, 2005.

Simone, AbdouMaliq. "Urban Circulation and the Everyday Politics of African Urban Youth: The Case of Douala, Cameroon." *International Journal of Urban & Regional Research* 29, no. 3 (2005): 516–532. doi:10.1111/j.1468-2427.2005.00603.x.

Simone, AbdouMaliq. *For the City Yet to Come: Changing African Life in Four Cities*. Durham, NC: Duke University Press Books, 2004.

———. "The Ambivalence of the Arbitrary." *Theory, Culture & Society* 28, no. 1 (January 2011): 129–137. doi:10.1177/0263276410387624.

———. "The Dilemmas of Informality for African Governance." In *Democratising Local Government: The South African Experiment*. Edited by Susan Parnell, Edgar Pieterse, Mark Swilling, and Dominique Wooldridge. Cape Town: University of Cape Town Press, 2002, 294–304.

Smillie, Shaun and Kanina Foss. "Peaceful Refugee Removal Next to Highway." *IOL News*. Johannesburg, July 29, 2008. http://www.iol.co.za/news/south-africa/peaceful-refugee-removal-next-to-highway-1.410178#.UE2-ekTdlJM.

Smith, Daniel Jordan. *A Culture of Corruption: Everyday Deception and Popular Discontent in Nigeria*. Princeton: Princeton University Press, 2008.

Soja, Ed. "Six Discourses on the Postmetropolis." In *Imagining Cities: Scripts, Signs and Memories*. Edited by Sallie Westwood and John Williams. New York: Routledge, 1996, 19–30.

Sontag, Susan. *On Photography*. New York: Picador, 1977.

Statistics South Africa. *Census 2011: The South Africa I Know, the Home I Understand*. Pretoria: Statistics South Africa, 2012.

Steinberg, Jonny. *Thin Blue: The Unwritten Rules of South African Policing*. Jeppestown: Jonathan Ball Publishing, 2009.

Stren, Richard E. and Rodney R. White, eds. *African Cities in Crisis: Managing Rapid Urban Growth*. African Modernization and Development Series v. 5. Boulder, CO: Westview Press, 1989.

Swilling, Mark. *Governing Africa's Cities*. Johannesburg: Witwatersrand University Press, 1997.

Swilling, Mark. "Building Democratic Local Urban Governance in Southern Africa." In *Governing Africa's Cities*. Edited by Mark Swilling. Johannesburg: Witwatersrand University Press, 1997, 211–274.

Thale, Thomas. "Drama as Police Swoop on Inner City Buildings." *City of Joburg*, September 25, 2003. http://www.joburg.org.za/2003/spet/sept25_hillbrowswoop.stm.

Tillim, Guy. *Jo'burg*. Johannesburg: STE Publishers, 2005.

Todaro, Michael P. *Economics for a Developing World*. 2nd edition. Essex: Longman, 1982.

Todes, Alison. "Housing Integrated Urban Development and the Compact City Debate." In *Confronting Fragmentation: Housing and Urban Development in a Democratising Society*. Edited by Philip Harrison, Marie Huchzermeyer, and Mzwanele Mayekiso. Cape Town: University of Cape Town Press, 2003, 109–139.

Tomlinson, Richard. "HIV/AIDS and Urban Disintegration in Johannesburg." In *Confronting Fragmentation: Housing and Urban Development in a Democratising Society*. Edited by Philip Harrison, Marie Huchzermeyer, and Mzwanele Mayekiso. Cape Town: University of Cape Town Press, 2003, 76–87.

Tonkiss, Fran. *Space, the City and Social Theory: Social Relations and Urban Forms*. Cambridge: Polity Press, 2005.

Tostensen, Arne, Inge Tvedten, and Mariken Vaa. *Associational Life in African Cities: Popular Responses to the Urban Crisis*. Uppsala: Nordic Africa Institute, 2001.

Turner, Victor. *The Ritual Process: Structure and Anti-Structure*. 2nd edition. Ithaca, NY: Cornell University Press, 1977.

Ulicki, Theresa and Jonathan Crush. "Gender, Farmwork, and Women's Migration from Lesotho to the New South Africa." *Canadian Journal of African Studies* 34, no. 1 (2000): 64–79.

Urry, John. *Sociology Beyond Societies: Mobilities for the Twenty-First Century*. 1st edition. London: Routledge, 2000.

Utas, Mats. "Victimcy, Girlfriending, Soldiering: Tactic Agency in a Young Woman's Social Navigation of the Liberian War Zone." *Anthropological Quarterly* 78, no. 2 (2005): 403–430.

Van Donk, Mirjam. *Local Government and Gender: A Reality Check. Survey of Selected Municipalities in the Western Cape*. Cape Town: Gender Advocacy Programme, 1998.

Vearey, Joanna. "Hidden Spaces and Urban Health: Exploring the Tactics of Rural Migrants Navigating the City of Gold." *Urban Forum* 21, no. 1 (February 2010): 37–53. doi:10.1007/s12132-010-9079-4.

Venkatesh, Sudhir Alladi. *Off the Books: The Underground Economy of the Urban Poor*. Cambridge, MA: Harvard University Press, 2009.

Venkatesh, Sudhir Alladi. *American Project: The Rise and Fall of a Modern Ghetto*. Cambridge, MA: Harvard University Press, 2002.

Vetten, Lisa. "Addressing Domestic Violence in South Africa: Reflections on Strategy and Practice." New York: UN Division for the Advancement of Women, 2005.

Vidal, Dominique. "Living in, out of, and between Two Cities: Migrants from Maputo in Johannesburg." *Urban Forum* 21, no. 1 (February 2010): 55–68. doi:10.1007/s12132-010-9080-y.

Vigneswaran, Darshan, and Julia Hornberger. *Beyond Good Cop / Bad Cop: Understanding Informality and Police Corruption in South Africa*. Johannesburg: African Center for Migration in Society, 2009.

Wa Kabwe, Désiré and Aurelia wa Kabwe Segatti. "Paradoxical Expressions of a Return to the Homeland: Music and Literature Among the Congolese (Zairean) Diaspora." In *New African Diasporas*. Edited by Khalid Koser. London: Routledge, 2003, 124–139.

Walker, Cherryl. "Gender and the Development of the Migrant Labour System c. 1850–1930." In *Women and Gender in Southern Africa to 1945*. Edited by Cherryl Walker. Claremont: David Philip Publishers, 1990, 168–196.

Walker, Cherryl. *Women and Gender in Southern Africa to 1945*. David Philip Publishers, 1990.

Wentzel, Marie, Johan Viljoen, and Pieter Kok. "Contemporary South African Migration Patterns and Intensions." In *Migration in South and Southern Africa: Dynamics and Determinants*. Edited by Kok Pieter, Derik Gelderblom, and John Oucho. Pretoria: HSRC Press, 2006, 171–204.

White, Luise. *The Comforts of Home: Prostitution in Colonial Nairobi*. 1st edition. Chicago: University of Chicago Press, 1990.

White, Naomi R. "Marking Absences: Holocaust Testimony and History." In *The Oral History Reader*. Edited by Robert Perks and Thomson Alistair. London: Psychology Press, 1998, 172–182.

Willis, Deborah. *Picturing Us: African American Identity in Photography*. New York: New Press, 1994.

Wilson, William Julius. *The Truly Disadvantaged: The Inner City, the Underclass, and Public Policy*. Chicago: University of Chicago Press, 1990.

Wirth, Louis. "Urbanism as a Way of Life." *American Journal of Sociology* 44, no. 1 (1938): 1–24.

Wits, Tufts and IFAS. "Migration and the New African City." Johannesburg: Forced Migration Studies Programme, University of the Witwatersrand, 2006.

Wolbert, Barbara. "The Anthropologist as Photographer: The Visual Construction of Ethnographic Authority." *Visual Anthropology* 13, no. 4 (2000): 321–343.

Wolff, Janet. "The Invisible Flâneuse. Women and the Literature of Modernity." *Theory, Culture & Society* 2, no. 3 (1985): 37–46. doi:10.1177/0263276485 002003005.

Young, Lorraine and Hazel Barrett. "Adapting Visual Methods: Action Research with Kampala Street Children." *Area* 33, no. 2 (2002): 141–152.

Zack, Tanya and Sarah Charlton. "Better Off, but . . . Beneficiaries' Perceptions of the Government's Housing Subsidy Scheme." Unpublished paper prepared for the Department of Housing, Pretoria, 2003.

Zembylas, Michalinos. "Agamben's Theory of Biopower and Immigrants/ Refugees / Asylum Seekers: Discourses of Citizenship and the Implications for Curriculum Theorizing." *Journal of Curriculum Theorizing* 26, no. 2 (September 12, 2010). http://journal.jctonline.org/index.php/jct/article/ viewArticle/195.

Zlotnik, Hania. "The Global Dimensions of Female Migration." *Migration Information Source*, 2003. http://www.migrationinformation.org/Feature/ display.cfm?ID=109.

———. "Women as Migrants and Workers in Developing Countries." *International Journal of Contemporary Sociology* 30, no. 1 (1993): 39–62.

Index

Page numbers in **bold** are references to photographs.

"adaptive preferences," 55
Adele, Congolese orphan, 108–9
Africa, public vs. private spaces, 74
Agamben, Giorgio, 97, 107, 108, 110
agency, of migrant women, 35–7, 74,
    78–9, 110–11, 116–22, 126
    see also co-constructed urban
        spaces
Agustin, Laura M., 120
AIDS and HIV, 16, 64, 74
Alexandra, Johannesburg, 96
America, *see* United States
antiforeign sentiments, *see* attitudes
    towards migrants
Anzaldúa, Gloria, 68
apartheid, impact of, 4–5, 7, 27,
    100–101, 114–15
apartments, *see* housing
asylum-seeker permits, 33–5, 88–9
    see also permits
attitudes towards migrants, 16, 78,
    88, 98–103, 110–11
    see also xenophobic violence
Australia, 66, 109, 122
Ayo, from Nigeria, 47, 49, 67

Bauman, Zygmunt, 17, 41, 66
belonging, *see* "home"
Berea, Johannesburg, 5, 7–8
Berger, John, 11
Betty, 30-year-old Kenyan woman, 58
binaries, 22–3, 25, 46, 73–5, 89–93,
    104–11, 120–3
Blanche, Congolese woman, 62

Bozzoli, Belinda, 57
brain waste, 58–9
bylaws, 13, 20, 32–3

camps, *see* refugee camps
Canada, 109, 122
Castells, Manuel, 16, 73
Castles, Stephen, 52
census data, *see* data and statistics
Center for the Study of Violence and
    Reconciliation (CSVR), 100
children
    in refugee camp, 98
    raising of, 83
Chipo, from Bulawayo, 56
church, role of, 48, 54, 85, 89–90
city bylaws, 13, 20, 32–3
"City Johannesburg" (poem), 4–5
Cleveland informal settlement, 96
Cleveland police station, 22, 95–6,
    99–101, 103–4
Clunan, Anne L., 25, 44
co-constructed urban spaces, 46, 75,
    129
    see also agency, of migrant
        women
Collins, Patricia Hill, 19
community participation, *see*
    participation processes
community ties, 16, **18**, 48, 50, 54,
    85, 88–93, 115, 127–9
Congolese migrants, 66
cooking, *see* meal times
Criminal Procedure Act, 31–2

cross-border trading, 57–8
    see also livelihood
CSVR, *see* Center for the Study of
    Violence and Reconciliation
cultural boundaries, 83–5
Curran, Sara R., 53

Das, Veena, 22, 107–8
data and statistics, 7–8, 34, 37, 52
dating, 83–4
De Certeau, Michel, 37, 116
De Kock, Leone, 121
Demissie, Fassil, 124
Democratic Republic of Congo
    (DRC), 57, 60–1
Department of Education, 101
Department of Home Affairs, 34, 98,
    101, 105, 109
Department of Social Development,
    98, 101
deportation, fear of, 36–7, 89–90,
    105–7
derogatory images of migrants, *see*
    attitudes towards migrants
Deutsch, Sarah, 75
Devas, Nick, 91
Dibwe, Donatien, 57
Disaster Act, 103–4, 107
domestic spaces, 7, 18, 21–2, 72,
    78–85, **80**, **81**, **82**, 92
    see also private spaces
domestic violence, 21, 72, 74, 85–93,
    86, **87**, 123
Donald, James, 115
DRC, *see* Democratic Republic of
    Congo

economic considerations in migration,
    13–14, 20–1, 51–2, 61–4, 68–9
Edward, Kenyan man, 96, 109, 122
Emma, street trader, 35
employment, 53–4, 58–9, 77
    see also livelihood
*End to the Neglect of the Problems of
    the Negro Woman!, An*, 71
Esperance, 26-year-old woman from
    DRC, 61–2

ethnic divides, 48, 54, 84–5, 93
Europe, 66–7, 73

family, 80–1, **82**
Fatuma, Congolese woman, 98
Fazila, from DRC, 1–2, 34, 36
fear of going home, 21, 48–9, 68
feminist standpoint theory, 19
feminist studies, xvi, 19, 71, 79–80
Fezila, from Congo, 81, 88–91, 93
Flore, nurse from Cameroon, 59
Florence, Congolese market trader,
    32–3
formality, 9, 14–15, 25–8, 32–3,
    38–9, 44–6, 101–3, 108, 125,
    129
Foucault, Michel, 41, 119
French Institute of South Africa
    (IFAS), 8, 56
Friedman, Steven, 124

gender roles, 18–20, 49–50, 62–4,
    73–4, 79–80, 120
Glenanda camp, xiii, 22, 103–4,
    105–7, 109–12
globalization literature, 16–17
Goldstein, Daniel M., 118
good governance, 9, 26–7, 46, 126
Gotz, Graeme, 90–1, 129
governance, *see* urban governance
government, *see* state, the
Granovetter, Mark, 53

Hall, Stuart, 118
Hanisch, Carol, 71
Hannah, street trader, 28–31, 33,
    35–9, 43
Harriet, Ugandan migrant, 76, 83–4
Harvey, David, 73
hawking, *see* street trading
Hellen, 28-year-old Ugandan woman,
    62–3, 67
Hellmann, Ellen, 19
heroines vs. victims, 120–3
Hillbrow, 5, 7–8
HIV/AIDS, 16, 64, 74
Hobbes, Thomas, 38

Home Affairs, *see* Department of Home Affairs
"home," meanings of, 72, 76–8, 130
hooks, bell, 79
Hornberger, Julia, 101
hostility toward foreigners, *see* attitudes towards migrants
Hotel Yeoville, 117
housing, 5, 47–8, 74
humanitarian agencies, 101–2, 106
human rights lawyers, 105–6
hybrid urban spaces, 9, 14–15, 20, 23, 42–5, 103, 125
Hydén, Göran, 33

identity building, xv, 64–5, 112, 118–19, 127
IFAS, *see* French Institute of South Africa
Ife, from Nigeria, 67
illegality, *see* legal/illegal boundaries
illegal trading, *see* street trading
images, *see* photographs
Immigration Act, 105–6
immigration market, 51–2
import-export businesses, 57–8
  see also livelihood
in-between city, 8–9, 15–18, 22–3, 28, 37, 76–8, 113–17, 123–30
inclusive decision making, *see* participation processes
informality, *see* formality
informal trading, *see* street trading
insider outsider, 97, 107, 111, 114
interstitial city, 8–9, 15–18, 22–3, 28, 37, 76–8, 113–17, 123–30
invisibility, 9, 33–6, 46, 118–19, 128

Jean, from Cameroon, 43, 65–6
Jeannette, from Rwanda, 80–1, 83
Jeganathan, Pradeep, 40
Jinnah, Z., 57
Johannesburg, xv–xvi, 2–9, 13–14
  maps, 3, 6
Jones, Claudia, 71
journeys to South Africa, 1–2, 10
Juliette, from Cameroon, 77, 84

Kasrils, Ronnie, 106
Kenya, xiii–xv
Khattak, Saba Gul, 76–7
Khumalo, Sergeant, 22, 98–103
Kiwanuka, Monica, 90
Kok, Pieter, 60
Kurgan, Terry, 40, 117

Labuschagne, Sergeant, 99–100
Ladi, Congolese student, 77
Landau, Loren B., 41–2
Law, John, 16
law enforcement, *see* police
laws, *see* legislation
legal/illegal boundaries, 20, 39–42, 45–6, 101–8, 111–12, 114, 125–7
legislation, 13, 20, 31–3, 38–42, 103–7
liminality, 8–9, 15–18, 22–3, 28, 37, 76–8, 113–17, 123–30
Linda, Zimbabwean woman, 21
Lindela deportation camp, 106, 111
Lindell, Ilda, 27
livelihood
  cross-border trading, 57–8
  employment, 53–4, 58–9, 77
  street trading, **10**, **12**, 20, **26**, 28–33, 35, 38–9, 42, **42**, 56–60, 108
local government, 26–7, 125–8

Malaquais, Dominique, 16
Malkki, Lisa H., 110
Mandela, release of, 7
Manichaeism, 25, 46
Mapisa-Nqakula, Nosiviwe, 106
maps, 3, 6
May, 21-year-old Zambian woman, 57
Mbeki, Thabo, 106
Mbembe, Achille, 107
meal times, 7, **82**, 83
Medicines sans Frontiers (MSF), 101
Memory, Zimbabwean woman, 64
methodology, xv–xviii, 9–23
migration economy, 49–52

Migration Model of Todaro, 51–2
Miller, Mark J., 52
Mills, C. Wright, 71
Mlambo-Ngcuka, Phumzile, 106
mobility, 35–6
    see also liminality; social
        mobility
Mohanty, Chandra Talpade, 79
money, see economic considerations in
    migration
moral boundaries, 43–5, 83–5, 126–7
Morris, Alan, 8
Mozambican migrants, 60
MSF, see Medicines sans Frontiers
multiple regulatory authorities, 27,
    45–6, 103, 114, 124–30
municipal bylaws, 13, 20, 32–3
myths, of migration, 63–8

Namwene, 29-year-old from Zambia,
    63–4
Ndembu people, 17
Neema, Tanzanian woman, 58
neoclassical economists, 20–1,
    51–2
NGOs, 99, 101–2, 106
Nigeria, 43, 67
nongovernmental organizations, 99,
    101–2, 106
notice to appear in court, 28–32,
    35–6, 38–42
Nqakula, Charles, 106
Nussbaum, Martha C., 52, 53, 55

objectivity, xvi–xvii
offenders vs. victims, 104–11
Ohler, Norman, 2
"other," construction of, 107, 110,
    121

participation processes, 123–4
Pat, Kenyan woman, 66
permits
    asylum-seeker, 33–5, 88–9
    section 31(2) of Immigration Act,
        105–6
"personal is political," 71–2

Personal Is Political, The, 71
photographs
    community ties, 18
    domestic spaces, 7, 80, 81, 82
    domestic violence, 86, 87
    family, 82
    street scenes, 4, 12, 15, 26, 42, 44
    street trading, 10, 12, 26, 42
    success, 65
    use of, 11–13, 40, 78–80, 117–19
Pink, Sarah, 79–80
police
    domestic violence, 86–90, 93
    law enforcement, 28–42, 125
    Red Ants, 95–6, 106
    roadblocks, 36–7, 40–2
    state law and, 38–42
    trust, 93, 100
    violence in everyday policing, 101
    xenophobic violence, 95–6,
        98–103, 106
policy making, 22, 45–6, 123–6
    see also urban governance
Ponte City, Johannesburg, 2
Poole, Deborah, 22, 107–8
poverty, 55, 98–103
power dynamics, xvii–xviii, 22,
    25–8, 37, 45, 80–1, 97, 110–11,
    120–3
private security companies, 38–9,
    86–7
private spaces
    domesticity, 78–85
    importance of, 21, 71–2
    "personal is political," 71–2
    public spaces vs., 73–5, 89–93
    see also domestic spaces; domestic
        violence; "home"
protection fees, 38–9, 86–7
Provincial Disaster Act, 103–4, 107
public spaces vs. private spaces, 73–5,
    89–93
Putnam, Robert D., 128

Ratha, Dilip, 51
Red Ants, 95–6, 106
Red Cross, 109

refugee camps, 22, 96–8, 103–8, 111,
    125
Refugees Act, 33
regulation
    multiple regulatory authorities, 27,
        45–6, 103, 114, 124–30
    urban regulation, 27–32, 38–46,
        93, 108, 113–14, 129
reintegration program, after
    xenophobic violence, 110
renewal strategy, see urban renewal
    strategy
residential buildings, see housing
resistance, see offenders vs. victims
respect, 83–4
Rifle Ridge camp, see Glenanda camp
rights of migrants, 97
rites of passage, 17, 60–9
roadblocks, see police, roadblocks
Rosine, Burundian refugee, 21, 34,
    47–9, 53–5, 84–5
Ruth, street trader, 43
Rwanda, 48, 81, 84–5

Saguy, Abigail C., 53
Said, Edward, 23
SAMP, see Southern African
    Migration Project
Sanford, Victoria, 40–1
Sarudazai, 45-year-old Zimbabwean
    woman, 63
Sassen, Saskia, 17, 66
Scott, James, 14, 37, 39, 41
section 22 permits, 33–5, 88–9
security guards, 38–9, 86–7
Sen, Amartya, 52–3
sending money home, 52, 56, 61–4, 69
Serote, Mongane Wole, 4–5
shame, 16, 21, 49, 54–6, 61, 64, 68
    see also fear of going home
Shaw, William, 51
Short, John R., 14, 119
Sibongile, Zimbabwean woman, 40,
    60–1, 85–91, 93, 121–2
Simmel, Georg, 91
Simone, AbdouMaliq, 13, 90–1, 124,
    129

Smith, Adam, 55
Smith, Daniel Jordan, 43
social death, 20–1, 47, 49, 68
social mobility, 20–1, 51–3, 60–9
social networks, see community ties
social stigma, 63–4
Soja, Ed, 14
Sontag, Susan, 119
South African Nursing Council, 59
Southern African Migration Project
    (SAMP), 56–7
standpoint theory, 19
state, the
    as anti-state, 38–9
    legal/illegal boundaries, 41–2, 45,
        104–8, 111–12, 125–6
    power dynamics, 22, 25–8, 37, 45,
        96–7
statistics of population, 7–8, 34,
    37, 52
status, see success
Stella, Ugandan woman, 126–7
stigma, see social stigma
storytelling, 63–8
street scenes, **4, 12, 15, 26, 42, 44**
street trading, **10, 12**, 20, **26**,
    28–33, 35, 38–9, 42, **42**,
    56–60, 108
    see also livelihood
stuck, state of being, 47–51, 60, 69,
    104, 129–30
success, 21, 48–51, 53–6, 65–6, **65**,
    68–9, 129

taxi ranks, **15**, 30
third country relocation, 104, 109,
    111–12, 122
"threshold people," 17–18
Todaro, Michael P., 51–2
Tonkiss, Fran, 13
trading, see street trading
Traffic Act, 106–7
transitional states, see liminality
Trinkunas, Harold, 25
trust, 100
Tufts University, 8, 56
Turner, Victor, 17, 23, 68, 129

"underclass," 55
United Nations High Commissioner
    for Refugees (UNHCR), xiii,
    103, 109
United States, 58, 66, 73, 109
University of the Witwatersrand
    (WITS), 8, 56
urban development, *see* urban renewal
    strategy
urban governance, 9, 13–15, 20,
    25–8, 37, 42–6, 96, 108, 114,
    123–30
    see also policy making
urbanization, 14, 73, 114–17, 122–3
urban regulation, 27–32, 38–46, 93,
    108, 113–14, 129
urban renewal strategy, 32, 45–6,
    129
US, *see* United States
Utas, Mats, 121

Vearey, Joanna, 89
Venkatesh, Sudhir Alladi, 127
victims
    heroines vs., 120–3
    offenders vs., 104–11
Viljoen, Johan, 60
violence
    domestic violence, 21, 72, 74,
        85–93, **86, 87**, 123
    in everyday policing, 101
    see also xenophobic violence
visas, *see* permits

visibility, *see* invisibility
visual diary group, 40, 85, 121–2
visual images, *see* photographs

Wangūi, Kenyan woman, 105–6
Wentzel, Marie, 60
"where are you from?" question,
    xiii–xv
White, Luise, 19, 57
Wilson, Julius, 55
Wirth, Louis, 91
WITS, *see* University of the
    Witwatersrand
Witwatersrand University, *see*
    University of the Witwatersrand
women, *see* gender roles
women's diary group, 40, 85, 121–2
work, *see* livelihood

xenophobic violence
    attacks of 2008, xiii, 22, 48, 95–8,
        111–12
    victims vs. offenders, 104–11
    Vignette 1: Sergeant Khumalo's
        Dilemma, 98–103
    Vignette 2: The Camp, 103–4
    Vignette 3: The Refugee - Bare
        Human Life?, 108–11
    see also violence

Yeoville, 5, 7–8

Zimbabwe, 10

Printed in the United States of America